Time Statues

Robert F. Morgan, Ph.D.

Winds of Change Press

Winds of Change Press
An imprint of Orenda Healing International
www.orenda-arts.com

Copyright © 2021 by Robert F. Morgan
All rights reserved.

For permission to reproduce any part of this edition in any format, write to
Winds of Change Press/Orenda Healing International,
1868 A Calle Quedo, Santa Fe, NM 87505
Or send email to Publisher at windsofchangepress@orenda-arts.org

ISBN: 978-1-73-359364-9

EPUB: 978-1-73-359365-6

Acknowledgements

I thank my past editors from different printing opportunities who encouraged me to write whatever I chose, even if without statistics, graphs, tables, footnotes, or scientific jargon. I was told to just call it *"Commentary."* Or just write it.

In this I think of Valerie Hearn, with the staff at the *Cambridge University Press*, and Valentine McKay-Riddell, with the staff at the *Four Winds Journal* and the staff at the *Winds of Change Press*. Especially Valentine whose careful care made this book's publication possible.

After decades of publishing about a hundred scientific journal articles and 14 books, it felt good to write freely and outside the confines of professional custom.

I thank colleague Charles Tart who shared his own writing strategy: *"Just write what you really want to say. Then, as needed, you can add any citations, references, footnotes, and anything else an editor suggests."*

Original material in this book is supplemented with my excerpts and illustrations from the *Four Winds Journal*, the Cambridge University Press *Journal of Tropical Psychology*, the *Bulletin of the International Association of Applied Psychology*: Supplement to *Applied Psychology: an International Review, Trauma Psychology in Context: International Vignettes and Applications from a Lifespan Clinical-Community Psychology Perspective, Opportunity's Shadow and the Bee Moth Effect: When Danger Transforms Community, Unfortunate Baby Names,* and the journal *International Psychology*. Cited references are found at the end of the book in a consolidated reference section.

As to the key mission of understanding the strange world we live in, and what we can do about it, I thank my Guides. Those include Robert Lee Green, Martin Luther King Jr., David Cheek, Michael Knowles, Rollo May, Nathan Hare, Fred Luskin, Sidney Farber, Robert Dattila, or mentors like Stanley Ratner, Bert Karon, Hans Toch, Lois Fisher, Helga Doblin, Cinnamon Morgan, Canadian-born Angel Morgan, Walter Milleson, grandchildren Akasha, Luke, Ava, plus the multitudes of my friends, teachers, parents and other relatives (my brother Nelson Morgan and sister Pat Norman come to mind).

Then there is both a former student and an instant colleague, friend and family, Dr. Benjamin Robert Tong. He can be found here and there in this book but his influence is much more profound.

Also Michael Butz, Ron Slosky, Len Elkind, and the other thousands of students in six+ decades of teaching who have taught me much in return.

Above all I should thank that amazing woman I met in Billings, Montana, so many years ago. She said that, for her, humor was sexy. Oh! I can *do* that!

Now we've been together about 30 years, it's time for me to thank Becky Owl Morgan. Not all my humor met the mark. She's put up with a lot. Her own sense of humor and grace keep us going. Luckily the fun and the love are more than enough.

Better than amusing, she is my Muse.

TABLE OF CONTENTS

Acknowledgments... i
Introduction: From Mammaries to Memories................ 1
Chapter 1. Time Statues................................. 4

I. On the Job... 52
Chapter 2. Batacas..................................... 53
Chapter 3. The Naked Latvian........................... 56
Chapter 4. Cleanliness in the Intensive Care Unit (ICU)...... 65
Chapter 5. Madstop: Grades as Personality.............. 69
Chapter 6. The Time Zone Defense....................... 88
Chapter 7. The Invisible MMPI.......................... 91
Chapter 8. Lifespan of a Cult.......................... 97
Chapter 9. The International Rise of Balloon Therapy....... 111
Chapter 10. Inductive Pathways & Best Way to End a Life.... 118
Chapter 11. Maidu Murder Mystery &
Paradigm Shift Epiphany............................... 123
Chapter 12. Unopened Gifts............................ 134
Chapter 13. Two Georges............................... 149
Chapter 14. Turtles, Dogs, and Eagles................. 154
Chapter 15. Elders with Anticipatory Trauma........... 158
Chapter 16. Close Encounters of the Anomalous Kind....... 167

II. Language & Influence............................ 199
Chapter 17. Language Malfunction...................... 200
Chapter 18. The Discovery of Poison Ivy and Quicksand...... 214

Chapter 19. Existential Exceptions to the Truth 215

Chapter 20. Fresh Breath Top to Bottom 219

Chapter 21. Insulting Introduction Equity 221

Chapter 22. Musical Contest 223

Chapter 23. Surfing the Tsunami 225

Chapter 24. Silent Language 250

III. Citizenship. 254

Chapter 25. Bastille Day 2020 255

Chapter 26. Actualizing Democracy. 256

Chapter 27: A Columbus Perspective 296

Chapter 28. Unknown and Known: Drs. Green and King 301

Chapter 29. Are We Team or Equipment?
Automation Windfall 331

Chapter 30. Forrest Gump on Today's Box of Chocolates 335

Chapter 31. Opening Night 2020 337

Chapter 32. Climate Change has Fingerprints 339

Chapter 33. Equity and Ice Fishing. 345

Chapter 34. Interview with Grover Hardscrabble 350

IV. Family: Non-Human Relatives 353

Chapter 35. Animal Clients 356

Chapter 36. L'escargot Sauvage. 368

Chapter 37. Guam & Singapore, Brown Tree
Snakes & Bee Moths. 374

Chapter 38. Lepidoptera Wars & the Month of the Moth 388

Chapter 39. Ritters Critters 392

Chapter 40. Puppy Unleashed 395

V. Family: Human................................ 416

Chapter 41. Tomato Soap, a Fantasy 418

Chapter 42. Who Killed Andy Curry? 423

Chapter 43. When Time Goes Faster...................... 429

Chapter 44. Another Golden Pond........................ 434

Chapter 45. A Life Owed to the Dime Movie............... 438

Chapter 46. Father's Day 441

Chapter 47. An Unpaid Bill 445

Chapter 48. A Mystery Even to this Day.................. 449

Chapter 49. Young Love 2020............................ 460

Chapter 50. Shaking Hands with Lincoln 461

Chapter Last. The Human Family Reunion 465

References 490

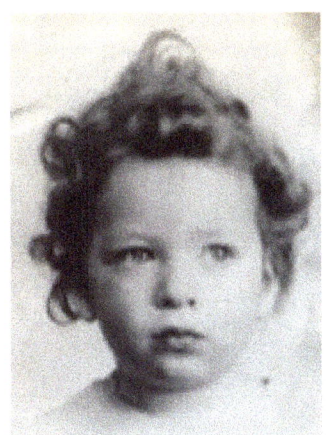

Introduction: From Mammaries to Memories

As a pre-school toddler, I already knew that I would grow up to be a writer. Everybody said I was a little Dickens.

We were secure and warm, growing in safety. Growing so large that we began to be cramped. Here were the beginnings of desire for a larger apartment. Not to mention that the gentle rocking had become earthquakes.

In that moment or many moments later we first emerged into a new world. A mysterious world. Whirling shapes and colors, rumbling sounds. Made no sense.

We can explore though. Because we had the safety of the cord connecting us still to the warm safety we had left. Our air, our liquid energy. The lifeline is still there.

Hey! It got cut! Gone. Find a new way to breathe! We better figure out this weird place we are in. That's the primary mission. Fast as we can.

It takes a lifetime. And then only a *little* bit understood. Too late to go back to the womb. (On Mother's Day she will emphatically agree.)

The newborn learns to breathe the alien place's air. For energy it can suck nourishment from a giant's huge breast. This perspective might lead to a lifelong craving that will never be fully satisfied. Males seeking ever larger breasts? Females seeking to *have* ever larger breasts? Here for some could be a primal critical period leading to wealthier plastic surgeons and silicon merchants. (What about bottle-fed babies? Maybe alcohol drinks would sell better in baby bottle shaped containers?)

Not us. We moved on. We need not climb the beanstalk to get to the giant. We grew up and *became* the giant.

Whatever else we learned to do, our survival still depends on the mission. To understand this strange world. Remember what we learn. The important stuff.

Time is a place. Each moment is a statue in time, always rooted in that time and that place. Memory allows us to visit them.

After eight decades of this, I have amassed a library of memories. Stacks after stacks of time statues archives.

So much that it can take minutes or more to access just one memory and only with patience. Elders do better at this when we imagine our search as an ordering at a restaurant. Then, usually, it will come. Arriving late? But it will come.

From the viewpoint of age, we can view these memories in their entirety as a grand tapestry. Not necessarily arranged in order, chronologically.

More by specific themes jumping temporal locations to connect in themes.

Chosen here: **On the Job, Language & Influence, Citizenship, Family: Non-Human Relatives, Family: Human**.

What is a good guiding strategy for navigating these patterns, this treasure in an elder's experience?

Maybe it's ones that were meaningful or fun. Sometimes both? Usually based on real past experience. Sometimes not.

All of these can be shared.

As in the chapters that follow.

Chapter 1. Time Statues *

"The future will be better tomorrow"
— Singapore T-shirt

"I never think of the future. It comes soon enough. The only reason for time is so everything doesn't happen at once."
— Albert Einstein

"It is just an illusion here on Earth that once a moment is gone, it is gone forever. And I asked myself about the present: how wide it was, how deep it was, how much was mine to keep. If I am going to spend eternity visiting this moment and that, I'm grateful that so many of those moments are nice."
— Kurt Vonnegut

If scholars from Einstein to Vonnegut are right, time is a place. It follows that whoever was alive in that time and place will always be there, alive, in that very specific time and place. In each moment of our experience, we create enduring dramas, statues in time, one for every moment of our life. Some of these statues are true art, testament to the greatest successes of the best life sculptors in our human family. Once a time statue is found, we have only to recognize the fourth dimension in which it resides. Then, when we choose, these statues can become a form of temporal vignette. A theater that we can see from an audience distance and, all, so far, seen through our memory.

Those we love will always be vibrantly alive in their own time and place. Those moments that we shared with them can be revisited as we wish, at least in our mind. As we live our life, scene by scene, we are all creative artists in this temporal theater. This complete life sequence of moments does of course include temporal vignettes that would *not* be happily visited by any time tourist. Then again, we can be very proud of other scenes that we have created, particularly if we become aware that, as we shape each moment of our existence, the results endure.

Suggested classic soundtracks for this chapter: https://www.youtube.com/watch?v=Wb9By-lODgk and https://www.youtube.com/watch?v=-uyV7tYJ56s

Some of these time dramas glow. Some are just fun. Some may highlight a new path forward. Here are some samples of temporal vignettes that I can recall clearly.

An Earliest Memory Exercise

Eventually somebody may challenge you to share your earliest memory. In the field of psychology, this is almost certain.

The first time this happened to me, I used auto-hypnosis for a few seconds and recalled that not long after the newborn moment when I realized my hand belonged to me. This turned out be too boring for my friends.

So I abandoned hypnosis and just reached to visit an early memory that came to mind, later verified by parents. Here is what that was: *When I was two years old I was allowed to go out and play by myself. But one Sunday it was raining and my father wouldn't allow it. He disappeared behind a newspaper and ignored me. So I went to the window and began tapping with the rhythm of the rain. Slowly my father's giant head emerged from behind the newspaper and said "STOP THAT." His head dropped back behind the paper. I considered this carefully. I wasn't bothering him. I wasn't allowed outside. I was just simply amusing myself by keeping tune with the rain. He probably didn't mean that. It wouldn't be fair. I went back to tapping on the window, faster as the rain had picked up strength. Again the head appeared above the paper and with a near roar said "DO **NOT** LET YOUR FINGERS TOUCH THAT WINDOW ANY MORE!" Okay. He means it. He can hit. Not fair but he can hit. All right then. No fingers. I got my little wooden hammer and went to the window. My last memory of this was flying through the air.*

Maybe that was the beginning of why he often called me a "Jesuit Lawyer" whenever I found command loopholes. Per the David Cheek method I had years of time to superimpose my hard-working father with who he turned out to be later in his life—a loving grandfather to my children and eventually very kind to me. But at the time, for that child, it was struggle.

Most people, confronted with this exercise, begin their earliest memories with the first year of school or age five. Before that, too traumatic to recall easily?

TIME STATUES

The First Day of School

My own first day of public school was at the age of four. I was surrounded with little people my size, only far from the rational giant adults I had grown used to. One boy needed the teacher's help to use the bathroom. A little girl danced around me humming and saying *"I'm a bumble bee!"* I wondered where I had been left and what was *wrong* with these people. In retrospect my adult mind projected the thought that it felt like I had been abandoned in a mental hospital's locked ward. Quite a temporal vignette to visit.

The only strong positive feeling for me in that time and place was the teacher. I never saw Miss Kelly's face that first day. I was too little compared to her. When she came near me and I realized she was there, I turned toward her but faced her knees. I heard her speak and it was a gentle, beautiful voice descending from the clouds above. An early crush but well beyond my non-existent pay grade.

As to non-memory evidence, a report card from that era surfaced not long ago. Educational goals were all marked "S" for satisfactory as opposed to "U" for unsatisfactory. The comment though read as follows: *"Robert is very dreamy. He sees no need to do anything at once."* My intense feelings may well have been unrequited.

A lot can be learned about yourself, people, the human family, and time statues with this exercise.

And it can trigger other temporal visits

Public School #8, Buffalo, New York

That earlier school memory took me to a later one, covering sequential experiences in grades 3-5 (age seven to ten) at Public School #8.

PS#8 was in a low-income community comprised primarily of Black families up from the South.

The school building had two separate entrances, one labeled "BOYS" and one labeled "GIRLS." We ignored these outdated labels and flowed into whatever door was closest.

The administration and teachers were all melanin-deficient white women in contrast to the majority of their students.

There was a dress code with all boys wearing white shirts and ties (pants & shoes too). Girls had more options but needed to wear their best.

At the weekly assembly, many memories here, we usually began with a song the teachers thought suitable, like *"If I knew you were coming, I'd a baked a cake."*

During the week our physical education included dance instructions. The teachers once again looked at us and decided that learning the aptly termed Square Dancing would be culturally appropriate. In this low-budget school there was no swimming pool so we never learned to swim.

Maturity came fast, for some too fast. By the end of the sixth grade some of the girls had become mothers. Some of the boys were no longer alive. Years later, too few of the children had survived. A few others had thrived. George Seay, my best friend in grade school, wound up as the "Voice of the Smithsonian's Wilson Center" with his 21 years of *"Dialogues"* radio interview show. It was George that said *"Never take the person sitting next to you for granted. When you get started in a conversation with somebody new, it's like discovering a whole new world. We're surrounded by remarkable people."*

About then, I was doing site visits for Head Start and its parallel program into the elementary grades called Follow Through. I took an opportunity to site visit PS8 in Buffalo, and see once again my own primary school. The day I arrived, a third grade teacher was having her retirement party. I reminded her that I had been her student for the last three months of her first year there. She took in my suit and tie and proclaimed to the room that I had been her student once. Then, based on that three months of contact when I was seven years old, she took full credit for all my subsequent life. I smiled and nodded. Such ambition deserved encouragement, especially on her departure day.

And another:

Buffalo, New York, 1942: The Broken Lamp

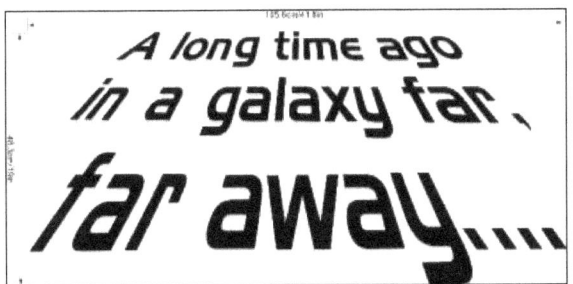

World War II was less than half over and who would win was unclear. When I was a few months short of my third birthday, my parents left to do some shopping. Alone in the rented apartment, I began an imaginary drama that included couch jumping, riding a tricycle over the carpet, and fast running around a lamp. My foot caught on the cord and the whole lamp crashed to the floor. Broken glass, cracked stem.

Not knowing how to fix it, I focused on other things, reading quietly, playing tribal war with a deck of cards. Probably an hour or two passed in this way before the parents, giants to me, came home. My mother stood over the destroyed lamp, knowing it would be a while before she could afford to buy another one. "Did you do this?" she said.

"Yes. Sorry. But it happened a long time ago."

The passage of time can lead to forgiveness, but it was not to be this time around.

(I remember my father saying to her "You're the one that is always so proud that he ran before he walked." This was true though another time he told me I was running away from my mother.)

> Michigan 1965: All right then, Focus on the Moment
>
> Then, Now, and Next.
>
> *"Time flies like an arrow. Fruit flies like a banana."*
> — Groucho Marx

When I was a graduate student, my instructor presented a case history of a behavioral intervention in stimulus-competition he attributed to an advance copy of Ulrich's new textbook (1966). It was felt this could well illustrate, for both couples and entire communities, the power of context, a dimension essential for the transformation of communities in stress, sometimes at the level of trauma.

In the case history, a married couple living in university housing complained of insomnia, marital conflict, sexual disinterest, and concentration difficulty when studying. All seemed to be signs of growing stress approaching the traumatic level. They were desperate.

It turned out they lived in a tiny studio apartment where the bed was the main and only major piece of furniture. It was on this bed that they studied, slept, argued, and had sex. The practitioner told them these activities all in the same setting were competing with each other. To differentiate them, it was advised that they purchase a lamp with three different light bulb colors: white for study, green for argument, red for sex, while lights out would do for sleep. The couple carefully followed this plan and reported care-free sleep, more effective study, less argument, happier sex. There ends Ulrich's case history, the conditioning a clear success.

Good for Then and Now, but what about Next?

When my instructor finished presenting this in class, I couldn't help but wonder: If the learning was truly effective, what will they do at traffic lights?

Washington, DC, 1966: A Memory of Ermon, A Woman for All Her Seasons

"It is a strangely irrational notion that there is something in the very flow of time that will inevitably cure all ills. Actually time is neutral. It can be used either destructively or constructively. I am coming to feel that people of ill will have used time much more effectively than people of good will. We will have to repent in this generation not merely for the vitriolic words and actions of bad people, but for the appalling silence of good people."
— Martin Luther King, Jr.

Now, these many years later, Ermon no longer shares our temporal stage with us. Still, her many gifts of the time statues she created in her lifetime endure and they are amazing. This one below though was in retrospect mainly fun. With consequences.

TIME STATUES

Washington, DC at the close of summer and the approach of fall. Outside the high-priced Watergate-style apartments, condos, and town houses, the city can look a lot like Detroit or Newark. But with much better weather. This afternoon showcased the Capitol District well.

Street people were very friendly, maybe the most that I had ever seen. Beautiful and friendly women, dressed sparsely perhaps due to the heat, seemed to be at every corner, always welcoming me to their city with offers of dates and intense friendship. But I had work to do and somebody to meet.

She was waiting for me in front of a restaurant that we both wanted to try. Ermon Hogan held a doctorate in psychology. Under Robert Lee Green, she and I were research partners for a U.S. Office of Education contract with Dr. Martin Luther King Jr's Southern Christian Leadership Conference (SCLC) organization. We were studying a whole rural Virginia county's four thousand children held back from school for four years to avoid desegregation. The outcome was powerful evidence that the IQ tests were measuring education experience far more than intelligence. Those out of school for years showed lasting damage; critical periods for specific learning in reading and math were also identified (Green & Morgan 1969; Green 1969; Green, Morgan, & Hoffman 1967, Green *et al* 1964a, 1964b).

Four years?!! Desegregation?

We had an hour for lunch so we went into the much celebrated restaurant at a time when it was nearly empty. Three in the afternoon is the best time to get served in normally busy eateries. There were only three other tables of customers for the one waitress, who was briskly delivering food to her customers.

The conversation was great as always. That may be why 60 minutes went by before we realized we still didn't have a menu and the waitress was clearly ignoring us.

Let's add some color to this picture. The waitress was white as were the other customers. As I am. Ermon was not. We could now see that an interracial couple in very Southern DC was not being served in an apparently all-white restaurant. Still, in a restaurant inside a federal district, the apartheid context was less obvious, one of quiet non-service really.

I stood up and called the waitress over. Loudly. She arrived.

With an appraising glance, she reappraised the situation. I was wearing a suit and tie. Ermon was dressed in an expensive down-to-business suit. Then she seemed to decide we might be important.

As they say in Singapore, the waitress seemed to think trouble might now be about to be knocking at her door.

She thought for a second, eyes looking left, and generated this vivid apology:

"Sorry I'm so... slow today. My whole family was killed yesterday in ... ummm .. an auto accident. The doctor said it would help me to come back to work today. Okay?"

Ermon was having none of this: *"If we don't get our menus, order, and food right now, you will lose the LAST member of your family!"*

It worked just fine. We took our time with the meal.

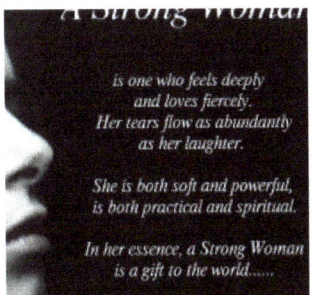

Note: Dr. Hogan went on to be the Education Director at the National Urban League in New York, following in her mother's footsteps, who had been on their Board. There she wrote effectively on key aspects of race and education. These included our work with Robert Green from the early 1960s on how teacher expectations and self-concept can predict learning success for their students (Hogan & Green, 1971). This anticipated the 1966 classic work of Robert Rosenthal and Lenore Jacobson on the same subject. From there she became a Rockefeller Foundation Fellow at Howard University. Next, in 1973, she moved to international psychology with the U.S. International Affairs Office, Department of Health, Education, and Welfare, where she chaired a task force on international adoption of Vietnamese children. At the African American Institute she coordinated study tours for French speaking educators from Africa. In 1977 she became the Director of the U.S. Peace Corps for the Ivory Coast. Marriage to Assane Kamara of Senegal expanded her name to Dr. Ermon O. Hogan Kamara. Her distinguished international contributions improved the lives of many in the 20th century. She is missed in the 21st.

Consequences Postscript:
Back to Wolfville, Nova Scotia, Canada, 1970

Janet Marshburn, an African American New Yorker, was new to San Francisco. She was beginning her psychology Ph.D. studies at the first free standing school of professional psychology. There in the early 1970s San Francisco campus, the roaring 1960s were still going strong. Personal space was out, everybody hugged at any time. New Yorkers still valued their physical privacy. So Janet declined to hug, consistently and continually. Finally a few of the women tried an intervention, demanding to know why she was so aloof. She faced them down, saying with conviction: "When I hug, I mean business!" This perspective was interesting and soon accepted. It even gave many some emotional room toward using affection only when it was wanted, the precursor to "No means no!" Thanks to Drs. Marshburn and Hogan, interventions toward genuineness reshaped cultures toward greater healthy autonomy. This could even be found in the Canadian Maritime provinces.

Dalton Vernon in 1970 was only the head of our small psychology department in eastern Canada's Acadia University. Today he is revered as a key pioneer in Canadian Psychology. Back then he was a recently retired Admiral who then became enthusiastically immersed in the client-centered approaches of Carl Rogers. This unusual blend of authority and generosity of spirit shaped his governance of us young faculty, now under his supervision.

An example was the marathon sensitivity training group required for psychology student majors that he required each of us faculty to lead on one weekend. No exceptions for any faculty or students. From Friday evening at 8 PM to Sunday noon, my group of ten students was to endure nonstop sensitivity exercises in my home. The other faculty had their own groups going at the same time with the same agenda in their homes. My colleagues reported that energy peaked around Saturday morning at the latest, with any progress or good will evaporating quickly after that. Dalton was not great at generating our motivation, but the Admiral was so sincerely kindhearted that we still complied.

Now, in my group, I felt we had gone about as far as we productively could by Saturday evening. And then I shared my experience with Dr. Hogan in Washington with the group. This they enjoyed. Ermon had inspired a new line of conversation. *"Why do these groups need to be 'sensitivity' ones? Why can't we learn to be '<u>in</u>sensitive' when that's what's needed?"* they asked. We decided the word that we needed was not 'insensitive' or 'aggressive' but an in-context 'assertive.' Now others have coined and publicized the assertiveness group approach, still going strong today (often allied with martial arts training).

But for my group at that time, we became an assertiveness group, focused on productive ways to fight back. Now the students had formed a cohesive and creative cohort, full of excitement despite the fatigue. As Sunday noon approached, I wound up the group by asking the existential question *"What will you do with all this energy?"* Then, being older than they were (almost 30), I went to bed. They were left plotting in my living room to actualize their assertive energy as they saw fit. When I woke that evening, they had all been long gone.

Our university was nestled in a quietly conservative town. The students were mostly from that region. Their parents were so fundamentalist in their beliefs that they rejected anything so frivolous as dancing or movies. The university administration was more progressive, but not by much. The students though were not immune to the youth currents at the end of the 1960s. They yearned to break through the constraints of past generations.

So, in their assertiveness energy, they descended on the campus Sunday evening. Going right to the psychology building, an understated quietly dignified gray wooden structure, they covered it in bright evocative tie-dye paint with sporadic wish-fulfillment comments. One said *"Chaste is waste."* As in this photo.

TIME STATUES

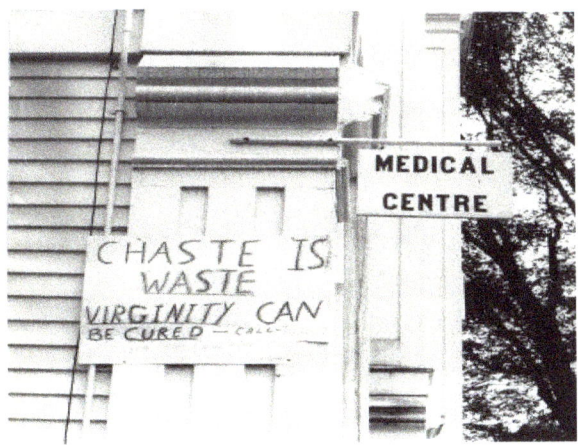

On Monday morning, faculty and students arrived to unexpectedly see a new psychology building, pulsating in all its rainbow glory.

Three outcomes became immediately apparent:

1. The university urgently organized a repainting of the building so by the end of the day it was gray again.
1. By the close of business hours massive numbers of students had switched their major to psychology.
1. Dalton Vernon notified us we would be having a department meeting the next morning before the campus opened or the sun came up.

Dalton was such a sincere and decent man, well, we all complied once again. Although I admit I did show up in robe and slippers. While we had our meeting, my family fed me breakfast. Dr. Vernon's scowl turned to a smile despite his best efforts. In the end, he agreed we had accomplished some new directions in psychology group process. We also accomplished the cessation of Dalton's mandatory marathon groups.

The next summer, Canada had its own Woodstock concert, headlined by Joan Baez. They had it in our valley. Attendance was 50,000 and it seemed like they all stayed in our house or at least our little town.

Thank you Ermon

Wolfville, Nova Scotia, Canada, 1970: The Case of the Power Words

All cats are Maoists. All horses are naysayers.

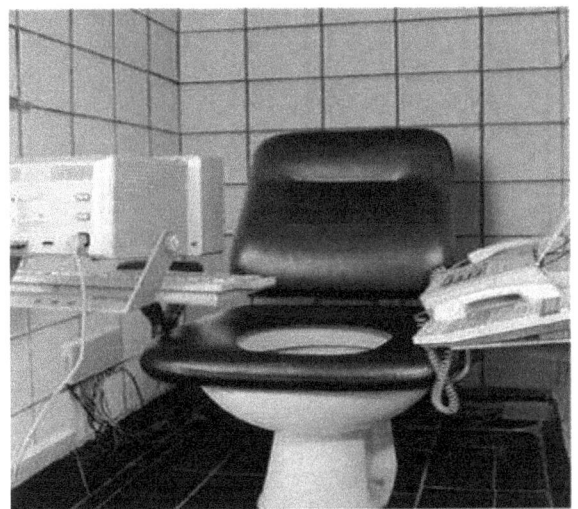

In Canada some years ago, a very conservative Nova Scotia University gave the students access to their new Computer Center with many stations. These computers were normally only for administrative use but the students had access every Monday and the faculty was allowed access every Friday (days of the week when usage would be less).

Strangely, the Center kept going out of order for an hour at a time, several times each Monday. Some students of mine asked me to look into it as they were getting no explanations on their own.

It turned out that the programming had a censor that closed all the stations down any time a student user typed in a prohibited or profane word. The head of the Computer Center excused this to me by insisting that, psychologically, use of a "swear word" on the keyboard meant that the student was angry and might then harm the computer. Shutting everything down was only a safeguard to protect the equipment.

The students responded to this by saying the real reason was to control their freedom of expression. This in the context of a fundamentalist administration that had little liking for any behavior outside a very constricted range.

My brother, then a new researcher at the International Computer Science Institute (ICSI) in Berkeley, took into account the antiquity of the Computer Center systems and estimated that more than a third of their computing capacity was dedicated to this censorship.

As an academic service to avoid shutdowns, I obtained a list of the nearly hundred words that were prohibited. And distributed them to the students so, among other things, they might avoid the shut-downs.

Word spread and very soon there were no more shut-downs on student Mondays.

On the other hand, suddenly there were torrents of shut-downs on the three days administration used the Center.

It would seem the students had learned to hack into the system somehow and use the magic words strategically.

Pueblo, Colorado 1975: Playing Outside the Box

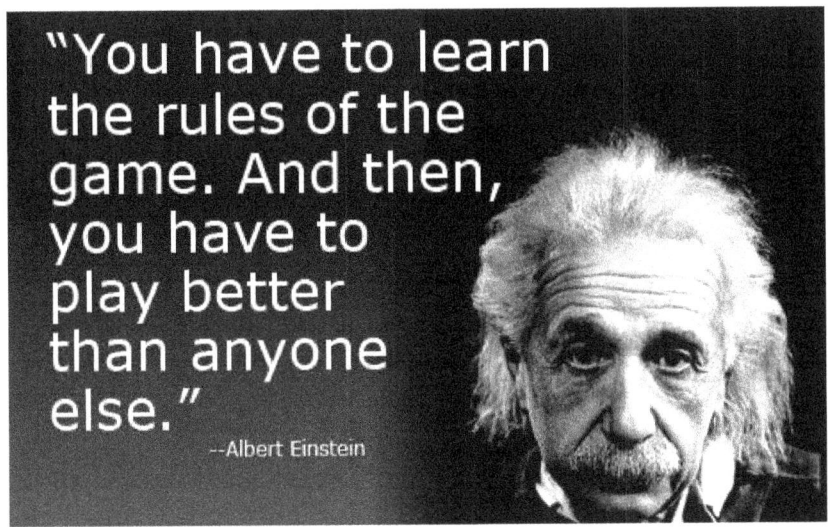

Alan Love was my Dean and supervisor at the University of Southern Colorado. He was well defined by his last name. Probably the kindest supervisor I ever worked with. His discipline was political science.

I lost no time in questioning the relationship between those two words. Alan liked the argument, particularly since he had a long-standing debate on this with the other senior colleague in his department (no, I don't recall his name).

This other Political Science professor was well connected with the state legislature and some very wealthy Coloradans. As such, he preferred a front-

"He wants to meet my new psychology department head," said Alan. *"He wants to prove that us science eggheads can't think outside the box and win a real down-to-earth life-centered game."*

Monopoly? Hmm. For these two it was more a contest of ego than buying and selling property.

But I was curious and I agreed. It had been at least 20 years since I had played Monopoly and never as an adult. I did have a theory though, stopping briefly at a department store to get the means to test it.

When the night came, Alan and I arrived at his antagonistic friend's house. There was a large, brightly lit dining room with a Monopoly board on a table and three chairs facing the action.

After introductions, again I was challenged with the current cliché of thinking outside the box. So we set to it. The intensity was clear—this was not only a game.

I was indulged in my preference for folding my share of the monopoly money, large to small, and keeping it in my wallet. *"Closer to life"* I told them. It took almost two hours, but eventually they were out of money and I had their property. Game over.

Alan was smiling and his colleague was puzzled. Both wanted to know the secret as to how I had won so completely.

I complied: *"I had a good theory. In real life, assuming no moral or ethical code (often the case in contemporary politics), there would be an overwhelming advantage in any competition where I had far more resources. I just had far more money than either of you had."*

Alan's friend demanded to know how this was possible. We all had begun with equal money, had we not? So I told him: *"I literally went outside the box. To buy a second box. I bought my own Monopoly game and put all the money in my wallet. The money from this board just added to it. Using it cautiously, not drawing too much attention to it, I still had an unlimited supply. In fact, most was still left in my wallet. You two were paying most attention to competing with each other, thereby not noticing what I was doing. Until it was too late. In a capitalist game, the one with capital advantage usually wins, especially when the rules lack any requirement for honesty. Just like in practical results-centered politics as you describe it."*

Turning to Alan, he said: *"Let's not play with a psychologist again."*

Nor did they. Alan laughed all the way to his car.

Auckland, New Zealand, 1978: Sprinkler in the Storm

"Show me a sane man and I will cure him for you."
— C.G. Jung, 1932

In the late 1970s I flew to Auckland, New Zealand, to consult with the university's Medical School.

They wanted some advice on bringing Maori students into the medical school since the government had noticed that this important group was inadequately represented in the medical community.

The Chair of Psychiatry had found my name (erroneously) listed in a Directory of Black Psychologists, possibly due to my publishing work in an earlier decade on Martin Luther King's projects, primarily with psychologist Robert Lee Green (Green & Morgan, 1969; Green et al, 1967).

As I met the Psychiatry Chair at the airport, he was less than happy to see my race was not as he had assumed it would be.

Further, he shared that he had fired his last American psychologist for that man's unfortunate practice of demonstrating the use of a penile plethysmograph to his class with his own erection.

Despite this traumatic time statue fresh in mind, he still scheduled me to meet with his Board of Directors. This gave me the opportunity and time to review the data available.

The answer to their problem seemed reasonably obvious.

Why no Maori medical students? There were no Maori physicians on the faculty.

Essential mentoring and recruitment might well be simply achieved by hiring some of the few but distinguished existing Maori physicians to join the faculty. And then, recognizing that this represented a likely departure from past practices or prejudices, how to present this very un-complex recommendation?

On the way to meet the Board at the university, it rained torrents, the intense horizontal wind-driven rain so common in the Pacific. Yet, there in the front of the medical school building was a university employee watering the steps with his hose. I asked him why he did this in the middle of such a storm. He replied that his job required him to water the steps and lawn every day at this time, needed or not. He agreed it was absurd but said he found losing his job to be much worse.

Now I had the perfect metaphor to focus the Board. And so I began my presentation with that observation. They were not amused.

My remaining two weeks in New Zealand were unstructured since the Board had no more need for my services. This gave me time to learn much from the rest of this beautiful country.

Still, I learned that they would then be hiring some Maori faculty.

Reno, Nevada, 1979: Two Guys from Italy

"I thought I had made a mistake, but I was wrong."
— Lucy Van Pelt aka Charles M. Schulz

It was the first anniversary of my divorce. To celebrate, I went to a favorite Reno restaurant: *Two Guys from Italy*. I ignored the rumor that the place was owned by the mob, since that was alleged about all Italian restaurants in Reno. The main thing is that the food was great.

So, bachelor unleashed, I went there for lunch while my daughters were in school. That day there was a vivacious waitress who seemed full of curiosity about me. I complied, feeling the same about her. Turned out that she was the daughter of one of the owners.

We agreed at the close of the meal that it might be a good idea to meet again outside the restaurant. I said I would get back to her.

Moving quickly to the nearest flower shop, I chose the largest, most dramatic flowers they had and had them sent to her that very day at her restaurant with my name on the card.

The next afternoon I went for lunch once again at *Two Guys from Italy*, same time, same table. I asked the waiter to let her know I was there.

Soon two very large individuals in suits came to my table. "Why are you threatening my daughter?" said the older of the two. "I'm not. I would not," I answered. The younger one said, "Then why did you send her those funeral flowers?"

At least I got to meet the two guys from Italy.

Reno 1979 again: Sammy Davis Jr. and a Disruption in Timing

When we lived in Nevada, my daughters were ages 8, 11, and 18. The 10-year-old had a weekly painful dental procedure that lasted several months.

To make this after school Wednesday appointment less unpleasant, it was followed up by the two of us going to a live show. By paying a strong tip to the staffer seating us, we always were able to sit right against the stage for a close-up experience with some performing celebrity.

TIME STATUES

Naturally the 8-year-old and the 18-year-old petitioned for equity. So one of them was my guest on a Tuesday night and the other on a Thursday night. No sacrifice on my part since they each got one child friendly show but I got three. This went on for about a year and was a valued family event.

One Thursday evening, the 18-year-old and I went to see the music, dance, and comedy performance of Sammy Davis Jr. As usual, we sat in the seats closest to the stage. Knowing that Mr. Davis had a glass eye, we sat in front of the stage area he could see. Close enough for me to relax my feet on the edge of the stage.

Sure enough, he came right over to us for the audience interaction part of his show. I nodded to my daughter, but Davis ignored my suggestion and a microphone was put to my face.

There were introductions, including my daughter. I recall him saying then: *"What do you do for a living?"* and my response *"I'm a psychologist."* He took a big step backward in mock horror. Crowd laughter. Then he leaned toward me and said: *"Are you also in show business?"*

Now I recognized that oncoming joke immediately. It's older than I am. Heading off his punchline, I pulled my feet from the edge of the stage, shook my head 'no' and sat upright. It was pretty reflexive.

He frowned and pulling our microphone back, said: *"Hey! You must have thought that I was going to say: THEN GET YOUR FEET OFF THE STAGE!"*

Smiling, he stepped back and said: *"Look. You're a good sport. Why don't you and your daughter come by my dressing room after the show to hang out and we'll have a bottle of champagne together?"* Then he went on with a truly entertaining show.

After the show we went backstage and found his room, star on the door and all. Standing in front of it was a large severe looking individual in a business suit.

He said: *"Mr. Davis sends his apologies but he won't be meeting with you tonight. He hopes this gift will be enough."* I was handed a bottle of champagne and an envelope. The note in the envelope said: **"NEXT TIME KEEP YOUR FEET ON THE STAGE!"**

**

Eventually my daughters became adults. I asked them one day what their best memory of their childhood years in Nevada was. I thought they would recall the months of stage shows.

Instead they agreed it was the treats under their pillow the year we were there.

I had been in the habit of putting some minor gift, edible or otherwise, under their pillow after they were asleep so they would wake up happy and valued to their new day. I had forgotten about that. But they said *"Except for the worst part."* Worst? *"After we moved, you stopped!"*

Palo Alto, CA 1989 and San Francisco 1972: In Search of the Journey

If you want something you never had before, you must do something you have never done before."
— South African Proverb, per Nathan Hare.

I went to a fundraiser at which the guests of honor were Men's Warehouse clothing magnate George Zimmer (*"You'll love how you look; I guarantee it!"*) and actor Leonard Nimoy.

Leonard was promoting his new book, one full of his own creative photography. He had retired from acting and now was enjoying this new career in his final years.

After the guests made their presentations, the whole large group moved into an adjacent room for some food. Leonard stayed behind for a few minutes to autograph copies of his book. I stayed last since I had lacked the foresight to buy a copy for him to autograph.

When we were the only two left in the large meeting room, I told him I had no copy to autograph but I could be his guide to dinner.

He smiled and said that would be fine.

He got up and seemed a little unsteady. I put my arm around the small of his back for his stability and we carefully walked out of the room.

Leonard was shorter than I had pictured him and he seemed very frail. I was impressed by how he as a younger actor had carried off the role of a powerful Vulcan. Today he was just Leonard Nimoy, a very fine human in his own right.

He asked me what psychologists like me thought about his "In Search of" television show, possibly wanting to hear nothing further about Star Trek.

I told him I had watched it because of the interesting topic choices and his presentation, all this despite the frustration about it being all search with nothing ever found.

I told him about my former student Roger and his own in-search-of (see next page). He laughed. We made our slow way in search of the dinner.

Which, by the way, we did find.

TIME STATUES

The original 'in search of' that I told Leonard about was an exchange with a graduate student I'll call Roger. It was the earliest days of the first freestanding California School of Professional Psychology or CSPP in San Francisco, 1971. In those first days, my class was held on the floor where we all sat on student-chosen harem pillows.

Roger was older than most (including me), maybe in his late thirties. He had a goatee and a pony tail, street boots, and a perpetual good-natured smirk.

Sitting on his harem cushion, he looked like a life-size garden gnome.

After my presentation on the need for outcome measures of success, Roger ponderously made this statement: *"Life is always just a journey. We may be in search of a destination but this we will not achieve. We must then appreciate that our journey is all that matters."*

Roger then returned to his third cup of coffee, as he sat impressively cross-legged on the cushion. I waited through his fourth cup of coffee while class continued, until he finally arose, turned, and started toward the door. I asked, *"Where are you going, Roger?"* Looking somewhat disappointed at my foolish question, *"I'm going to the bathroom!"* he said. I asked: *"Will you ever get there?"*

San Francisco again, 1994:
Ceremony for the Lifespan of a Marriage

"Life isn't a matter of milestones, but of moments."
— Rose Kennedy

TIME STATUES

> You are regretfully invited
> to the wedding between my perfect son,
>
> *The Doctor*
>
> and some
>
> *Cheap Two-Bit Tramp*
>
> whose name escapes me right now.
>
> The biggest disaster in my
> family's history will take place at
>
> *9pm on Saturday, September 8th*
>
> and no doubt end in divorce,
> hopefully in time to still be eligible for an annulment.
> The overwhelmingly disappointing heartbreak of a ceremony
> will be followed by dinner, where nuts will be served
> because whatsherface has an allergy.

One technique used in marriage ceremonies was called the burning envelope method. Each person to be married privately wrote down on paper all their reservations, concerns, dislikes, and foreboding about the person soon to become their spouse. Nobody else saw this paper which was sealed in an envelope. As part of the ceremony, both sealed envelopes were burned, symbolizing the release of doubts.

A beautiful gesture. Still, the two of our good friends married in this way did eventually divorce.

What if there were a ceremony for the divorce? Would this bring closure to the feelings of hurt or loss?

What if we had held a memorial service for our friends following the final divorce process? A time to recall the best and most troubled parts of their time together and release tension.

This could be somewhat more dynamic if one or both of them pulled out an envelope, declaring: *"I kept a copy!"*

Berkeley, CA, 1997: Artificial Intelligence and the Soul

"The full development of artificial intelligence could spell the end of the human race"
— Stephen Hawking, 2014

When my younger brother directed the International Computer Science Institute (ICSI) and taught at the University of California Berkeley, he encountered some interesting arguments against funding the development of artificial intelligence. Not so much the current warnings from Hawking and others that eventually robotics will generate intelligence that will replace humanity as a dominant species. No, there were some who thought that entering a living person's memories, personality, and intelligence into a robotic clone might be an attempt to replicate the human soul and avoid the life after death heavenly judgment some believers expect. Therefore they thought this research should be blocked, definitely not funded.

The key question my brother asked me was: *"If all my memories, personality, and abilities were stored in the electronic brain of a look-alike robot and I died, would the robot and its consciousness still really be me?"*

My words came from my mouth before my cortex had time to consider them, a common event: *"No it wouldn't be you or your consciousness. You'd be dead and gone. But, thanks to the robot, we wouldn't miss you."*

He probably won his argument without any help from my consultation.

"If that's all there is, let's keep on dancing." (Peggy Lee, 1969)

TIME STATUES

A Gift of Time from the Western Pacific, 2001

My own golden rule of proportionality continues: I still try to solve more problems than I create.

When you fly commercial air from Washington DC to San Francisco you cover about 2,500 miles in six hours. Fly from there to Honolulu and it's another 2,400 miles in five more hours. Fly from Honolulu to Guam and add 3,800 miles for seven hours.

That's a total of 18 hours in flight to cover the 8,700 miles of travel to get to an island in the deepest ocean on the other side of the earth.

Of course, doing this travel for the years I lived in Guam did chalk up the frequent flyer miles.

It was 2001 when I taught a course in Saipan, Guam's Western Pacific neighbor, I advised these future psychologists to not divulge their profession to an adjacent traveler on such a long trip. The conversation will soon become a month's worth of unsolicited psychotherapy, devoid of any compensation. I told the students my own fantasy was to carry a small taxi meter on board. Then I could lower the meter flag and the person beside me could view the growing cost. Might shift the conversation to lighter moments or even a gentle silence for reading.

The class seemed to go well.

Maybe it was the friendly seminar atmosphere, soft lights, a Fiji water and dark Ghirardhelli chocolate per person per class.

Maybe it was the Saipan culture.

Whatever it was, the class pooled resources and gave me their best version of my taxi meter fantasy as a thank you gift.

A handmade wooden hourglass with sand designed to flow for exactly the 50-minute therapy hour.

Temporal Compassion in Southeast Asia, 2011

"The second mouse gets the cheese"
— Unknown, definitely not mouse #1

He paced back and forth, agitated and muttering to himself.

He was the chief administrator of an Australian university campus in a Southeast Asia country. He was gesturing at the workmen dozing on his grass, their construction work temporarily set aside.

Though this country was not Malaysia, the workers were all Malaysians. There they were, lying on the ground, exhausted and sleeping though their half hour noonday lunch.

Probably working two or more jobs, this one in the hot sun, rather than use lunch time to eat, they chose rest.

I walked up to him and asked why he was upset.

"Look at them! Sleeping where they stood! When will this work ever get done?!"

I said: *"They look wiped out. Haven't they been making progress?"*

"Not nearly as fast as they should. I wanted this all done by now. Only halfway there at best. They're just so slow!"

I thought of saying some things he would never understand in defense of the poorly paid and physically stretched Malaysians, or other words that would only accelerate his anger toward the workmen even more than to me.

Instead I said: *"Are you paying them by the hour?"*

His shoulders shrugged off the question and, without turning away from the sleepers to face me, he said: *"No! I'm paying them by the day!"*

His temporal distinction, while missing the point completely, was worth my telling my New Zealand colleague a few minutes later. An experienced diagnostician, he asked: *"Did the little cretin know he was embarrassing himself?"*

The answer was obvious.

Best I could do at the time was to smuggle bottled water and dark chocolate bars out to the workmen when the coast was clear.

To close, we go back in time to Michigan 1963: A Student's Solvency by Lie-detecting Annelids

"He that will not apply new remedies must accept new evils."
— Francis Bacon, 1624

It was a new year and the onset of January.

I began my psychology Ph.D. program at Michigan State University. At the age of 21, I had just started a family with a wife and her three young children, all of whom needed to be fed, clothed, and sheltered. The best solution for us all was a National Institute of Mental Health (NIMH) Research Fellowship.

My supervisor was Professor Stanley C. Ratner, an exceptionally decent person and a brilliant expert on animal behavior (Ratner &

Denny, 1964, 1970). He urged me to immediately apply for the NIMH support. It would pay my tuition, give a stipend for every member of my family, and provide research funds. All I had to do was send NIMH a research proposal, one I would use some of their money for.

While at that time I was on an experimental psychology degree path, the NIMH research application seemed to me to require an applied mental health component. I chose something original: clinical application of the auto-kinetic effect.

This effect was done by putting a volunteer (always undergraduate students in those days) in a dark room with a spot of light projected on a wall in front of them. They would be told to say out loud what words or sentences the moving light would spell. In fact, the light spot never moved or spelled anything. The volunteer's moving head would create the illusion of movement. This, plus the expectation that a perceptive volunteer would see words, often led to enunciation of nonexistent sentences.

I thought this could be a very interesting projective test for clinical practice. So I developed that proposal and submitted it to NIMH with my application. It was so original an idea that I could find no clinical research references to cite.

The response was fast. Rejected. The proposal had no clinical research references. Too original.

The reviewers did sent an encouraging note though.

I was asked to realize that I was only a low-level trainee and originality was not the point nor expected. On the other hand, if I submitted a proposal that fell within the research scope of my much published and cited supervisor, they would fund me. Hmm.

Professor Ratner at that time was doing research on the simplest animal with a central nervous system. This turned out to be *Lumbricus terrestris*, also known as the "night crawler," an earthworm.

Not high on my own evolutionary scale of clinical interest. But family to be fed.

(Rollo May came to give a talk at our MSU psychology colloquium that year. Following his discourse on the meaning and application of existential psychology, Stanley Ratner arose and asked *"How would existential psychology apply to earthworms?"* Rollo considered this carefully and then responded with only *"That is a very interesting question."* Two decades later when Rollo was a friend and godfather to my daughters, he still remembered Ratner's question; he advised that acknowledging the question was the best answer when you had no answer. My wife, Becky Owl Morgan, has her own Cherokee-Choctaw alternative to this dilemma: *"That is a mystery even to this day."*)

The earliest publication on the perceptual world of the earthworm was by Charles Darwin. He put one on top of a piano and noted that it contracted to the vibration of a piano key. Well, I knew that I could do this research better than Charles had.

I had already done a quick study with the galvanic skin response or GSR, a measure of electrical resistance of the skin (low tech: a simple ohm meter would work). Startle a volunteer, they did get course credit, and the GSR would jump. The understanding was that immediate reaction perspiration on the surface of the skin reduced the electrical resistance. This had become a key component of lie detection because it was assumed to measure anxiety.

(Lie detection equipment used then by law enforcement never measured lies—just anxiety level changes in response to questions. Police equated anxiety with falsehood; sometimes it led to a confession while other times it just misled everybody).

I used GSR to compare the efficacy of the multiple page questionnaire Taylor Test of Manifest Anxiety (TTMA) with a five-point scale responding to the question *"Are you anxious?"* My five-point scale correlated higher with the GSR than the TTMA and was much faster. Also somewhat disrespectful to the author, Janet Taylor Spence, an eventual American Psychological Association president, or so I have been told.

Still, I thought my GSR research might have some application value for this NIMH proposal I needed to submit.

It was reported anecdotally in the literature that earthworms could not see the red light portion of the spectrum. Fishermen hunted earthworm bait at night more successfully with red lights. What if I tested this assumption with the GSR?

Professor Ratner (animal behaviorists tended to have last names like Fox, Wolf, and Ratner but I found that none agreed that their name had anything to do with their chosen career path) liked my idea and the proposal was submitted. NIMH approved it and my family was saved.

Now I had to do the research.

First, per my supervisor, I must read all I could about earthworms.

They turn out to be essential to the fertility, porousness, and reduced toxicity of the soil, all essential for the world's human agriculture. An essential element for tropical food production.

They have eye spots all along their very sensitive skin (salt is corrosive to them). They breathe through this and so need to be constantly hydrated.

They do have a primitive central nervous system but with a lump of neural cells, a brain if you like, on either end, with the smaller one in its posterior. If they are blocked going one way, they could switch to their posterior brain and still move forward but in the opposite direction. Interesting animals.

I got stewardship of a refrigerator in the basement of the psychology building. On the lowest level would be placed an earthworm on a moist sponge surrounded by their (delicious?) edible moss. A biology friend of mine sewed thread around its mid-section to keep it on the sponge. She was amused but made it clear that I owed her bigtime. All worm subjects (participant or volunteer doesn't seem to fit ethically well here) had the same treatment in turn. GSR electrodes were gently placed on the worm.

At a higher level of the refrigerator, a white light bulb was ready to flash.

Now: for the first worm. A white light flash led to a GSR jump. Did that prove the worm perceived it?

Not necessarily. Ratner had taught me to look at alternate explanations and then control for them.

What if the GSR reaction was to the heat of the light and had not anything to do with the worm?

Removing the worm, I flashed the light and still got a GSR reaction to the empty sponge.

So, had to control for heat. Or assume the sponge had a life of its own.

I put a bowl of cold water between the light and the sponge and flashed the light. No GSR now.

Leaving the heat control bowl of water there, I retested the earthworms on sponges. GSR showed they could perceive white light flashes but, when a red bulb replaced the white one, there was no response. This was a consistent finding.

For this proposal, NIMH funded my graduate years all the way to the doctorate. This study became my M.A. psychology thesis. With Ratner's urging, we published the earthworm research (Morgan 1964, Morgan, Ratner, & Denny 1965). Based on the 1964 publication, I was surprised to learn that very year that I had been made a Life Member of the Michigan Academy of Science. But none of this kept my interest in any further research on *Lumbricus terrestris*.

(Serendipity note: Following my study, the eventually deceased earthworms were left in a jar of water in the refrigerator. I had meant to dispose of them but, well, you know how life can be in graduate school. After a month had gone by, I was summoned by another student who demanded I clean out the stench from the jar in the refrigerator. The smell was so overpowering that nobody would go near it. Sure enough, even a drop of this wormy potent potion would easily empty an auditorium. We did find a use for this but that is another story, best avoided in print or in the presence of authorities.)

I was gladly done with night crawlers and never went back to *Lumbricus* research. My next big project was a doctoral dissertation. For that, I chose instead to focus on the psychology of time, but only for humans (Morgan 1965, 2005a). That interest in the psychology of time never faded. As you can see.

Menlo Park, California, 1990, and then Our World today: Finding another Path

"We stand in life at midnight; we are always on the threshold of a new dawn."
— Martin Luther King Jr., 1964

Decades later I was invited to give a luncheon talk at the Menlo Research Institute (MRI). For these celebrated scholars and luminaries, I was asked one more time to share my research on anxiety, lie detection, and earthworms. So I did.

There it was I began to see at least a metaphorical usage.

The early career understanding of earthworms helped me in these later years to put a modern group in an understandable context. These are individuals among us, including in leadership roles, who deny our climate is well on the way to a full global torrid zone, one that will be barely inhabitable at best. Despite all science to the contrary, and often in ludicrous defense of lucrative but destructive greed, walking down their temporal path jeopardizes the survival of our entire human family.

How do the primitive central nervous systems of earthworms assist us to understand the successes and excesses of climate change deniers? This in the face of obviously increasing global hardships now inflicted upon so many struggling countries, particularly at the sea level of tropical regions. As they strategically apply overwhelming amounts of money to accomplish this denial and destruction, not excluding their own, they do routinely create an illusion. The illusion that they are leading us forward, progressing, while actually they lead an accelerating retreat in the opposite direction. Much like the earthworm, they may be led in this by a smaller secondary brain located in their posterior.

We have much to do to move forward on a better path.

If that succeeds, remember: ***"The future will be better tomorrow."***

I. ON THE JOB

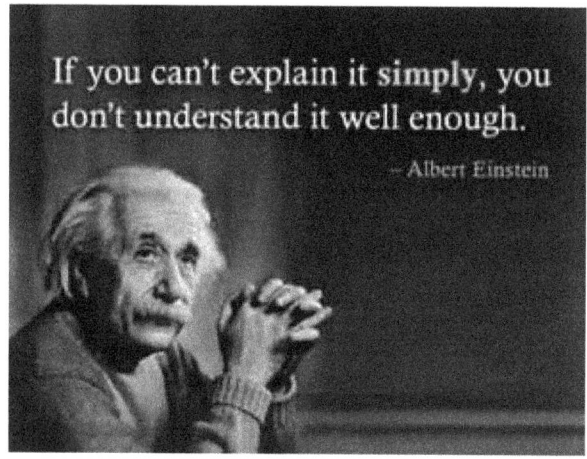

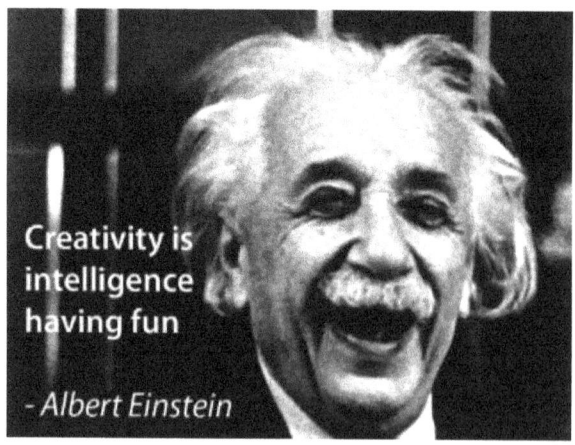

Chapter 2. BATACAS

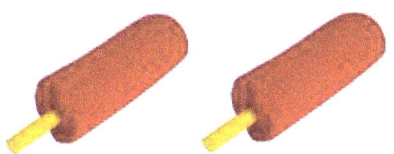

Clinical Psychologist George Bach introduced his "Fair Fight Training" couples therapy to our San Francisco professional school in its earliest years. By our year of 1972 it was popular with students and even a few faculty.

George began his therapy group for couples by telling them to raise their hand when they thought of something that their partner would want to know but they had been afraid to tell them.

When enough time had lapsed for group pressure to work, all hands were raised. Then George would say the group could begin: one by one each would tell their secret. Always a lively group.

George had a process for resolution. Each couple would begin negotiation by releasing pent-up hostility.

This was done by belting each other with foam rubber covered bats, ostensibly unable to damage participants. These were called Batacas.

Once exhausted or timed out, real vocal negotiations could begin. At their close, a sign of affection was expected.

One of my students brought a pair of Batacas into our classroom, explaining they were safe.

Another student was Lou Engel, a martial arts enthusiast. Lou held a Bataca high, gathered his brick-breaking Ki, and brought it down with such force that it cracked a wood desktop.

Harmless?

(After class, Lou asked me if I too pursued a discipline in the martial arts. I was hearing this term 'martial arts' for the first time, much less a required affiliation. So I just shared that I followed a non-violent path, a discipline I named Martial-Mellow. Best roasted on a non-foam stick over a fire. Followed next the generational delight of Bruce Lee movies. All was soon made clear.)

I was at the time involved in a troubled marriage, well within its final years. She eventually brought home a pair of Batacas so we could release our hostility.

Remembering Lou's demonstration, I declined. But she insisted. Now I did not want to hit her nor did I desire being hit. This I said. But she ignored this and attacked with her Bataca.

My solution in the moment was to treat this as a martial arts exercise (by then I was hooked). I would neither hit her with the Bataca nor allow her to land any hits on me.

In those, my young days, I had more speed than most. So as hard and fast as she attacked, I blocked it every time. Neither of us was ever hit. After many frustrating minutes for her, she threw her Bataca down.

I let George know that in this, my in-the-moment technique, as any psychologist might have expected, I had raised her hostility exponentially.

I also told him about Lou Engel's demonstration.

George was a good listener, highly practiced at it, but clearly was far from impressed.

Never saw Batacas again.

Or George either for that matter.

He died in Los Angeles in 1986 but no evidence that it was from Batacas.

Chapter 3. The Naked Latvian

"Results! Why I have gotten a lot of results. I know several thousand things that won't work."
— Thomas Edison, 1930.

"You can tell a poacher by how he orders his eggs."
— Uncas Slattery, 2000.

We ask psychological assessment tools to guide us in the three aspects of description, prediction, and communication. We ask of evaluation much more. The longer we have been in the field, the more experiences come to mind, a regular buffet of associations. Here are a few.

Personnel Selection

While a visiting professor in Canada, I was asked by a local bank president to assist him in a personnel transition situation. I agreed to develop a battery of computer scored tests that might add a dimension of understanding to the administrators being evaluated, but with the caveat that an actually hiring or promotion decision should include a personal interview and actual performance data.

He asked me, as a consultant, to just do a pilot try for him with only the test results. So he submitted the responses of three administrators to me and the computer digested them, regurgitating impressive charts and graphs. I then met with the bank president and his key staff to go over the findings.

I decided to go with the most uncomfortable one first. "This person's results suggest a person who is highly likely to depart from accepted ethical practice and would be a hiring risk" was my kindest interpretation of the sociopathic pattern on the charts. The president grinned widely and everybody looked relieved. "Yes" he said "we had him take this test just before we fired him and had him arrested for embezzlement. I told you this testing was the way to go. Why, look at how much trouble we would have saved if we had known this early on!"

So this was a test of the test. Hmmm. I moved on to the second set of results. "This person is a highly creative and intelligent individual that should be highly successful at whatever he undertakes" I said, hoping it was not another felon. "Right again!" said the president and all grinned, especially the highly successful vice president who had taken the test and was sitting right there in the group.

At that point I had a feeling I should quit while I was ahead (or "Quit while you are behind" as my youngest daughter liked to say). The probability of a third and final success seemed remote, particularly now that it was clear that all three sets of results were already well-known employees.

But, following many caveats again, I was ready to move to the last of the three protocols, an apparently straightforward one. "This person is normal in all respects, stable and reliable. His only low scores are in creativity and independent thinking. As long as ideas come from others and the situation is well structured, he would do well, possibly in accounting or maintenance." Following a long silence, the president said "Well, I suppose that is about right. Thank you professor." Of course, the third set of results was from that president.

My departure was cordial enough, all things considered. It was Canada after all.

I was not invited back.

Preconceptions

While still there in Canada, my colleague Don Marum and I were called in to consult with the regional hospital's psychiatric staff. The affable chief psychiatrist (it happens) took us to the only locked ward.

There were a variety of developmentally disabled adults engaged in various desultory activities. The Chief took us to the far corner where an immense naked man sat, his arms folded and his lips in a pout. He probably held the weight of two men and reminded us of how close we humans are to primates as he sat there in pink skinned obesity and hairy belligerence.

We were told that he was from Latvia and spoke very little English but was assumed to be of very low intelligence. Because of his size, staff was reluctant to force him to keep his clothes on and had turned to us.

Dr. Marum immediately noted that the patient must have a huge appetite. He suggested that he be put on a behavioral reinforcement regime where he would be fed a treat for every article of clothing he put on.

While the Chief was mulling this over, I asked him "Why do you think he doesn't want to put his clothes on?"

Marum and the Chief seemed to think this question was not helpful and ignored it, so I asked a more specific one: "*When* does he put on his clothes?" That was easier to answer: whenever he is allowed out of the locked ward to go on a walk.

Once it was determined that he was no danger to anybody I requested that he be moved to an unlocked ward. Once this was done, the naked Latvian posed no further problems.

The Chief psychiatrist was so pleased with this outcome, he invited me back to see if we might do some evaluation research together. I chose to evaluate their use of electroshock treatment (ECT) and, to my pleasant surprise, he agreed. This was before we could prove definitively in an evidence based way with MRIs etc. that ECT was such a high risk procedure that it should never be used. (Morgan, 1999, 2004a).

As to measures, he wanted ward behavior compliance and I wanted measures of cognitive function and brain damage. Despite our different expectations and interests, we did agree in the end to use all the measures we each wanted.

And then came the research design. I wanted him to randomly choose half those who were going to get ECT and withhold it from them so we might have a control group. He vetoed that approach, saying withholding treatment would not be ethical, and wanted to assign ECT to a random group of patients who would not ordinarily get it. This I vetoed.

Clearly our expectations of what this invasive treatment would or would not do, prohibited any research. It would take modern MRIs and CAT scans to prove the issue of damage, although it still remains a psychiatric tool despite the proof. Our ECT research was never done at that hospital but we did make a naked Latvian happier.

Validity

First I have learned to agree on the *purpose* of assessment, such as the *question* to be answered or the *mission* to be achieved. Then use the measure most likely to yield clear data that can be usefully interpreted. All else is inductive from there.

Student feedback on the effectiveness of their instruction and instructor is often littered with 10 point scales and hard to interpret questions. One might think this was a deliberate way to obfuscate the results, particularly from administrators trying to quantify impact on ordinal scales.

A simple percentage satisfaction score is probably the most interpretable (Morgan, 2005). I also very much lean toward dichotomous choices if it is a dichotomous question and, in general, brief and concise measures. The 12 point scale may *look* more valid but if it is truly a yes or no question, what in the world will three decimal points add?

Nor do the number of pages in a psychological test add to any genuine validity.

Exceptional Assessment Measures

Some test items seem somewhat strange but I suppose if the numbers show reliability and validity, being counter intuitive is fine. I am waiting though for items like: *"Sometimes I feel like none of the questions on this test have anything to do with me."* or *"When sweets are served do you feel lonely and desserted?"*

We also know that time is an important variable in testing (Morgan, 2004b). It used to be assumed, for example, that the older adults get the lower their tested intelligence scores. Even before the contemporary differentiation of fluid and crystallized intelligence, Nancy Woodruff demonstrated that removing the stopwatch from the intelligence testing procedure allowed IQ scores to increase with age rather than decrease. As we get older we get smarter but slower (Morgan & Wilson 2005).

Albert Ellis (1984) told me once that he would like every journal article that is published to be followed immediately by a rebuttal. He felt this would lead to a better evaluation of everything. Or, at the very least, a good argument.

I am tempted to include here some of the more interesting applications seen along the path, such as a brief non-invasive standardized test of human aging (Morgan 1968a, Morgan & Wilson 2004), efficiency percentages as ways to clarify assessment impact beyond statistical significance (Morgan 1968b), the most powerful genetic assessment technique to get at the roots of gender differences (Morgan 1968c), and an overlooked central tendency method for test item analysis (Morgan 1968c). (More on this in the chapter on Unopened Gifts.)

Evaluation remains the bedrock for organizational and administrative change and has brought about the empowerment and enhanced effectiveness of many an institution.

Now, the most powerful assessment study I can recall was that of the more than 3000 children deprived of public education in Virginia. Our finding, above and beyond critical periods of learning, was that tested intelligence *depends* on education; it varies with the quality of the learning environment (Green & Morgan, 1969).

The implications of this study impacted many countries even to this day- Bermuda comes to mind (Morgan & Fevens, 1981; Morgan 2004a).

But Bermuda, John Exner and the Molokai Peace Corps project, the invisible MMPI scale, and other such digressions are better left for other chapters, so I can wind this one up sooner.

My favorite offbeat assessment measure for psychologists was done by California psychologist S. Don Schultz when he held responsibility for the California State psychology license exams. It was before the current national exam.

California back then elected to score an essay exam. A major question on the essay exam, Don's favorite, asked us test takers to discuss Public Law 379 as it applied to child custody determination.

There *was* no Public Law 379 on child custody determination. The correct answer was *"There is no such law."* An acceptable answer was *"I don't know"* or *"I am not familiar with this law but in other states..."* A failing answer was to discuss it knowledgeably as though it really existed, to fake it.

This item reliably failed the few psychologists taking this test that should never practice.

I got the right answer and Don later told me he knew which paper was mine when he corrected them even though our names had morphed into numbers for the correctors.

"How did you know?" I asked. He said *"When you answered the question on how to deal with an invasive government form threatening your client's well-being and privacy by writing 'Answer abusive bureaucratic forms with bureaucratic forms of your own: send them*

an extensive form to fill out to justify their request', I knew it was you." Informal days, those.

Observation versus Perception

Lightner Witmer, considered the founder of applied clinical and professional psychology, ran afoul of American professor William James, considered a co-founder of all psychology in parallel timewise with European professor Wilhem Wundt.

The issue was assessment (McReynolds 1997). James considered assessment as a form of research. So from that perspective, norms are meaningless unless procedure is held constant.

Witmer preferred to follow Galton's path (Galton 1907) and vary his techniques assessing children based on individual differences, a dichotomy still at times separating researchers from practitioners. In other words, procedures were flexible depending on the child's needs.

I advocate following James when collecting data and Witmer after the data are collected. Since most intelligence tests end on cumulative failure, I usually continue with children on easier items long after those data are in so as to make the whole testing experience much less aversive. They end the experience with getting answers right, not on ending in failure.

Also in that era, we have Joseph Bell mentoring Arthur Conan Doyle when Doyle was a medical student and Bell was the Royal Surgeon. Bell's highly perceptive attention to detail and mannerisms have been considered the model for Doyle's eventual Sherlock Holmes novels (Booth, 1997).

One medical demonstration attributed to Bell and passed down through medical school classes for generations was as follows: *Bell marched into the lab followed by a flock of medical residents. He turned to them and said "Diagnosis uses all your senses, Ignore any at your peril. And do not shy away from what must be done for full perception. Here is a beaker of the urine of a patient with a very specific ailment. Let us test your perception and your courage." With that, Dr. Bell dipped his finger into the urine saying, "I will now taste my finger for clues. Then it is your turn." One at a time each intern dipped their finger into the urine and tasted it. When all were done, Bell said: "If any of you had watched carefully, you would have noted that the finger I put in the urine was not the finger I put in my mouth. Do not just observe: perceive." (Farber, 1956).*

Here is a more modern Sherlock Holmes story:

"Sherlock Holmes and Doctor Watson went on a camping trip. After a good meal and a bottle of wine, they fell into a deep sleep. Some hours into the night Holmes awoke and nudged his faithful friend. 'Watson, look up and tell me what you see.' Watson replied 'I see millions and millions of stars.' 'What does that tell you?' inquired Holmes. Watson pondered a moment. 'Astronomically, it tells me that there are millions of galaxies and potentially billions of planets. Astrologically, I observe that Saturn is in Leo. Horologically, I deduce that the time is approximately a quarter past three. Theologically, I can see that God is all- powerful while we are but small and insignificant. Meteorologically, I suspect that we will have a beautiful day tomorrow. What does it tell you?' Holmes held his silence for a moment, then spoke: 'Watson you idiot! Someone has stolen our tent!'" (Slattery 2000, Morgan, 2008).

Chapter 4. Cleanliness in the Intensive Care Unit (ICU)

"As you ramble on through life brothers and sister, let this be your goal: Keep your eye upon the doughnut and not upon the hole."
— Mayflower Doughnut Shoppe, Buffalo, New York

Friday night. The ambulance took 8 hours to arrive.

Once inside though, they did deposit me quickly at the hospital.

My surgeon had been waiting but left, saying he would operate in the morning.

Instead, I was rushed to the ICU where five nurses waited for me in a large friendly room.

Flashback to my Christmas stay 20 years ago in the Stanford Hospital ICU. They had all the hallways and room art blocked so as to wrap them each like Christmas presents. I was brought in to share a room with another patient. He was a 400-pound man who had been constipated for a week. As I got settled in my own bed, he was completing his own first successful enema. Unforgettable.

But this Albuquerque ICU was to be different.

The one male nurse stepped forward and said, to protect the unit from outside bacteria, I needed to be sanitized right away.

I was ordered, in friendly tone, to strip and lie on the bed. Nobody else agreed to do the same, but I complied.

While the female nurses watched, the male one anointed me head to toe with antiseptic.

Still, the shortest nurse, a Nepali woman, pointed out that the male had omitted anointing my genitals.

She decided to step in and fix that omission, taking a full 15 minutes to leisurely bathe and massage my genitalia in some soapy substance while the others took note.

Before I was discharged days later, the ICU non-medical administrator, Chris Gonzalez, asked me if anything had stood out during my stay in his unit.

So I shared this first cleansing experience from the night I had arrived.

I could tell he was reading this as a complaint. Not so.

I smiled and added: *"No, Chris! That was the best hospital welcome I ever had."*

It was.

Which reminds me of another way earlier hospital time statue. I learned this during my internship at Hawaii State Hospital in 1966.

Love in Hawaii

A psychiatrist claimed to cure locked ward patients from a distance at the Hawaii State Hospital in Kaneohe.

He sat in his office with his patient files, never meeting them, and practiced existential extremism: he assumed their traumatic pathology stemmed from him, apologized, and wished them love.

He reported that his patients got better while the patients treated by the other psychiatrists and their standard methods got worse.

This got a lot of play in the media.

Well, if this marvelous effect can be validated, it could mean more than a psychiatrist finding ways to avoid patients and collect a paycheck, interesting in its own right.

It would assume a certain existential narcissism: That psychiatrist is the cause and the cure of the trauma of others.

Of course, it might also be that the normal treatment of psychiatric patients in a locked ward is iatrogenic.

By withholding treatment (no ECT or psychiatric drugs) or other psychiatric intervention and staying in his office, he is demonstrating the control group power of placebo, moral treatment, or just leaving people alone (Morgan, 2005a).

On the other hand, if all the current problems of our human community truly come from him, he needs to start apologizing and sending global love without delay.

Love in New Zealand

During my three-week consultation there, I met a very beautiful Maori woman.

On our first date, I asked her what she thought about this: a recent sociologist's published assertion that cannibalism, something historically attributed to the Maori among many other cultures, was only a form of mental illness, a rare perversion, never an accepted part of any culture.

She explained that Maori warriors stuck out their tongues before a battle to let the enemy know they would wind up as their buffet.

She laughed when later showing me her grandmother's recipe for pickled human thumbs.

This was carefully considered by me during the later more intimate and confidential moments of the evening.

Chapter 5. Madstop: Grades as Personality

My first two years of college were as a Physics major in an engineering college.

Clarkson College, now Clarkson University, was in North America's coldest spot at the top of upstate New York (yes, I lived in Alaska and Clarkson's town, Potsdam, was worse). The temperature was usually about 20 degrees below zero during the day, rising to 40 degrees below zero at night.

"Madstop" was how we pronounced it (Potsdam backwards).

Clarkson College's motto was *"The workman that needeth not to be ashamed."* Though often our mentors could have used a *little* shame. My mechanical drawing prof was a fine example.

Professor Myron Mochel taught using free hand diagrams designed to create products for those who chose to build them, often by his own demonstration. I'm not an artist and this was validated often as I did my best to recreate his personal masterpieces. Ones so complex most of us never really did them justice when we tried to reproduce them.

This probably didn't help. One day he dared us to bring any two-dimensional drawing into class. He would then show us how effectively and rapidly he'd put it on the blackboard, exactly scaled and detailed such that anybody could build it.

When he said he was ready to pick a student's contribution, I deliberately yawned and looked out the window. So of course he took my drawing first, an object that was an illusion much like Escher's. After many heroic but futile attempts to schematically draw the illusion so that it could be built, he finally realized that it could not exist in real space.

The class laughed loud and long.

Mochler though overlooked the comedic aspects completely. So I was not his favorite.

More telling as to his character was his grading scheme.

His measurement of our work products, and ultimate grade, was on this scale: A, B, C, D, F, 2F, 3F, 4F, and 5F. This since, clearly, a single F could not accurately or fully express his overwhelming disdain for our work. The grade of 5F counted five times an F for a single work product grade and, by sure and certain design, devastatingly impacted each overall class grade.

In this measurement constellation, an average student's final grade would be "F." Maybe some pride in that as a grade from the middle of the range?

By the end of the class I anticipated such an average grade at best.

And yet, he passed me!

Pushing my luck, a common action, I asked him how I could have earned a passing (above the average F) grade in his class, given his measurement system.

He scowled and said he just didn't want me to take his class again.

TIME STATUES

Situation Reversed

Not many years later I was the instructor doing the grading. I took it seriously, even in classes numbering more than 300 students. In such large groups, I could not know each person as I always do now in smaller seminars. I could and did share item analyses with the class. I dropped any exam question that everybody missed from grading scores as likely due to my own lapse in teaching clarity. I had students at the very beginning predict their final grade. They usually made the prediction a self-fulfilling prophecy.

Only twice in more than five decades of teaching did any student ask me to give them a higher grade than they had earned.

The first was an international undergraduate student from Andorra. He wanted his average "C" grade raised to an "A" and wondered how much money he needed to give me for that. I knew that Andorra was a tiny country snuggled in mountains between France and Spain, a place I always wanted to visit. Andorra was also known for smuggling between its neighboring countries. Taking this into account, I patiently explained that grade bribery was unethical in my country. So: No way. He sadly let me know his family ran Andorra, or so he said. As he walked away, I crossed Andorra off my tourist list.

The second was another international student, this one from Israel. He was a high-ranking Army officer there, recruited to complete his doctoral degree with us by our school's president. That very president had sent him to me, saying it was my decision whether his test grade should be raised. Turned out that he had missed a passing grade on his final exam by only one question. His request was simple: raise his score by one question. He had to return to his country in a month and needed the favor. The president had already let me know that a retest on a parallel exam was an option but his preference was that I just approve the upgrade. Instead I said I would get him a tutor to prepare for the retest but I would not give him a grade he hadn't earned. I pointed out that raising his prior score by just one question was likely not much of a challenge for somebody of his experience. He turned and walked away quickly. Went back to the president and complained. Went to the Board of Directors and complained. When to his ambassador and complained. When none of this worked for him, he came back for another meeting. Now he was quite friendly. He was ready to work with the tutor and retake the test. I asked him why such a change in his attitude? He smiled and said that he respected my decision and integrity in making it. Always had. He just felt he would be remiss if he had not explored all the other alternatives. Now he knew that he was on the only best path. He did pass the retest. I was pleased to see him leave.

The Generational Secret of Clarkson College

It was the Spring of 1959 in Potsdam. The snow was almost gone.

The school semester still had some months to go until the end of my first undergraduate year in this remote Engineering College.

Classes were begun six mornings a week. Dodging man-size Damocles style icicles on the way to class was the usual gauntlet. Hard to breathe in this alien world of low temperature, ones found throughout the nine months of school. The slippery ice along the way for those morning trips was soon countered by shoes with massive treads at bottom, ones insensitively called "Guinea Ground Grabbers."

Why was I here?

I had been one of a few high school seniors that had won a New York

TIME STATUES

State scholarship through high scores on a competitive written exam. There was a catch. It had to be a college in New York State.

Gone were my dreams of going to a university in the brand new state of Hawaii. Climate paradise for anybody growing up in Buffalo. My parents thought of the University of Hawaii as only teaching basket weaving and hula dancing. I had done research and knew better. My Hawaii plan had no backers though (later to be ruined by public awareness from the TV show *Hawaii 50*). Now the scholarship bound me to New York. So where there?

At 17 my career plans were more or less to actualize the best of science fiction. Learn the true nature of the cosmos. For this I chose to be a Physics major.

By chance I met a graduate of Clarkson College. He said he had loved it there. And it was a great place to study the mysteries of Physics.

Never mind the cold climate and the all-male student population (shaving and bathing in the absence of females was sporadic). He thought that if I had survived 17 years in Buffalo weather, I could survive anywhere.

Finally, he shared the generational Clarkson secret.

"Don't tell them unless they can't figure it out for themselves" he said. *"Give them some time"* he said. So I was sworn to temporary secrecy. And went to Clarkson. Well, the state was paying for it, most of it, so I gave it a try.

Took me awhile to realize that no cosmology or actualized fiction would be taught there. Instead it seemed to be training us as electricians and plumbers. *"Workmen that needed not to be ashamed."*

Also, not yet having mastered mathematics, or even having been casually introduced, I was in a strange country without knowing the required language. My only high grades were in "Liberal Studies" classes consisting of everything not Engineering or Physics. A message there.

I did enjoy doing a weekly satirical radio show on WNTC called **"Earaches."**

My opening theme was Bo Diddley's *"Great Grandfather,"* followed by *"My name is Morgan. Yours I don't need."* Between early rock & roll music breaks were my Stan Freberg style satire pieces and taped interviews, usually done in the spacious but busy dormitory restroom for the echo effect, barring flushes.

The satire pieces got me kicked off the air a few times. I had liked to have fun with our funding sponsor, Winston Cigarettes. Each time that happened I talked myself into being back on the air. So my listener base grew, eventually reaching near 100% of the students for that hour.

My favorite interview was with the Mayor of Potsdam who was being charged with gross embezzlement by a grand jury. He argued that as Mayor he was responsible for a million-dollar operation, so that fact alone should mean he had better not be distracted by such charges. There was still a lot of money left. He refused to resign. As I recall, he finished his term still not in jail.

I was having fun in this little carrier current radio station, rooms sound-insulated with empty egg cartons on the walls.

The show eventually lasted the two years I was at Clarkson.

Although in year two I moved from all Rock & Roll breaks to playing Hawaiian Music while urging every listener to move to that warmer climate. Vic Dawley, in the class a year behind me, continued this good work after I left.

Future Roomies

I would leave after my second year at Clarkson, to transfer to Michigan State University (MSU) and a better choice of major: Psychology. Ironically, it was there that I finally learned math and how to use it. Too late for Clarkson. At MSU, even though I was a junior there, all students in their first year, transfer or not, were required to spend that year in a dormitory. I got the one for administration-defined misfits: foreign students, returning vets, transfers, discipline problems. A truly creative mix. Here I will just include a nod to my roommates in *that* dorm, Bryan Hall.

The first was Gilbert Moore, a poet from Montreal. He realized by the close of the first term there that his poetic future was somewhat ignored in Michigan. He needed to be back in Montreal.

Without a roommate, I began the second term gifted with a late-entering freshman, a local and very young Alan "Mike" Mikesell. Mike's father promised that if his grades for that beginning term were all As he would be gifted with a car. A gift for the rest of us on our dorm floor too, we realized. We needed a sure thing. I had Mike enroll in the least challenging football players courses: Golf, Exercise, and "Ice Cream." The last class provided complete information on the history, manufacture, sales, and variety of the dessert. Mike got his As. But not the car. His father was not impressed with Mike's courses. Golf? *Ice Cream*? Mike got sent home, hopefully to try again eventually.

My third and last MSU roommate was Arthur David Otterbridge Hodgson. He was without a roommate too and we consolidated by moving into the same room before MSU could choose for us. Arthur had no roommate because he was not the white his original roommate had been.

The original roomie's mother would have none of that and yanked her son out of the dorm. Arthur was a soccer player and head of the Campus United Nations. From Bermuda, it was his ambition to go back there when he graduated and lead his country to independence from England. Looking like a young, athletic Malcom X, I believed him. He had two strategies for this:

1. Sign up to give a speech at the real United Nations in New York. Any citizen of a member country can do this, but the wait is years. For Arthur, he had it timed for graduation.

2. Apply for a Rhodes graduate award in his major of Economics. This would involve an apprenticeship with the head of state of a developing country followed by a more settled democracy in Europe.

As to the first, his timing was on target. As a member of his minority political party in Bermuda, their party leaders, faced with the reality of his speaking for them at the UN, appointed him forthwith as their representative on the (British) Governor's Council. Despite this prestigious and very visible role, he drove a cab during the day, dressing down in T-shirt and jeans. He wore the same clothes to the governing Council, which delighted the younger generation. Moreso when he dressed up in suit and tie for his sister's wedding to make his values clear. Arthur was a fine orator and did a great speech advocating freedom from colonial status. As to the second, his Rhodes fellowship came through. He would wind it up studying economics in Scandinavia. First though he would be off to study with Fidel Castro, the new head of an independent Cuba. Castro was too busy it turned out, shunting Arthur off to Cuba's Finance Minister, Che Guevera. Arthur eventually went back to Bermuda and did his best to achieve independence. That hasn't happened yet—even in this century—despite his best efforts, though some more autonomy has been established. Arthur is listed in various history books as *"Arthur Hodgson is a former Cabinet minister, Rhodes Scholar and graduate of Oxford University in England, where he studied philosophy, politics and economics."* Today he is a retired judge in his home country. Bermuda remains the oldest British colony with Queen Elizabeth still the head of state. Bermuda has great beaches.

Before all of this though we both had one more year, outside the dorm at last, to graduate. Having become friends we rented a place together.

Back to Clarkson in late 1958

Still, when 1959 was getting closer, I wondered: should I announce the secret?

First this: When I had left for Clarkson in the Fall of 1958, I was a tall skeletal teenager weighing 145 pounds. The food at the college was terrible but the cold weather and unrelenting pace made us ravenous for it.

Sure we found pennies and hair in the food. The "mystery meat" remained a mystery. The cook's dog helped lick the used plates clean for her. Despite all this I arrived home for Thanksgiving heavier by forty pounds of muscle now weighing in at 185. My mother couldn't believe it. Or didn't want to.

Let's explore this for a minute.

Food in the Fireplace

My mother was one of fourteen children.

Five of her nine brothers became medical doctors. Her brother Sidney (with help from Ted Williams) was a founder of Boston's Dana Farber Clinic. There his patients were children fighting leukemia, a death sentence in those days. Every night he tucked each one of his child guests into bed, doing all he could think of to have them survive another day. He invented the first drug treatment for this, becoming the "Father of Chemotherapy."

Another brother, Harold, became the President of his own insurance company. The eldest son, Marvin, became a philosophy professor, bringing the European phenomenologists to our country just in time to avoid being gassed to death by the Nazis.

My favorite, Dan, was an adventurer, successful at enjoying life fully.

How did Simon Farber, the immigrant stevedore father of these 14 children, get so many sons through school? He worked multiple jobs as long as he could and, as can happen in a large family, the older children helped the younger ones.

This included my mother, Evelyn, who always sent home as much of her salary as possible until she married at the advanced age for the day of 30.

What career paths for her and her four sisters? Or any women living a century ago? Evelyn, wanted very much to be a doctor too. But she had been born in 1908 and women in her day had only a few career paths other than "housewife." These alternatives usually were nursing or teaching. Evelyn got her teaching credential and continued through graduate work in Microbiology.

But her family needed her help, so she began decades of work as a teacher. At this she was successful, even teaching a high school Microbiology class. She was so loved by her students that, for several years in a row, their yearbook was dedicated to her. Then she retired.

Microbiology was as close as she ever formally got to being a medical doctor. Still, retired, she now had time at home to increase her informal medical practice without a license.

Her husband and two sons were the hostage patients. Other than that, her new post-retirement career mission was to be a great cook. Food was soon integrated into her realm of home medical practice, allowing what she considered to be healthy or restorative components to every meal. Sadly, by her age she had been deprived of substantial taste bud competence. Her food then tasted awful. Who knew what she had added in any given meal? She was a great fan of laxatives for one thing.

My father worked hard and needed sustenance. He too came from a large family, his of nine children. He ate fast. He ate anything. He ate whatever we did not. This made him her star patient when it came to the culinary practice.

Not so for my brother, though it may have helped him survive the streets during his Haight-Ashbury years.

As for me, I continued as a skeletal teenager, surviving on TV dinners and meals at the homes of friends.

I also used every opportunity to make my own meals from whatever was available. Complete feasts that way would be tomato soup and grilled cheese, a thinly sliced chip steak on a slice of toast, or the World War II specialty understood as *"Shit on a Shingle"* (ham and peas on a slice of toast).

When we ran out of hot dogs, I learned that a hot dog roll filled with relish, onion, coleslaw, mustard, and ketchup tasted just fine without the dog.

Summer trips to Canada taught me that fries go fine with vinegar (try it) if you have no ketchup. The beverage of choice was tap water or Vernors Ginger Ale.

In later years I learned to make a few special dishes like leg of lamb slow cooked with green maraschino cherries or fried bananas with lemon sauce. Or omelets purple with grape juice.

When cooking for my two daughters though, they preferred to each do their own cooking. Maybe it was the green food coloring I added to scrambled eggs or most other things I served. I did green eggs and ham before Dr. Seuss made it known.

My mother *was* good at making deserts though. They were delicious and a staple.

So our nutrition was impaired as well. Years later I was invited to a home office party in San Francisco. My charge was to bring "green food." I brought green ice cream and green treats from the "Citizen Cake" store. Childhood strikes deep.

The grandchildren felt much the same as my brother and I about their grandmother's cooking. On holidays we would all gather at the home of my parents. Grandchildren waited until Evelyn had stepped out of the room to dump their plates of food in the fireplace, covering it with ashes. Eventually, at one holiday family gathering years into this clean plate technique, my father started a long overdue cleaning of the fireplace. As he worked through the years of holiday meals past, he was good natured about it all. Finally finished, he stood and announced to us: *"That was like an archeological dig!"*

So Clarkson food was a step up. Not a great step. But up. Back to the story of Clarkson College, later renamed as Clarkson University. Maybe photos might help. These are on the next page.

**Photo A. A typical dormitory shot.
Hygiene was sparse in all male dorms.**

An earlier roommate of mine was from Japan. Hirofumi Matsusaki. Japanese are tightly packed on an island country. They tolerate this by daily bathing and devoted cleanliness. Not so in our dormitory. For me, growing up poor, the once-a-week bath was on Saturday night; so-called sponge baths with a wet washcloth were done other days. Hirofumi and I definitely influenced each other. For me, though it didn't take until a year or two later, I eventually arrived at a devoted daily bathing regime. Dating maybe had something to do with this. But no women to impress, or not repulse, in the Clarkson dorm. Hirofumi for his part did not return after the first Thanksgiving break. Looking him up on the internet in this more current century, I found him to be celebrated in Japan as an inventive chemical engineer successful with fragrance products. Maybe I had a little something to do with that career choice.

My substitute roommate that first year was George Zabriskie or "Zips." He was a great fan of Chet Atkins who I heard nonstop in our room for the rest of the year. Zips plastered the bulletin board over his dorm bed with Playboy Playmate pictures. We had a desk in the middle of the small dorm room, between the separate beds, so when we studied we faced each other from our respective sides. This gave me a scenic view of his Playmate photos.

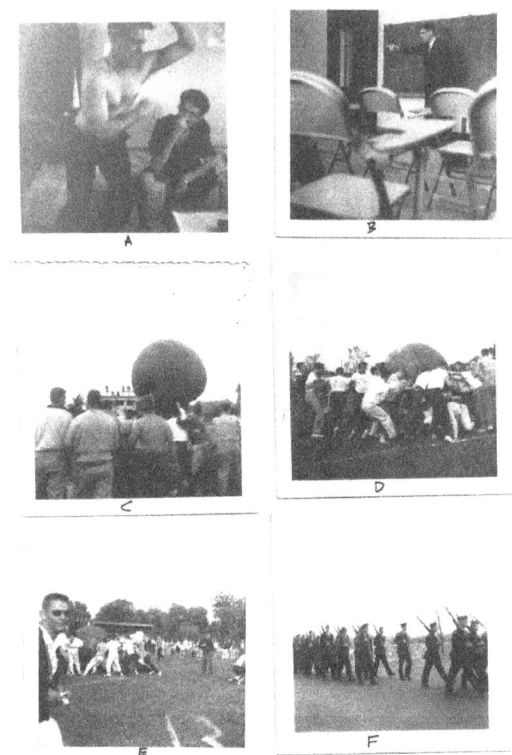

To fill my own Bulletin Board, I posted a large very colorful chart my mother had sent me called *"the infant stool cycle."* Zips found this hard to view, despite the Chet Atkins perpetual soundtrack. Periodically he would lean back and throw himself at an angle so he could look at his own Bulletin Board. Zips became a good friend. I missed him when he didn't return for the second Clarkson year.

About 40% of the rest of our class weren't back then either.

That year, I had the best Clarkson dorm roommate: Douglas Griffin, seen in Photo <u>A</u> sitting and holding his nose while our neighbor from the next room shared armpit fragrance in his typical gesture of sharing.

I'm still in touch with Doug, even though I was one of those not returning in year three. Doug went the full distance, got his degree, and did a career with IBM.

(I found a hole in the middle of my dorm mattress but, rebuffed for a better one, got used to it. I joked with Doug that the hole was for easing my sexual tensions though it was far too small. When his father came to visit, he asked to see my famous mattress hole. Left me impressed by the great relationship he had with his Dad.)

Most in the dorm were learning to be engineers. Different subspecialties could be competitive. For example, I announced on my show the rumor that the urinals were all about to be raised a few inches so as to keep the double Es (electrical engineers) on their toes. Apparently they were deemed to be shorter.

The dorm had many characters, too many to expand on here. The largest among us, for example, was Karl Trout who naturally was nicknamed "Guppy." Required to post our own shortened nickname on our room door, a neighbor, Spargo, posted "Sir."

The last I will recall here was Lynn Pagliarro (not sure of spelling). He had been dating a girl named Maureen whenever he went home for breaks. During one Visitors Day, Maureen's parents came by to have a look at (and judge) their daughter's new boyfriend. In this way I got to guide a very stern looking Ronald Reagan and wife to Lynn's room. Not sure how it all worked out. Even Death Valley might have smelled better for Reagan than our own swell dormitory home.

Photo B. Clarkson College faculty were, if nothing else, undeterred by the bone chilling cold.

A hardy lot, many had arrived from equally chilly or desolate places elsewhere on the globe. This is a photo of our Economics Professor. From Switzerland, he spritzed substantially and with impressive range, when he lectured. The students were huddling in the last rows of the classroom, one with an umbrella as I recall, but the lecturer continued on oblivious.

Photos C, D, E. The death of hazing: Clarkson's g enerational secret emerges.

The hazing of freshmen by Sophomores was continuing month after month with no end in sight. Freshmen could be ordered to streak without clothes from one dormitory building to another. This was a short run but at 40 degrees below zero risked pneumonia, certainly some respiratory damage. Freshmen could have their heads shaved for disobedience. In a good day, they would at least be stopped routinely and harassed. We got the freshman to walk in groups of five or six to or from class. It felt more like High School than College.

The few law enforcement individuals were nowhere to be found once summer ended. Rumor had it that they were "Snowbirds" migrating to warmer Florida to leave the snow behind. So a lawless place with little recourse.

Except for the one that needed in time to be realized. A secret passed on through the generations. I knew what it was. Should I announce it on my weekly one-hour radio show? Was the time right? Why not? This had gone on long enough.

TIME STATUES

On my next show:

"Have you ever noticed that the sophomores returning this year are a lot fewer than last year? They are down to less than 300 now. This means the freshmen class at more than 500 outnumbers them. So why is hazing continuing so long? Let it fill the whole year? Notice that no stop date has ever been given by the College? Here is the Clarkson secret passed on down through generations of hazing. **It stops when the freshmen SAY it's over***! That's all it takes. We just declare it done and it's done. Then the College gives us a little weekend ceremony to end it traditionally. How about it? Is it done?"*

Back at the dorm signs saying HAZING IS OVER were everywhere. So it ended then and there.

Except for that College ceremony promised for the next weekend to come. Fine for the freshmen to declare hazing over. For the sophomores a more vivid experience was called for to make their new situation clear and final. A ceremony was designed for exactly that.

The sophomore 300 lined up on one end of the football field and the freshman 500 on the other end. In the middle was a huge canvas ball. Officially the rules were to push the ball into the opposing goal posts. But with no referees to be seen that day (true to the Potsdam and College spirit of the times), 800 males met in the middle, more or less where the ball was, and conflict ensued. This blew off steam, followed by a more relaxed campus situation. Some bruises and bandages but no fatalities (a gentler time). They all moved on.

This is what photographs C-E captured.

In my second year I tipped off the freshmen after just one week of hazing. They organized quickly. Hazing ended the second week, a

Clarkson record.

Some of my classmates were not happy about this. They had looked forward to getting even with their oppressors from last year by taking it out on the new students this year. Way to pass on sadism over generations, prophetic of Eduardo Duran's intergenerational trauma insights so many decades later.

Well, I was against hazing then and I am against it now. Phil Zimbardo has shown how bad this inequity can get. On the other hand …

When and *How* the hazing stopped was a rite of passage for Clarkson students. They gained the maturity of learning their own power to make change, to protect themselves by group action when no adult force was there to do it for them. Sure enough, those passing through this ritual seemed to mature substantially. More self-sufficient, more independent critical thinkers. Less likely to succumb to dysfunctional authority. Very useful for citizens in our challenging world of today.

Photo F. Our Army ROTC marching stroll every Thursday.

We were scheduled for the Army ROTC training our first two years, though an equal time of Physical Education (PE) could be substituted. Out of curiosity I stayed with ROTC. Turned out a very Clarkson/Potsdam approach to the Army. The commanding officer was Colonel Clarence Campbell. He later ran the pro hockey league, a big sport in snow country. But back in the late 1950s, the Colonel was more of a front lines kind of leader. He made sure we knew how to shoot, how to do the manual of arms hefting the surplus M-1s we carried.

As to precision marching, he had disdain for that. Didn't think it would keep us alive in a shooting situation. So we marched as in coming back from the Front. When most are not in step, synchrony disappears. See photo F. Individuation very much in literal step with the Clarkson/Potsdam (CP: opposite of PC) spirit. I marched, more or less, the first year. The second year I drew on my High School newspaper editor experience and offered to be the photographer and press liaison. The Colonel agreed. A very good man, that Campbell. The second year no more marching with M1s every Thursday. I just hefted my camera.

A few years later, in the time of impending draft, I was in the USAF Officer Training or OTS. They assumed my Potsdam marching experience with ROTC was a plus. I did prove true to my Clarkson CP experience, marching at shifting cadences and directions when it intuitively suited my legs. Too boring for them to conform indefinitely to what everybody else was doing. Did not go over well though.

I did eventually get to Hawaii where I did my postdoc internship.

After leaving Potsdam, it still had taken me six years to get there.

Chapter 6. The Time Zone Defense

"A girl must marry for love, and keep on marrying until she finds it."
— Zsa Zsa Gabor

A married woman, approaching her mid 30s, was referred to me by her physicians.

A series of tests had found no apparent somatic reason for her poor appetite and stomach aches. She had moved to sunny San Diego from an overcast London 17 years before.

I asked her to describe her typical day and diet. She drank only a six-pack of Pepsi in the morning, followed by two packs of cigarettes by 2 pm in the afternoon.

TIME STATUES

It was tempting to have stopped right there, upset stomach explained. I kept going, asking her when she ate real meals. She got hungry twice a day, but never when anyone else did.

Using time-zone calculations, it seemed she was still stuck on her original London time zone when it came to the two daily meals she had enjoyed when there.

I told her she was still on London time. Jet lag should not last 17 years.

Unconsciously, she was making an existential choice to be in a safe familiar place. One far removed, since her California marriage had turned out to include severe continuing problems.

We agreed on an intervention. In the following months she gave up Pepsi and smoking (diagnosed emphysema made the latter mandatory).

But her husband continued to give her his second-hand smoke, even at the risk of her life.

She said that he was still angry about her affairs at her bartender job (*"I get asked for sex a hundred times a week and I usually turn 99 of them down,"* she argued). The husband refused to join us in the counseling.

Based on many sessions, she realized that marriage problems were the main source of her escalating trauma. Consequently, she decided on a more fundamental choice: she needed not to be married to her present husband.

Counseling now was to assist her through her divorce.

On the day this divorce was final, she at once became hungry three times a day at regular hours for her time zone of residence. She now lived on San Diego time.

Our follow-up sessions taught us both that a finished divorce may not guarantee a finish to a bad relationship. Her husband continued to control her decisions, blocked new friendships, and any other paths to safety and happiness without him.

Realizing she was allowing this, she found her inner strength to make her own choices and eventually moved on successfully.

Her stomach issues now left completely (Morgan 2004b).

Chapter 7. The Invisible MMPI

Psychological tests are used to describe, predict, and communicate human behavior. Their non-psychology pre-history includes efforts of dubious validity albeit fair reliability (repeatable results). These read head bumps as in phrenology, posterior topography as in rumpology*, and character interpretation associated with breast analysis as in the classic 450-page book BISBA (Burr, 1965). Of more scientifically credible tests in the era of psychology, the MMPI stood tall.

New Zealand Psychologist Charles Wrigley, was on the verge of a great discovery.

The United States Peace Corps was in its earliest years and he had access to the MMPI data from all the country's trainees. He had all but confirmed the patterns that predicted successful completion of training and their success in the field.

This was no mean feat given the quality of the main frame computers of the day. Contemporary psychologists, students and faculty, now have easy individual access to PCs, I-Phones, I-Pods, I-Pads, and even the predicted multi-faceted Maxi-Pad. Wrigley had primitive equipment and yet, he needed only one more validation run to confirm the success patterns he had been charged with discovering.

Peace Corps in its first decade was very scrupulous in both training and the avoidance of error. They wanted no international incidents from poorly trained or poorly selected volunteers.

—

* "Rumpology or bottom reading is a pseudoscience akin to physiognomy, performed by examining crevices, dimples, warts, moles and folds of a person's buttocks in much the same way a chirologist would read the palm of the hand. The term rumpology is a neologism. The American (late) astrologer Jackie Stallone (Sylvester Stallone's mother) claims that rumpology is known to have been practiced in ancient times by the Babylonians, the Indians, and the Ancient Greeks and Romans, although she provides no evidence for this claim. Stallone has been largely responsible for the supposed "revival" of rumpology in modern times. Rumpologists have a variety of theories as to the meaning of different posterior characteristics. According to Stallone, the left and right buttocks reveal a person's past and future, respectively, although she has also commented that "The crack of your behind corresponds to the division of the two hemispheres of the brain." According to blind German clairvoyant and rumpologist Ulf Beck, an "apple-shaped, muscular bottom indicates someone who is charismatic, dynamic, very confident and often creative. A person who enjoys life. A pear-shaped bottom suggests someone very steadfast, patient and down-to-earth. The British rumpologist Sam Amos claims that "A round bottom indicates the person is open, happy and optimistic in life. However, a flat bottom suggests the person is rather vain and is negative and sad." Rumpology can be performed either by sight, touch or by using buttock prints. In addition to live readings, Jackie Stallone will perform buttock readings using e-mailed digital photographs, and has claimed to predict the outcome of Presidential elections and Oscar awards by reading the

bottoms of her two pet Doberman Pinschers. Ulf Buck claims he can read people's futures by feeling their naked buttocks." https://en.wikipedia.org/wiki/Rumpology and http://www.jacquelinestallone.com/rumps.html

So the trainees did not become Peace Corps Volunteers (PCVs) to disperse around the globe for a 2-year commitment until they had trained for 3 months in the US and had been approved by the selection team.

In Hawaii, those training for Micronesia placements underwent 3 months in the undeveloped rugged island of Molokai, where they were trained by experts from the islands they were slated to go to, and evaluated for suitability to go at all by a team of psychologists.

The leader of this team was called a Field Selection Officer (FSO) and ours was a young John Exner, still working on his first Rorschach book. The FSO supervised Field Assessment Officers (FAOs) who each focused on a group of about 30 trainees going to a specific island country.

I was a post-doctoral intern at Hawaii State Hospital from which Exner had recruited all of the psychology staff for part-time FAO duty. In my case that meant flying in Wednesday night, working with my 30 trainees all day Thursday, and flying home Thursday night. John also had two psychiatrists on hand for referrals.

One of these was very competent and helped immensely; the other took to shining flashlights in tents at night to make sure people were sleeping with the appropriate partners (he did not last long).

John was very relaxed in his structure: our mission was to identify, by any means necessary, those who should go and those who should be "de-selected" and sent back to their home. There was a review of each trainee at the midpoint and the end of the 3 months.

I chose to spend my Thursday in Molokai meeting with three groups of 10 each; each group met with me for 90 minutes and reviewed their weekly progress. I did a modified Social Distance test ("Name up to 5 trainees you would like to serve with and up to 5 you would not like to serve with") the outcomes of which were shared and discussed in the groups.

In the end all but three of my 30 went to their destination in Ponape as PCVs.

One was so hyper-motivated that she washed out quickly. The women in her group complained that she was wearing a bathing suit in their shower and urged her to not be so shy; the following week the same women complained that she would no longer wear any clothes at any time. A very nice but very gullible young woman, the fishing trainers from Ponape were telling her to eat the still live fish off her spear and otherwise embarrassing her. She was too gullible to survive and, sadly, was "de-selected."

The second casualty was a woman in her mid-twenties who had a personal mission to have sex with every male trainee and every male Ponape trainer. The married women were unhappy and George, the psychiatrist with the flashlight, could not keep up.

As an exercise, I asked her to not sleep with anybody for one week to see if it could be done. The following Thursday, on my arrival, her bags were already packed. "I tried but I couldn't stop," she said. Declining to return to her hometown, she let Peace Corps fly her to Honolulu where she took on a job at a local pub, ultimately visited often by her many (male) friends from the Molokai project.

The third and last "de-selectee" was the only one of the three I wanted to send to the Peace Corps project.

Jamie was a young man of 19. He had bonded easily with some healers from the island he was slated to work in. Each day he would sit for hours in meditation. The Ponape healers considered him "an old soul."

But when Exner saw Jamie's Full Field Check (FBI review of his life up to that point) he was concerned that Jamie had been arrested in a protest march. Now many of us had participated in such events but Exner worried that the trainee would try to protest while a PCV in another culture and might be beheaded.

So Exner had the competent psychiatrist give Jamie a Rorschach. The results were normal except for what Exner noted as the many "flame responses" in the lad's stories and this was interpreted as possibly suppressed rage. I interpreted this as an artifact of being given a Rorschach at night next to a campfire. Exner shrugged and said "Maybe- but we are taking no chances." Jamie was given a chance to do training all over again but he went home instead and eventually became a distinguished television celebrity.

And, oh yes, the abbreviated Peace Corps MMPI was presented to every trainee on day one. Following this, the profiles, once viewed by us, were sent to Wrigley for analysis.

At our level at first we saw no pattern other than a consistent "fake good" score which was understandable given the stress trainees were under to present their best face.

But Charles Wrigley had found the MMPI patterns that would revolutionize the prediction of success in nearly any country or culture.

Based on the sheer volume of data he was ready to share his findings. Until an event beyond his control took charge.

In Washington, the MMPI had been misused as a screening test for federal employment. A young woman not receiving her applied for secretarial job went to the press, pointing out that one of the items asked her to rate her sexual satisfaction. There was a congressional inquiry. In response the government stopped using MMPI for standard screening.

The head of Peace Corps went even further: "We never use MMPI" he said. Now, when somebody in high authority says something untrue, those working for him are expected to make it true. Wrigley's data was shredded and he was ordered to maintain a lifelong silence about his discoveries.

I had taken a class from Professor Wrigley at Michigan State University before his Washington adventure and we had stayed in touch. I was saddened by his loss, and of course the loss for all of us. Except for what we had finally found on Molokai.

Whenever a Trainee refused to take that MMPI on day one, they were still allowed to continue. This was confidential and during the training none of the trainers knew which ones had declined the test. Yet when it was all done, we found that those who had declined to take the MMPI *always* failed to successfully complete training.

We named this predictor the *Invisible MMPI*.

Chapter 8. Lifespan of a Cult

"Oh what a tangled web they weave, when first they practice to deceive. Yet now the web's swept out of sight: they practiced till they got it right."
— Sir Walter Scott updated. (Morgan 2007)

"Rollo May often said that both optimism and pessimism were classic mistakes and that only hope made sense. For example, the optimists see the glass as half full and the pessimists see the same glass as half empty. When it comes to the world today, it may be more realistic and still hopeful to see our glass as 10% full."
(Morgan, 2012)

Werner said in a voice so soft only those of us in the first row could hear it:
"Do NOT open your eyes yet. That could be dangerous!"

Jay dreamed of killing Werner Erhard. This upset him no end.

It was the Spring of 1973. Jay, a large man in his thirties, had never hurt anybody. Fresh from his 10-year stay as a chronic mental patient in another state's mental hospital, he had come to San Francisco for a new start. A gentle man, he was overwhelmingly anxious around others, easily feeling hemmed in.

I met Jay when, as a new psychologist, I was observing how intake interviews were done at a San Francisco Mental Health Center devoted to "special" problems for clients not normally served by the regular agencies: typically criminal justice, sexual life style, and drug-related issues. There were three of us in a small interview room and Jay finally asked if one of us would leave. I said "of course" and left, following which Jay insisted I be his therapist.

In our first session, Jay shared that he had come to San Francisco hoping to find an extended family. In this he had succeeded, joining a commune of congenial people.

But one day they participated in an up-and-coming human potentials weekend workshop called "EST" led by a young charismatic former encyclopedia salesman named Werner Erhard. Jay was not allowed to go with them as EST excluded former mental patients, reportedly for liability reasons. When Jay's communal family returned, they had changed. They dropped their jobs and responsibilities to join Werner's "movement," along with 500 other San Franciscans who had taken EST. To Jay they seemed hypnotized or medicated. Worse, they began to ignore and even to shun Jay as somebody who just didn't have the "it" that the EST experience grads thought they had acquired. They asked Jay to find another place to live.

He had come to therapy for help in finding a new home but what he really wanted was to somehow protect and reclaim his former communal pre-EST family. He had dreams of killing this Werner, this "master hypnotist," and saw this desire of his as a scary urge to rid the world of a budding cancerous cult, possibly in time to save his friends. This was before the laws for mandatory reporting of possible harm from the client to self or others now found in many countries, but it was clear I needed to do some risk assessment.

Jay had come in voluntarily, had no history of violence, and was appalled at the idea of murdering anybody for any reason. I decided I would first help him ventilate his anger safely in counseling, find a new location to live, and take his "Shadow" on myself: I therefore promised to investigate Werner and report back to him, but only if he in turn would promise to focus solely on his own progress, abandoning any intention to harm Werner or anybody else. He agreed to this therapeutic contract with relief.

By the second session he had found a room at the Jack Tar Hotel just within walking distance from our clinic. Soon Jay was volunteering at a charity he cared about and, by the end of the year, he had forgotten Werner and EST. He was now a paid part-time employee at his charity setting. In fact, he spent the rest of his awake time having so much fun (chess in the park, Tai Chi at sunrise) that at times I envied his lifestyle. Finally, after a few months of counseling, he had an opportunity to move into a collective setting with new non-EST roommates. Yet he hesitated to do so, still mildly intimidated by fear of failure in this transition.

Eventually it occurred to me to point out that the name of his hotel home, Jack Tar, spelled backwards sounded like "Rat Cage." This seemed to be a catalyst for Jay, who was a great believer in the symbolic power of words. The next day he made the jump to new quarters with success. His dreams of Werner were gone and, based on a follow-up a year later, never came back, even after I had given him, as promised, my report. Now, as to that report.

I was a dean at the birth of the San Francisco campus of psychology's first free-standing professional school, the California School of

Professional Psychology. There I taught an advanced seminar for students finishing their doctorate in community/clinical psychology.

Meeting one night each week, we would invite a guest speaker. In the beginning Fall trimester, these were mostly famous psychotherapists. My students soon learned to ask them my rude question: *"How do you know you are successful?"*

(Years before outcome-based accreditation or "evidence-based" therapy; i.e. the good old days).

Some guest dignitaries answered this with grace, a few even had decent client follow-up procedures, but most were affronted. These invoked the Bad Restaurant defense:

"My patients never came back"

or the Holiday Season defense:

"They send me Christmas Cards every year."

Once the Spring trimester began, my class seemed more interested in the self-help and human potentials field. Transpersonal and Humanistic Psychology was taking off as a Third Force in psychology. Many wise and valuable practitioners in this genre joined our seminar, some even to go on as part-time faculty.

One week, by student request, I agreed to schedule a moderately successful human potentials salesman named Alexander. He was a highly confident individual, even to the verge of bombastic. His presentation was of value, not so much in what he said, but in the opportunity we had to understand the presenter and his process with psychological clarity. As we approached the break time I went to get our speaker a cup of coffee, as I had done each week for guest speakers.

On my re-entry into the room, a student asked the Question:

"How do you know you're successful, Mr. Alexander?"

He answered: *"By the immediate result!"* and, whirling in my direction, he pointed at me: *"I willed that man to bring me a cup of coffee!"*

I never liked coffee much and still don't but at that moment I drank his, saying

"And apparently you willed me to drink it."

After the class was through laughing, Alexander good naturedly said he would ask his newly famous former student, Werner Erhard, to join us at a future seminar meeting. He said Werner was more a match for us than he was. He enthused: *"Young and full of energy, Werner has discovered all the best hard sales techniques you can find in Zen Buddhism."*

It was more than a month before Werner sat in my classroom. First he hired one of our graduate students as an assistant at his workshops. Then, fully informed about us, he came in for a preliminary interview. He wanted to teach a class at our school. Up to that point, his young movement had only accomplished academic exposure at Sonoma State University, and Werner wanted to claim us as well.

Well, we had a process including an interview with a committee of three faculty, three students, and me. Werner showed up without his usual entourage of supporters who normally would "testify" on his behalf. He appeared alone and in shirt sleeves but with unusual contact lenses designed to add sparkle to his otherwise ordinary blue eyes.

With quiet confidence, Werner shared how positive an experience his class at Sonoma had been for all but saying that since Sonoma State was also *"known for teaching levitation,"* he wanted the added experience and prestige of a psychology school (this was amazing to us as we were in the first year of a then not yet accredited graduate school). Any students enrolled in his course, faculty too if they wished to come, could participate in EST training for free for one weekend, spending the rest of their in-class time on campus to discuss the training. Werner would charge the school nothing to teach the course. Some faculty thought this overpriced.

I too thought his price was far too expensive but, to my surprise and bemusement, the majority of the screening committee wanted him to come teach the class. One of the faculty, Murray Tondow, had already agreed with Werner to do some personality testing of EST participants before and after their weekend training. At least one of the students said he had voted yes because he wanted to see me *"sell this to Nick Cummings,"* our President. (It wasn't difficult: free was the correct price for Nick, and our San Francisco campus had much hard-fought autonomy at the time.) The screening committee dissenters, those in the losing minority, were appalled.

I met privately with Werner, and told him that before I approved this recommendation, I wanted him to come to my seminar and do a demonstration. He of course already knew of the notorious seminar from Alexander but readily agreed.

By now I had made my pledge to Jay and I saw this as an opportunity to keep my word. Werner said his mission was to bring EST training to the international world and to expand his EST community exponentially. He insisted his assertive form of distorted existentialism could transform humanity, putting both responsibility and fresh interpersonal tools in the hands of EST's graduates. I told Werner that I saw him more as the charismatic leader in a community cult phenomenon much like Father Divine or Daddy Grace (a few years too soon for Jim Jones) rather than a human potentials facilitator. With an estimated 500 San Franciscans already following him devotedly at the expense of family and career, I was curious as to how he generated such reckless loyalty. He thanked me for my candor and agreed to come to my class.

The night of his appearance, my seminar had to move to a room that could accommodate the more than a hundred additional members of our community, students/staff/faculty, who wanted to sit in and watch. Werner again arrived in shirt sleeves, a short energetic man with light splashing from his special contact lenses. He gave a brief description of the training and his philosophy of unilateral responsibility and power, there for the taking, just a workshop away. He was also asked about the workshop finale in which several hundred participants learned to diagnose at a distance for somebody they had never met. This was the "magic" of human potentials promised by EST, so of course the audience pressed Werner to give a brief illustration of some sample of magic that psychologists could use to help others. After a few seconds' thought he agreed, saying: ***"The power to abolish headaches should be helpful. This will be done with a volunteer. Who here has a headache?"***

Having asked the question, he sat back on the table behind him and waited expectantly, confidently, for a volunteer with a headache. He sat looking at more than a hundred people as though he had hours of patience, no rush. I had never seen one person bully an entire group before, much less do so quietly.

The pressure seemed to build for minutes. But in fact it was probably less than 60 seconds before one of the faculty, a Gestalt practitioner named Elaine, stood and walked up to Werner, saying ***"Well, I have a headache NOW."***

The audience laughed and the tension was broken.

Werner had Elaine sit and told her to shut her eyes: ***"First I will ask you to affirm that you have the ability to abolish this headache. Elaine: do not answer me with words. Just let your arm rise by itself fully when you know that you will succeed in this."***

He said a little more but it was clear to those of us just trained by David Cheek that he was using a standard hypnotic challenge but without the fundamental respect Cheek built around such unconscious communication with the participant's ideomotor finger signals (Cheek 1968, 1993; Rossi and Cheek 1994). Further, being faced by a hundred of her students and peers put tremendous pressure on Elaine. How could she not declare herself as capable? In any case, eyes shut tight, Elaine's hand rose slowly but fully.

"Now Elaine, your arm can relax again."

It did.

"You know I'm sure that 'thinking' can get in the way of success at times and is not as essential as 'feeling.'"

Elaine smiled at this as her perspective in psychology did in fact stress the primacy of emotion over cognition. This was exactly what Elaine taught her students. Werner continued: ***"But even 'feeling' is not as important as 'seeing'!"***

Elaine frowned, clearly not following this, nor did we.

"Use your powers of description now as you can actually see this headache. As it becomes visible to you, tell us what shape it is."

A few seconds went by and Elaine described the shape: *"Like a slow moving meteor or frying pan."*

"What color is it?"

"Red and Orange like a flame."

"How is it moving?"

"Diagonally up to the right."

"Now what shape is it?"

And this went on for about another minute of description, until Elaine declared: *"I can't see it any longer. It kept getting smaller and now it has disappeared."*

"And your headache is gone."

This was Werner's flat statement, no question. But Elaine answered anyway: *"Yes, it is"* she said with a smile.

This was a useful demonstration of stimulus satiation applied helpfully to mild headaches, a technique we gladly incorporated into our bag of tricks, neuro-linguistic programming or NLP for example, for decades to come. In fact, the metaphor of facing headaches directly and shining a light on them until they are overcome is also central to positive community transformation.

If the demonstration had ended then, it would have been more than sufficient. Graduate students seek the magic techniques (before learning the true magic is in the relationship between people) and here was the promise of many of these magic tools. The demo was a success. It could have ended then, it should have ended then, in fact most thought it had ended then. But it did not.

Werner said in a voice so soft only those of us in the first row could hear it:

"Do NOT open your eyes yet. That could be dangerous!"

Elaine's face crinkled with surprise and she frowned, but complied, eyes still tightly closed. Then Werner quietly counted her back from 10 to 9 to 8 and ultimately to zero, telling her in between each number that she was becoming more awake and relaxed and safe, until at zero she was told that her eyes were free to open. Except for the introduction of the "danger" crisis, this had been a standard hypnosis re-entry technique. Elaine returned to her seat with earned applause for her courageous volunteer work.

During his count back, most in the audience just saw Werner whispering to her. Only those close enough to touch them could hear Werner throwing Elaine into unnecessary and unexpected traumatic stress, the perception of danger, and then rescuing her from it. When done en masse at an EST workshop, did this transform the participant's confidence and ability to a higher level, or did it also transform a substantial few into the growing cult community of Werner's followers?

Erhard's class went as scheduled. I didn't join it but Werner began by acknowledging me in absentia for allowing him to share his work on the campus, particularly since I clearly did not endorse him. Made me wonder. But I was told it went well. The weekend workshop was full of our students and even a few faculty, none paying the stiff EST admission for the experience.

A pregnant faculty wife, nine months along, demanded to be let out of the room to empty her pressured bladder. Two imposing guards refused (this technique was to demonstrate the power we have over our body by not urinating for hours): Werner intervened, recognizing her as a special guest, but said it was to be the only exception of the day. Four hours later, she understandably had to relieve herself again but this time was told if she left she would not be readmitted for the rest of the workshop. By then, she had heard enough of Werner's philosophy and, grabbing one of the microphones set aside for audience input, she loudly shared her dilemma followed by her solution: squatting on the floor she emptied her bladder on the hotel carpet, microphone catching the gentle sounds of running liquid. There was a moment's silence and then Werner declared, in his microphone, that she had **"Got It!"** With his approval in tow, everybody cheered. Werner had deflected a challenge into a win for both. No telling how the hotel staff felt about this triumph.

Other exercises included more hypnotic counting, a self-confidence piece where each participant took turns facing the whole crowd to realize that each one of them in that turn had the same fear of group approval. Then, eventually, the grand demonstration of telepathic diagnosis at a distance. Several hundred EST graduates entered and each one paired up with one of the new workshop participants. With so many people just like them, a fraud did not seem likely. And yet.

Each graduate had a typed card with demographic and personal physical or mental health information about somebody at a distance who was unknown to the new participant. The participant had to "*go into their space*."

(They had learned this trauma reduction technique in which they visualized a safe place already in another of our graduate courses. David Cheek taught it as a standard trance device for clinical hypnosis, but in his teaching it was always preceded by automatic ideomotor finger signals. This allowed for respectful permission from the participant, a key element missing in Werner's method. An excellent more recent brief therapy hypnosis resource on this would be Rubin Battino, 2006, or David Rossi with Cheek, 1994. Cheek's methods, based on respect for the autonomy of the individual client, represent a clear antidote to international cult formation today.)

Back to what seemed to be diagnosis at a distance. Once achieving this visual space, eyes shut, the participants began to see a person. The EST graduate then asked their questions and verified correct answers. Usually all hundreds of participants, each paired with an EST graduate, succeeded at this final demonstration of their newly acquired EST magic. How could this be?

The faculty husband of the pregnant woman mentioned earlier found a discarded instruction sheet for the EST Graduate questioner at the close of the weekend sessions. It was vintage Milton Erickson hypnosis but lacking his ethics. Oppositional statements were merged in a confusing but consistent direction. Near the top of the page it said:

"*Do not lead the participant, success must be their own.*"

This was followed by:

"*If the participant appears to give an incorrect answer, do not say they are wrong but rather rephrase the question so as to make it possible for them to view correctly,"* and *"Be mindful that their performance is your responsibility, you are the cause of the outcome."*

So if somebody visualized a male and it was a female's information on the card the graduate would just say to look closer and refocus until a female came into view. Opportunity and opportunist are such similar words.

In 1974, Murray Tondow's unpublished personality data suggested the EST participants did become more self-confident, assertive, and had higher self-esteem, but no ESP abilities were assessed, nor was gullibility.

In following years, Werner did go on to expand globally as he had planned. Alan Watts when asked about Werner Erhard, smiled and was reported to say only: *"Ah, that rogue!"* (Bartley, 1988).

Our students and faculty did not abandon all to join Werner's intentional community, but some found the techniques useful, both as what to do and also what not to do (Morgan 2008, 2012).

Eventually, EST morphed into an organization that claimed it would combat world hunger. It also came to light that there was no "Werner Erhard"—just a sad but charismatic man who had abandoned his young family to take on a new name and identity.

In rescuing those he had himself placed in the illusion of danger, he led many to abandon their own families for the new cult, an important key in understanding our own era. Was Werner acting out his guilt at the betrayal of his own family or just sharing a more modern destructive for-profit life pattern?

In any case, he had absorbed charismatic salesmanship, faith healing, and hypnosis, read a little Gurdjieff (Thomson, 2002), borrowed from seminars with Alan Watts (Bartley, 1988), and built his intentional community on the here-and-now foundation of a Latin present tense: "EST" or "It is." He had successfully sold the opportunity for a lot of magic and transformation, delivered substantially less, and made millions of dollars.

Sound familiar? Organizational, social, and community psychologists can find these cults today, still growing like mushrooms in rain. Some national or international.

Well, once EST became past tense, the man calling himself Werner Erhard disappeared from view with, I would imagine, Jay's long-awaited substantial satisfaction.

For many Decembers after our EST seminar experience, I got Christmas cards from Werner Erhard signed: "*Love, Werner*."

I didn't respond and eventually the holiday cards stopped.

Like a satiated headache, his unrequited love was gone.

Chapter 9. The International Rise of Balloon Therapy

When the American Psychological Association (APA) first developed electronic access to journal articles, PSYCHLIT, it began with psychology publications only from the 1970s forward.

This concerned me, knowing of the substantial international contributions since the birth of psychology in 1879. Also, I had published a lot in the 1960s: my narcissistic impulse objected to it being lost from access. Then too, I have been and continue to be concerned with a student and publisher zeitgeist that assumes that only work with the most recent publication date is of value—the notion that all worthwhile knowledge begins with the reader's existence, not before. I agree with author Alex Haley who was quoted as saying that the death of a single elder is like the burning of a library. The death of a library's earliest collections, or in this case a large portion thereof, is like the burning of memory.

So I set out at every annual national annual APA convention to visit the booth demonstrating PSYCHLIT. Once there, I argued that extending the beginning of its journal purview earlier in time would become exponentially easier since the number of journals and articles would decrease as they added in past years, eventually reaching the founding of our young discipline. I was listened to politely. There was agreement that discovery and data are not necessarily linear over time; in fact pockets of important studies might be lost to new research if the electronic access failed to go back far enough to find it. But for many years, the start date remained locked into the 1970s.

Eventually, with or without my argument, APA did extend back to the beginning of psychology's history, even adding books to journal articles. The first annual convention after this first occurred, the demonstration booth ran my name to show me how effective it had become with psychology publication lifespan.

The staffer snatched up the printout before I could see it, gathering up all the rest of the APA brethren available. "Look!" she said, "It's the *Balloon Therapy* piece!" Turned out that my Canadian article had been a favorite back in Washington DC and had been posted on APA office bulletin boards.

I had mixed feelings about this. I really appreciated the accolades this brief satirical piece was getting but with a body of work now spanning five decades, it seemed I was known to APA only for an imaginary therapy. I once had a graduate student sum up all of Sigmund Freud's contributions as "introducing Cocaine." Not being Freud, nor an advocate of Cocaine, I finally decided to thank the staff for their kind applause and move on.

In a subsequent decade, I was a Dean at the California School of Professional Psychology (now Alliant International University) in California's Fresno. There the campus staff honored the unique cultural holiday of April Fool's Day (April 1st) each year by arriving at work early and filling the offices of all administrators with toilet paper. An earned vicarious release, it was tolerated glumly by my administrative colleagues. For my part, I had no complaint. This was because they chose to fill my office full of balloons instead of toilet paper. This time I gladly appreciated the notoriety of my article in psychology circles.

The original article in *Canadian Psychology* (Morgan, 1982) was reprinted in a Canadian/American text used by clinical students: *The Iatrogenics Handbook* (Morgan, 2004). In very recent years, my students and colleagues at an Australian university in Singapore, James Cook University, apparently took notice of this.

(Note: The books of clinical psychotherapies originally satirized are naturally now outdated. Corsini and Wedding (2010) do a more modern review, despite a paperback cost rivaling a home mortgage, but the multiplicity and redundancy of approaches persist, disputes on what is evidence-based notwithstanding.)

Singapore is a rich blend of four cultures originating from China, India, Malaysia, and Everywhere Else. On my campus, this was then set in the British education version filtered through Australia.

Many of my best students, most multilingual, initially tried to understand *Balloon Therapy* as a genuine clinical intervention, albeit from the seemingly bizarre USA perspective. Humor (Humour) was not an expected element in the psychological literature they were accustomed to. Once this was understood, these highly disciplined and impressively well-educated students took to the modality with energy and zest. The very next food-oriented celebration, of which multi-cultural Singapore has abundance, I was drenched in balloons. All colorful (colourful) and with welcome laughter. A tradition that may have outlasted the end of my Visiting Professorship in Singapore with, hopefully, some influence on applied psychology in the United States, Canada, Australia, China, India, and Malaysia. You never know.

Not sure if it made it to Great Britain as well, but if you see international psychologists being drenched in balloons anywhere, it may possibly be traced to the article that follows (modified excerpt reprinted with permission):

"Balloon Therapy"

The balloon therapy technique described in the following paragraphs should only be done under medical supervision. **Do not do this at home. Or anywhere else.**

There have been some excellent paperback guides available to catalogue the many therapeutic techniques available to a growth-oriented public. Among the earliest, Chris Popenoe's <u>Wellness</u> *(me-ness, you-ness, we-ness), (1977) includes hundreds of pages of brief descriptions of healing techniques from "Flower Remedies" to "Cold Sheet Treatments," from "Psychodietetics" to "Tibetan Medicine." Richie Herink not much later edited* <u>The Psychotherapy Handbook</u> *(1980) which lists and describes over 250 psychotherapeutic systems and techniques from "Creative Aggression" to "Vector" therapies, with an introductory caution that the list was likely far from complete.*

Now, many of these techniques may well be quite effective, particularly when applied systematically, with ongoing feedback, to disorders that have been scientifically determined to best fit the approach. Further, careful reading shows that the general approaches (with the underlying theories) may be distilled down to but a very few unifying perspectives. Most of these fit well, in turn, into recognizable views giving differential priority to thoughts or feelings or choice or eclectic blend. Why then, such variety of title, such smorgasbords of technique? One must realize that often a professional career rests on such personalized labeling of generalized phenomenon. To attempt to unify and integrate a system is to risk de-individuation of one's reputational self-actualization (i.e., the big bucks follow those who stand out from the crowd). Since everyone must individualize their own system, I have evolved a hypothetical technique neither Popenoe nor Herink have catalogued yet: **Balloon Therapy**.

Method

Client has two large helium-filled balloons fastened on, one to an ear (in the event of only one ear, use only one balloon). The shape, filling, color and design of balloon will vary with the judgment of the therapist (messages of client scripts might conceivably be purchased from transactional analysts or psycho-dramatists; the message must be securely fastened to the balloon and should not exceed the vocabulary of the people likely to be encountered). Client wears these fastened balloons twenty-four hours per day for an entire week. At the end of the week, the client returns to the therapist and the balloons are removed.

Benefits

1. *Relief of depression: client feels elation at no longer having balloons on the ears.*

2. *Bolstering of self-confidence: client, having survived this, can survive anything.*

3. *Advertising: few clients completing this procedure will fail to rationalize it as extremely beneficial (the alternative to be defended against is that they are, to some infinite extent, gullible) and the technique itself draws notice.*

4. *Reducing social isolation and withdrawal: not only are balloons a conversation piece but there would be immediate identity with anyone else undergoing this therapy (without breaching confidentiality, clients would be able to recognize each other anywhere).*

5. *Relieves anxiety neuroses: everything relieves anxiety neuroses.*

6. *Particularly suited to autistic and catatonic disorders: these clients immediately adjust to the unusual balloon presence, never once objecting or complaining. In several years, only one catatonic asked us to get the balloons the hell off his ears and we responded by certifying him cured.*

7. *Sexual dysfunction: relieves obsessional performance orientation or, in fact, performance.*

8. *Alcohol abuse and dependence: clients are refused service.*

9. *Significantly reduces discomfort from any disorder reimbursable by insurance or directly payable by client.*

Points of Therapeutic Expertise

1. *Deciding on characteristics of balloon (see Method).*

2. *Choosing between glue, clip, tape, magnetic or natural honey fastenings.*

3. *Selecting the best point of attachment for the balloons – using body parts other than the ears may be appropriate with several types of client.*

4. *Matching length of strings to client characteristics.*

5. *Fee structure.*

Contra-indications:

1. *This technique is not recommended when the client:*

2. Has poor sense of humor, combat experience or an attorney.

3. *Is financially insolvent.*

4. *Can spell "iatrogenic."*

Chapter 10. Inductive Pathways & Best Way to End a Life

If you want something you never had before, you must do something you have never done before."
— South African Proverb, per Nathan Hare (2002).

Inductive Pathways

At Michigan State University in the 1960s, walking paths on their huge campus were determined inductively. Undoubtedly the original paved walkways were planned carefully by some artistic or logical pattern. Yet in my six years there, we students often deviated from the appropriately paved areas to travel the most useful routes to our immediate destinations, often across carefully manicured lawns. Soon these alternate routes became well-worn dirt paths connecting buildings amidst pampered grass. In other places and times, fences might have been erected to halt this desecration. Warnings and penalties might have been tried. Instead some administrative genius, unknown by name to us, decreed that every dirt path be paved over to become a new and approved pathway. It worked well. Soon the grass was safe and the traffic pattern highly functional. Travel was conflict free.

This of course is exactly how applying psychology should work.

On the other hand, this same university in the same era had other administrators doing more rigidly deductive approaches, ones less aware of the predilections of human behavior.

The university library budget routinely carried replacement costs for stolen books. In an attempt to trim this expense, an investment was made to add great mechanical and human security at each exit. Warning signs appeared like mushrooms after a rain. Purses and backpacks were carefully searched for every patron. Quite the challenge for bright young people. By the end of the academic year, the budgetary cost for stolen books had tripled. (*I knew this as a member of my family worked in the library; I chose to show her an example of how the system was flawed by simply dropping a book of her choice out the window of a restroom and, reclaiming it from the outside lawn below, went back in and presented it to her as evidence; she was not amused.*)

Detour to Chico

Chico was overlooked by the town of Paradise, a town which despite its happy name burned to the ground not long ago at the start of the ubiquitous California wildfires. Chico was more fortunate. It still exists, though it remains a constant target for mountain-living outlaws who regularly raid the Chico "Flatlanders." We moved completely into our Chico home in 2004.

It was a friendly place to live with inductive path shortcuts standard. Everywhere we needed to get to, movies or shopping or woods, all was within easy walking distance.

Brunch was usually down the street at the *"Sin of Cortez"* restaurant (great crêpes). A short drive away was another fine brunch place, *"Morning Thunder."* Name reminded me of brunch back home when I was a boy. Yet the food at Morning Thunder was great and the ventilation sufficient.

The best way to end a life

Illustration: Leilani was a very bright and successful former student from my days as a psychology professor in an island community. One traumatic day her children and husband were lost at sea.

Unable to work, even after six months of mourning, Leilani increasingly slipped into an overwhelming depression. She no longer had anything to do with relatives or friends.

Ruling out a psychiatrist's recommendation for ECT (I told you she was bright), Leilani did agree to take a powerful antidepressant.

Like most such drugs, it had a manufacturer-proclaimed success rate of 95%. But she was in the 5% that experienced enhanced feelings of harming herself or others, magnified by the excessive marketing and usage of these high-risk prescriptions.

In her case, it was suicidal urges. When Leilani realized the drug was making her worse, she chose to stop immediately.

But once her body had adapted to the drug, sudden cessation of the antidepressant created a typical boomerang effect and Leilani's depression deepened (such drugs must be tapered off gradually and often within the care of psychologists specializing in withdrawal from hazardous prescriptions; a growing specialization).

In recent years suicide prevention and grief therapy techniques have become more diverse, sophisticated and accessible (Neimeyer 2012, Morgan 2012). Leilani existed in an earlier time.

Deciding to kill herself, and with her family gone, Leilani contacted me to say her goodbye. Since I was a few thousand miles away, I could not see her directly. She declined my suggestions to see a psychologist near her home or to undertake any more therapy.

I told her I understood completely why what had happened made her so unbearably sad. Everywhere Leilani looked she was surrounded by reminders of those she had lost.

Accepting that her chosen way to deal with the unending trauma in that place was to end her life, I suggested a way she could do that if she was willing to try.

Leilani said she was grateful to get my help in this, saying *"Yes!"* she would follow my instructions exactly.

I told her that a best way to end her life was to end the life she no longer wanted.

She should leave that place and move as soon as possible to a brand new universe. Universe?

Some place far away and completely unlike anywhere she had been before.

After a few more discussions over the next week, she had chosen such a place.

It was a long road to get there. She persevered.

A year after settling into Fairbanks, Alaska, Leilani let me know that her depression was gone. She still sometimes had sadness, but her new life, her universe, was working for her.

She said the Northern Lights always made her happy.

Chapter 11. Maidu Murder Mystery & Paradigm Shift Epiphany

 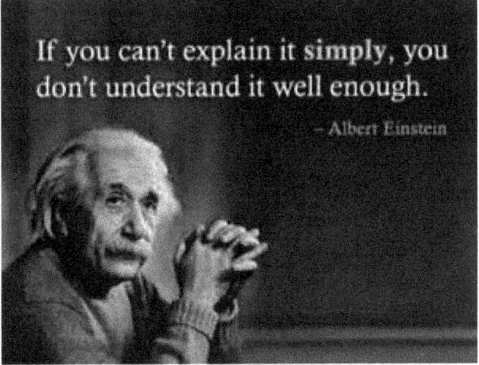

Since the 1962 publication of Thomas Kuhn's Structure of Scientific Revolutions, his term *"paradigm shift"* has been widely used, hotly debated, and substantially modified. The fundamental meaning is that of radical or sudden change in underlying beliefs or theory, normally applied to scientific research and its theoretical basis (Kuhn, 1996). In more modern times it has been applied to massive change in education or business. Today though, given an emphasis of applied psychology on the individual, this term might well be adequately descriptive of a person's ability to create an unexpected sudden paradigm shift in others. One might consider it as a way of creating a healing or amusing epiphany (McKay-Riddell, 2014) to secure a fortunate outcome, possibly an applied tool fitting within positive psychology.

Used in a challenging or potentially traumatic circumstance, one might consider it a very useful tool for safety or defense. Not so much a mechanism of defense as described by Anna Freud (1936, 1979), where even the best defense still failed to resolve the original conflict, the Paradigm Shift Epiphany (PSE) is used to secure a satisfying and favorable outcome. With PSE, when people fall, they land higher.

We can see examples of paradigm shift for individuals in disparate phases of psychology and contemporary life. In the clinical and transformational realm, we see neurolinguistic programming and Ericksonian hypnosis use the reframing of content and context (Bandler & Grinder, 1982; McMullin, 2005) (Erickson *et al*, 1984). Yet, these are highly specialized skills for clinical issues. Archer (2013) has more recently brought this perspective into a verbal application of the martial art of Aikido. You can find this in literature: Australian James Clavell's classic 1986 historical novel *Shogun* reframed the entire 1152-page book by reading the very last page.

Outside psychology, this PSE experience may be similar to the Hindu *"bodhodaya"* or the Zen *"kensho,"* a sudden twist revealing a surprising new improved perspective on previously challenging context. (I realized the answer to the *"What is the sound of one hand clapping?"* challenge can simply be answered by bending a flexible hand to clap with itself, although this can be experienced as passive aggressive and has not yet been shown to create any healing or amusement.) (Sigh.)

Charles Tart (2001) advised the rest of us faculty colleagues to approach a challenging event by shifting our physical posture, to literally see a puzzling circumstance in a new way, one often leading to insight. (I tried it to see into an illusion by magician/psychologist Arthur Hastings, and it worked). Arthur Conan Doyle based his

TIME STATUES

Sherlock Holmes character on his former medical supervisor, Joseph Bell. Bell, a forensic science innovator, developed great techniques for reframing context through perception and deduction (Edwards, 2013). The bent-over or sideways glances of Holmes and modern variations (eg. the current Sherlock Holmes television show "*Elementary*") exemplify Tart's suggestion for obtaining your own paradigm shift, at least on an individual level. Nor would much of humor work without the unexpected epiphany twists we count on for laughter.

A key psychotherapy phase, sometimes overlooked, goes beyond the intra-psychic understanding found in the occasional Freudian Association Round Table Society (acronym not stated) to move into an action phase, the goal being an external real-life resolution of challenges now better understood. In the 1970s this might have been called "Radical Therapy" but now it is a very important option for therapist and client. Rollo May's existential psychotherapy used the same key listening skills as Sigmund Freud and the same regard as Carl Rogers but, once the insights were fully available, Rollo might typically ask "*Now what will you do about it?*" In my own work, my version of this question might go: "*Now what will we do about it?*" Either way, the PSE becomes a very useful tool. So how can an individual apply this outer-directed PSE tool for that satisfying and favorable outcome? Possibly some illustrations and vignettes could be helpful.

****

It was a quiet day in the Kasbah.

Devastated and almost without hope, she turned in to a small storefront shop for a palm reading.

The fortune teller held her hand gently and peered carefully at the creases, delicately ignoring the flecks of food and sediment as her gaze drifted past them.

Finally she spoke in her authoritative but reassuring Gypsy voice:

"You can find happiness but there are four things you must know and remember when seeking a man.

First, find one who makes you happy and has a great sense of humor.

Second, find one who has much wealth and can see to your welfare for the rest of your days.

Third, be sure to find one who is handsome and satisfies all your sexual needs."

They palm reader paused to see if her customer was following. She was, and impatiently said: *"Tell me the fourth part, the last thing I need to do!"*

The palm reader smiled slyly and said:

"You must never let these three different men meet."

She left the palm reader laughing and feeling renewed without knowing why.

****

Some signs, taken literally, can be misleading. At the Australian James Cook University in Singapore, my wife's title on her library door was "**Head of Librarian**." The "**No Eating**" sign there might have better added **"in the library**." Taken literally it could lead to fast anorexia. Practically speaking, only the CEO there might take it that way. My favorites are huge signs in many countries that say "**Child

Abuse Week" or "**Teen Pregnancy Week**" or "**Cancer Week**." The addition of the words **"Prevention of"** might be more helpful. Working with children (as well as hypnotists, logicians, and existentialists) helps you look through their eyes at the literal meaning of words. This approach may qualify as a useful PSE or, at times, just annoying.

Recently, I found an excellent example of a PSE that can be used to enhance discussion with elders or their spouses and caretakers for a productive context reframing ... or satisfying cathartic ventilation:

The Job Interview

Potential supervisor: "Tell me your worst quality."
Elder: "Honesty."
Supervisor: "I don't think honesty is a bad quality."
Elder: "I don't give a damn what you think."

****

This is a true story:

At 16, Tom was a new recruit in his country's Coast Guard. The older sailors spoke a different dialect, enjoyed very different music, and found it amusing to give young Tom the worst details available. This was particularly true of the Captain of the ship. Although he occasionally worried that they were going too far with the bullying and might traumatize their recruit, he gained much amusement in pushing Tom to the limit of his youthful endurance.

Eventually, the Captain assigned Tom to permanent latrine duty. Here, day after day, he cleaned the well-used toilets, only to be berated when the Captain conducted a white-glove inspection of his work at the close of each shift. With another month at sea to go, Tom found himself increasingly angry, depressed, and withdrawn. Yet, one day, he awoke with an idea. A PSE that might create the empathy he needed from his shipmates.

Tom secreted a small portion of peanut butter from breakfast, wrapped it carefully in Saran Wrap, and headed to his shift. There he carefully cleaned and re-cleaned every porcelain fixture as needed until all sinks, floors, and toilets shone with maximum possible cleanliness. As his day there ended, the Captain and senior officers all entered for their regularly humiliating white-glove inspection.

Despite himself, the Captain was impressed. As Tom stood at rigid attention, everything in the latrine proved to be spotless and sparkling. Until the Captain came to the last wooden toilet seat and spotted the ball of peanut butter Tom had placed there.

"*Tom!*" the Captain bellowed. "*Get over here! Look what you missed, you…*"

Tom ran over to the seat, picked up the peanut butter and swallowed it.

"*Sorry Sir! Won't happen again!*" he said, and stood at attention.

He was sent to sick bay to recover. Tom spent the rest of the trip in the relaxed supportive care of a worried but chastened Captain and Crew, their reframed perspective intact.

****

Here is another example adapted from a case history published a few years ago (Morgan, 2011) and its subsequent application to grief therapy techniques (Morgan, 2012; Neimeyer, 2012). View it here as an illustration of the Paradigm Shift Epiphany.

A Paradigm Shift Defense intervention for Factitious Grief in a Maidu Murder Mystery

*"Now that my husband has shot him,
I don't know what to do with the body."*

Clients: At the International Congress of Applied Psychology in San Francisco in 1998 (Morgan, 2008), our organization introduced presentations from "nations-within-nations" recognized by the United Nations. These are often indigenous people such as the Maori in New Zealand, the Senoi in Malaysia, the Aboriginal People of Australia, and the original tribes of the Native Americans, Canadians, and Mexicans. A sense of humor can be found in these varying world views, often used as a test of trust. For them and for those clients from any culture where humor and irony are to be found, the initial rapport so essential to psychotherapy can be enhanced as a treatment for either genuine or factitious grief.

Contraindications: not to be used when the timing or client well-being would be compromised or the sense of humor is absent.

Method: When an apparently spontaneous or unrelated intervention occurs to a psychotherapist, it is important to do an immediate triage of barriers to use: Is it legal? Ethical? In the client's best interest? From Hippocrates on we know we must above all "do no harm."

The entire field of prevention of iatrogenic practice rests on violations to this standard (Morgan, 2004). Yet, if none of the triage barriers apply, it is often very useful to go ahead with the intervention. Intuitive humor or irony certainly falls into this category and can be an effective treatment, particularly in reframing seemingly overwhelming grief. This is one of my favorites (Morgan, 1982).

On the other hand, a client may present factitious or pseudo-grief as a test for safety and as a cover for more genuine grieving to be accessed later in treatment.

This is not unknown as a client-produced method from native peoples and the therapist's response needs to be congruent. Intuitive humor can be one such response.

In the mountains of Northern California, in counties where only one or two psychologists may be found at best, live the Maidu Indian people, side by side with scatterings of settlers from European cultures.

The nearest town to Greenville, where we had moved, is Reno, Nevada, about a two-hour drive from there.

We moved to Greenville because my wife was promised a job as the sole librarian for the town's tiny library. Being an American Indian herself (Cherokee-Choctaw plus some Irish) and with an accredited graduate library degree from the University of Washington, she was assured that the other 18 applicants, holding no such credentials or experience, would not be hired. She was needed.

We moved there. Only to learn that, while she was the only strong candidate, the job had been given to the non-American Indian county library director's non-American Indian girlfriend, a nice person with no experience in libraries of any kind. As I recall, she was the dentist's wife.

So there we were, moved into a small community and completely unemployed. Not an unusual situation for many, sadly.

Knowing that there were absolutely no psychologists in the area, I walked into the tribal health center, one covering the needs of the residents of that remote but beautiful half of the county.

TIME STATUES

Did they need a psychologist to help out? Yes, they did. Desperately. And a substantial amount of money was promised for every hour of service. A good cause and a way to pay the rent. I agreed immediately and was given an empty office just off the waiting room.

A day went by. No clients. No hours, no stipend, no rent.

I asked the Director if she would be willing to run an announcement in the local paper to let potential patients know I was there. No need, she said, they know you are here.

Interesting. No patients the next day either. By the morning of the third day, I was walking to work with some real concern. I was prepared to be the psychology equivalent of the country doctor, a real need there, but the clients were not apparent.

And then, within sight of the health center, a woman in her forties walked up to me and asked if I was Dr. Morgan. I was.

She asked if she could ask me a question. I said yes- did you have another question?

Clearly this was an out-of-the-office free consultation coming up, but it beat having no clients at all. She cleared her throat.

"My husband shot our dog today."

"Why?"

"Well, the dog is a loving dog and walks the children to their school bus every morning. But our neighbor hates children. So when they come by his house he yells at them and throws things. Once the children are safe away and on the way to school, our dog goes on this neighbor's porch and relieves himself in front of his door. Then the neighbor keeps

calling my husband and complaining. Says his front porch is not a bathroom for puppies. My husband got one telephone call too many and so he took the dog out in the back yard and shot him to death."

As she said this, her nonverbal behavior was completely incongruent. She was smiling, almost seeming to hold back laughter, and her "tells" suggested less than an honest description.

Of course, this can be a trap. If you smile back in the midst of a sad story, your client might feel you are not taking them seriously. The normal response for a clinician is just to point out that the smile doesn't match the story and is that how they feel?

But I wasn't sure about this culture. Maidu and many other tribal people have a rough sense of humor, somewhat akin to that of the inhabitants of Manhattan or Auckland. So I asked a question instead.

"Well, that is very sad. What do you want to know?"

"Now that my husband has shot him, I don't know what to do with the body."

Humor can be a very powerful way to help clients in trauma (Morgan, 2012) and even as a grief therapy (Neimeyer, 2012). Or, badly timed or thought through, it can create both trauma and grief. For both of us.

But, after internal triage, I took a chance that the story was a complete fabrication.

I said: *"Well my advice is to take the dog's body and leave it on your neighbor's porch with a suicide note. Sign it with a paw print."*

She studied me for a minute and then said *"You're not from around here, are you?"*

She turned and walked away slowly. Just before turning the corner, she started laughing.

That afternoon, the waiting room was full and I never had a shortage of clients thereafter.

(Note: For herself, she soon came to terms with her genuine loss and anticipated loss. These were both true and overwhelming. It took a year for her to surmount them but that she did. In a five-year follow-up she was still doing quite well. It is crucial to have some understanding of the client's individual culture and values, particularly when it may be so different from your own experience. Then there will often be a test for safety and trust, occasionally with fictitious information, even pseudo-grieving. Humor and un-defensive patience can move you quickly past that point and into useful therapeutic work with the genuine grief.)

Sample Fantasy Paradigm Shifts

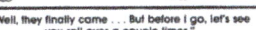

"Well, they finally came... But before I go, let's see you roll over a couple times."

Chapter 12. Unopened Gifts

Hypnotic anchoring of prescription drugs, measures for non-invasive human aging measures or alternative outcomes, empowerment methods, and impertinent questions.

At the end of a long life, many express regrets. Less than for things they wish they had not done, they regret more things they wish they *had* done. "Sins" of omission rather than commission. As their scope of opportunities narrow with age or physical limitation, it is missed options that come to mind. If asked what age they would be if they could return to any age, a frequent response is to be forty or fifty again: young enough to do anything, but old enough to choose wisely.

International psychologists often live long lives, full of productivity to the end, retirement untouched. Yet, regrets exist for us too and they include unopened gifts of professional opportunity. It may be useful for those of us not yet at an end time to reflect on what we are overlooking or postponing. We can identify these better choices now while it's not yet too late, rather than postponing them to those shadows of later. We might, with or without the aid of auto-hypnotic trance, imagine we are in our final hours and allow the images of what we wished we had done to emerge. When I tried this exercise, I recalled these possibilities that had some useful application.

1. Hypnotic anchoring as a prescription drug substitute

TIME STATUES

A few decades ago, Arthur Hastings and other psychologists were excited about the therapeutic potential of MDMA for clinical change. Combining mood elevation with hallucinogenic insights, it had the potential for clinical healing within a protected professional setting, more effective than the earlier use and misuse of LSD and, clearly, an approach to dealing with trauma—something increasingly important today. However, MDMA (aka "Adam" or "Ecstasy") was also sold, possibly adulterated, on the street for enhanced pleasure and exploration. Whether in the spirit of Mencken's definition of Puritanism, *"the haunting fear that someone, somewhere, may be happy,"* or because of concern for the unprotected safety of buyers, MDMA was classified in the United States as a dangerous drug. One consequence: most research and application came to an immediate halt.

In 1994, Arthur first published a way to replicate the effects of MDMA, ethically and legally, without actual use (re-use) of the substance. If MDMA had been used at least once in the past, Arthur's approach via hypnosis reproduced the effects. (See more recent work from Farber in 1999 and Hastings in 2000.)

After reading the 1994 article, I went to see Arthur, whom I had met once before, to explore the broader impact of his approach. Above and beyond MDMA, *any* drug might be replicated via this hypnotic technique. The pharmaceutical companies need only supply a prescription once and after that they would no longer be needed, possibly without the dangerous side effects common to the psychiatric drugs of our day (Breggin, 2007; Morgan, 2005).

It was clear that the drug corporations would not welcome profit losses, but the savings to the patient, including autonomy, could be immense.

We were not sure if the original drug's physiological response was being replicated or only the memory of it. Clearly this deserved further research.

I joined Arthur then at the Institute of Transpersonal Psychology (what is now known as Sofia University) in Palo Alto. But there his path and mine both diverged from this research and its potential application.

Arthur's research accomplishments are legendary from that time to now (Hastings *et al*, 2002) but we left the full implications of this specific drug substitution hypnotic application unrealized.

Professor Hastings died in the years after our work together and is still much mourned by his many students, peers, and friends.

My hope is that his work, including this application, can continue beyond his time with us and find fertile soil in many countries.

2. A non-invasive human aging measurement tool for autonomous self-discovery

Many of us have heard our physician tell us that we had the body of a much younger or older person. Doctors not just speculating may be referring to the carefully collected norms many countries have developed.

As a student in my first psychology course back in 1960, I realized that norms for measures systematically advancing as adults grow older could yield an estimate of individual body age. My instructor, Stanley C. Ratner, was encouraging. He suggested I develop a formal procedure for gauging this along the same lines of rigorous standardization, reliability, and validity demonstrated in our better psychological tests.

I chose to forgo the more time-consuming or ponderous measures (dark adaptation was one) or measures requiring specialized expertise (many blood aspects might fit here). Instead, I chose brief non-invasive measures that individuals might safely and simply do for themselves, consistent with the view that autonomous responsibility for one's health and longevity is best made available to all those who want it. The first article (Morgan, 1968a) was followed by more research and publications on the subject (Morgan, 1969-1994) and books (Morgan, 1976, 1981a, 1981b; Morgan & Wilson 1982, 1983, 2004) that included a standardized test manual complete with procedure and norms for a brief noninvasive set of do-it-yourself body age measures: the Adult Growth Examination (AGE).

The decades following these publications saw various practitioners applying this methodology in specific psychological settings. The impact of dietary, exercise, or health changes on aging could now be evaluated on an individual basis. Prevention and wellness campaigns in Australia, Singapore, and other countries made some use of the test. One university used it to show the positive impact of meditation on aging (Wallace *et al*, 1989, 1986, 1982). Alternative age measurement approaches without the strong procedural reliability and validity of the AGE began to appear in commercial exercise programs and were popular.

At the University of Southern Colorado, I developed an aging research lab. A prototype for a portable AGE measurement instrument to assess the non-invasive near vision, high frequency hearing, and (an average of three) systolic blood pressure measures was used to determine individual aging, particularly in response to health interventions.

An issue might not only be whether or not a specific vitamin combination or smoking cessation would reduce measured body age in general, but how this might impact the specific person being measured. In deference to the focus of individual differences so important to applied psychologists, each person using this tool had important information to steer their own specific care: a better existential choice than relying on generalities from population samples.

Still, the mass production of a portable test instrument, to go with the manual, has not yet occurred. Most of our colleagues have no idea this option exists, particularly without the portable instrument. In these days of better-informed self-help and prevention, there is an opportunity to make this steering mechanism available on an international scale. But not so far.

3. Alternative applied research outcome measures

I suppose these are sometimes called "hit-and-run" publications because, having published them once, the author abandons them and moves on. Many of my own hit-and-run publications were done in graduate school or shortly after.

Efficiency Percentages (Morgan, 1968b). Often psychological and other scientific results are reported in the press as a significant effect, usually at the 5% level. Rarely is the percentage of this effect that applies to the population sample given. This can be very misleading.

If country A has a significantly higher rate of alcoholism than neighboring country B, the public assumes country A is abundantly supplied with alcoholics. But what if country A has an incidence reflecting 5% of the adults while country B has 1%? If the sample is sufficiently large this could be a significant difference, meaning that we estimate more alcoholics can be found in country A than country B. But the public, without being told that 95 % of the adults in country A are *not* alcoholics, assumes that country A is an inebriant's paradise. From this may come a sad national stereotype. Some very disappointed but undesirable tourists could result.

The serious point, of course, is that we need to be very clear in our communications that a significant difference is not necessarily a majority description. From today's perspective, we might not choose to call this "efficiency percentage," as "efficiency" may be more commonly applied to statistical power. I suppose we could better refer to it as "validity percentages," inferring our goal from the sample is an accurate description of a population.

M/I Frequencies (Morgan, 1964a). A technique for choosing the best items in standardizing a psychological test by weighing median scores over means: medians per item (M/I) may often be the more accurate approach.

4. Effective Verbal Adaptation (EVA) (also 1964).

While a graduate student attempting to secure as many side jobs as possible to support my family, I was approached by an associate professor in the business leadership department. He was being considered for promotion but needed at least one visible publication or test. In particular he was looking for something that businesses could use in hiring or personnel screening. His plan was to supervise from afar, giving me full flexibility and creative freedom. He would provide volunteer groups to take the test once I had it developed.

I decided to have some fun and still develop a strongly grounded innovative test.

First I wrote nine challenging or embarrassing scenarios (*"This is your first day at work and the boss, who had you stay at your desk alone after hours, enters, locks the door behind him, and swallows the key. What would you do?"* I also recall a pedestrian in trouble with a traffic cop because of an insulting parrot).

After each scenario, the volunteer had three minutes to write as many responses as they possibly could. Then they turned to a second page and had three minutes more. By using the Bousfield-Sedgewick (1944) word association tables, we could calculate how many responses the test-taker would make if they had an infinite amount of time. This number, called a *"BS #"* referring to Bousfield and Sedgewick, would be summarized for each of the nine vignettes as an overall median.

And now for the empowerment of the individual business test reviewer: this employer would cross off all responses seen as less than effective or not what they were looking for in the person to promote or hire. Then the new scoring's overall median would fit the individual expectations of the specific business. I developed two parallel forms of the one-hour test and otherwise standardized it. The business professor, still afar, did help set up a reliability testing for two groups of volunteers: one from staff of the department of motor vehicles, one from an order of Catholic nuns.

(The nuns had fewer responses than the DMV people but showed more humor. One, in response to the key swallowing vignette, wrote: *"I would say: 'That will hurt more coming out than it did going in.'"* I would definitely hire her.)

In the end, the reliability and validity studies were robust and the test was done. Our professor was promoted and turned over all rights to the test to me, possibly not wanting to be associated any further with it. The test was called EVA for Effective Verbal Adaptation.

I had always meant to use it in some personnel screening way, but the years turned into decades with my attention elsewhere. My copies of test and manual burned up in May 2013 in an apartment complex fire. EVA may still be out there somewhere, waiting to be discovered.

5. The Auto-kinetic Effect (Schweitzer 1857, Adams 1912, Sherif 1935)

As shared in Chapter One, this was a projective test. In a dark room, a small stationary pinpoint of light appears to move but this illusion is only a reflection of movement from the observer. In my pilot study at Michigan State University in 1963, specific instructions to say what was being spelled out by the light led undergraduate volunteers to discern whole illusory sentences, occasionally of some significance (or embarrassment) to them. I wrote a research plan for testing this as a psychological projective procedure and submitted it to the National Institute of Mental Health for a clinical research graduate fellowship. They turned me down on the grounds that this work had never been done before. Instead they suggested I submit a proposal that fell more properly within the published expertise of my major professor, a very supportive but non-clinical animal behaviorist.

In the end I got the full fellowship, making my family financially secure during my graduate education. The research NIMH-approved topic involved earthworm perception (they can see white light but not red) using a lie detector (GSR) component (Morgan 1964b, Morgan *et al* 1965). The earthworms produced no evidence of auto-kinesis.

6. Sensory Deprivation Hallucinations as Therapy or Growth Opportunity (Morgan 1965, Morgan & Bakan, 1965).

We discovered that the three key elements needed to produce visual hallucinations within an hour were: an ambiguous perceptual field, a reclining position, and securing the head in a fixed but comfortable position. For one chronically hallucinating and distressed participant this turned out to be a clinical opportunity. Dr. Bert Karon was consulted ending with a productive outcome for the participant.

The study provided evidence that such hallucinations (no conscious control of an externally perceived event) were situation-specific waking lucid dreams and not a response to stress.

The utility of this as a catalytic clinical or transformative experience in the moment was apparent: an immediate hallucinated dream rather than memory of distant dreams or memories. The equipment was unobtrusive and inexpensive. Possibly someday it will be used in this way. Note: The Arthur Hastings *et al* (2002) "Psychomanteum" research does use some of these components, but for the very different purpose of grief resolution. CF. Morgan (2012) and Neimeyer (2012).

7. Impertinent Questions.

First one: A large San Francisco mental health center in the 1970s specialized in work with drug addicted clients. Almost all the medical staff were psychiatrists and psychiatric nurses. In addition, I supervised a group of psychology interns while a similar cohort of social workers rounded out the treatment staff.

The staff had their own (legal) addictions, particularly to strong coffee which was consumed throughout the day. The one non-psychiatric physician decided to add a non-smoking program as an addition to the client drug addictions already treated. He asked me to develop an inviting form to solicit staff involvement.

Beyond demographic and other information requested, I added these two yes-or-no questions: *"Do you smoke?"* and *"Do you believe smoking is hazardous to your health?"*

The physician thought these were not useful since all the health staff must know smoking was addictive and hazardous. But he reluctantly agreed.

It turned out that he was correct about responses from psychology and social work staff. On the other hand, all the nurses and all the psychiatrists turned out to be smokers and denied this was hazardous to their health. The frustrated physician abandoned his plans and had some coffee.

Second one: This was a consultation with 13 universities with predominantly Black student populations. Robert Lee Green and I, working with Dr. King's SCLC, agreed to evaluate a summer program designed to bring open-admission entering students up to college entrance performance levels (about a two-year jump). The teachers were given a questionnaire before they began their training and their program. At the end of the questionnaire I added this question: *"What % of the students in your class will reach college entrance levels by the end of this summer program?"*

At the close of the summer we tallied up the success rates. The Rosenthal effect was in full force. Those predicting failure were obliged by their students; those predicting success had successful students.

(The other robust predictor, based on graduation from college success, was measured motivation by the student. When teacher and student both reached for the same goal, it was usually successful.)

8. Empowerment Methods.
Here's another impertinent question:

At universities in Canada, Guam, and another in California, I recommended a different approach to electing faculty to the respective Faculty Senate or Union.

Why not let representatives be elected by petition?

Let's say we have 100 faculty with a goal of up to 10 Senate seats to be filled. To be elected, a Senator would only need to present a petition signed by 10 faculty (no more, no less). Nobody can sign more than one petition. Once the signatures are validated, we have representatives. This was also a way to move away from colleges or department regional representatives so as to foster cross-disciplinary representation. With each signatory endorsement so essential, representation would be strengthened. The faculty had no interest in this idea and to my knowledge it has never been tried.

I had done this in earlier years (1971-1975) while a Dean at the California School of Professional Psychology, San Francisco. Everybody, including all administrators, staff, and faculty, were evaluated annually as to their continuity with the results publicly available to the community. Overall the reviews were highly positive and morale improved.

These days it is now normal for faculty to be evaluated by their students. At a different level, supervisees evaluating supervisors (when done at all) is often spotty, secret, overly intricate, and hard to interpret. An annual concise direct review of supervisors by supervisees can improve morale, enhance productivity, and solidify a healthy work environment. It would be good to see more of this.

Finally: an unpublished survey of psychologists done by psychologist Dr. Gene Orro found that of 32 possible applied functions we can do, the most satisfying was: **to supervise**. The least satisfying? As you might have guessed: **to *be* supervised**. No point trying to herd psychologists either.

9. Bonus Gifts. (These are new. The first one actually works.)

A. Displaced Staleness: Marie Antoinette and Dorian Gray

This may well be two centuries old. My mother used it and got it in turn from her mother's usage in the 19th century. If you have fresh cake or scones or other food that might go stale quickly, just lay a slice of fresh bread over it, cover it, and let the good times roll. When you lift the cover again, the slice of bread on top will be stale and hard. Under it, everything remains fresh. Kind of a Dorian Gray process where the bread slice gets old but the cake does not. Marie Antoinette was said to have alienated French bread makers with the phrase *"Let them eat cake"* (also reputed to come instead from her mother Maria Theresa). Had either of them said *"Let them eat bread,"* France might still be a monarchy.

TIME STATUES

more at: Nana's Kitchen

Free Home Bidet Production

With the rise and fall of toilet paper availability, the Bidet has become much more attractive for downloaders. Still, it can be expensive and is not there for purchase in many zip codes. One solution involves turning the home shower into a free Bidet. This is done, carefully, by standing on your head in a water streaming shower such that the jet acts as a powerful Bidet. Caution: make sure to brace yourself during this process as it could be a falling hazard. Further, invite creative home engineering solutions to the problem of gravity forcing a downward runoff. Cover face with waterproof mask.

Chapter 13. Two Georges

It was my first year as a university professor and on an Autumn Thursday George was the first student to occupy my office with a desperate problem. As he sank down into a deep leather chair, he shared that, although he was not (yet) a Psychology major, his faculty advisor from Engineering thought he should talk to me. A bright student, used to high grades before coming to this university, he was failing all his first-year semester classes. He said he felt lost, unmotivated. He wasn't sleeping or eating well and he had a very difficult time focusing on anything. He found his first experience in university overwhelming and traumatic.

When I asked why he had chosen Engineering, he insisted he had not. His father was paying his bills and his father thought he should be in Engineering.

I asked then if George's poor grades were meant to fail his father.

On reflection, somewhat surprised, he agreed.

What would he choose if he took responsibility for his choice?

The notion that he <u>had</u> a choice needed to be digested for a second session.

In the meantime, I asked if any of the courses he was taking held any interest for him. Yes, his creative writing class did, but then again his procrastination at turning in a required paper had earned a poor grade here as well. I suggested a paradoxical intention: Why not, taking all he had learned in this class, write the worst paper his instructor had ever read? He was delighted and agreed. The following Thursday he came into my office gleefully waving his Creative Writing paper. At the top his instructor had written in red:

"This is the worst paper I have ever graded: you have violated every standard I gave this class: F!"

Then George flipped it over to the last page where it said, in a more neutral color:

"Now that you have told me that this is a psychological exercise from Professor Morgan, I realize that you must know the standards quite well to have reversed each of them so skillfully: A+."

George decided he wanted to switch to a joint major between English and Psychology.

By our 4th Thursday meeting he had broached this with his father and, to his great surprise, his father had agreed. George reported that he was sleeping and eating better,

and his focus was fine. In fact he looked forward each day to getting up and learning.

I thought that would conclude George's visits but every Thursday thereafter, for the entire semester and into the Spring, he arrived in my office at the same time, sank into my leather chair, and despondently broached a new potentially traumatic problem to solve: which with some assistance he always did.

TIME STATUES

Finally one sunny Thursday, on the way to my office, I saw George vault out of his top-down convertible, kiss his girlfriend goodbye, and head to my office, all smiles.

Yet ten minutes later, there he sat, deep in leather cushion, complaining despondently.

"*George!*" I said, "*I just saw you, only a few minutes ago, completely happy. What's going on?*"

He looked at me with surprise that a psychologist with my training would not understand, and said "*Well, sure, I'm happy all the time now. And that's because I know I can save up all the disappointments, stress, and unhappiness of the week and pass them on to you every Thursday.*"

And so it was that George taught me the essence of private practice. Also the need for planned termination.

The other George was an advanced psychology doctoral student ready to begin a clinical internship. I had been his dissertation Chair and instructor in several classes. He was a very sociable person, laughing companionably in his conversations with others and therefore was seen as endearing by most.

On the other hand, he had chosen a very challenging internship with imprisoned and dangerous patients: serial killers and rapists. Although he would be working there at a great distance from my campus, he asked if he could check in with me by telephone while he got settled. By then I was in my third decade of mentoring and knew that a transition bridge often made sense, particularly in the traumatic atmosphere he had chosen to do his internship in. I agreed.

He called the evening of his first day on the job. George had met in group session with his patients and asked them, as warm-up, how they would spend their Saturday night if they were free and what feelings came with that. His first respondent had said he would feel lonely, *"walking around watching happy couples and all I had to come home to would be the human heads in my basket."*

George was not having an easy time. He shared some symptoms of encroaching trauma, which were understandable although he would ultimately adjust and make a successful career of it. After hearing him out and being supportive, I asked if he had a supervisor on-site. Yes, he said, but she is a little overwhelming. Compared to the stress from the prisoners? Yes.

George described her as about 250 pounds, a foot taller than him, and a great believer in coffee enemas as a cure for all human ailments. She said she not only used this methodology often herself, but recommended the interns do so as well. George thought her psychological technique to be scarier than his patients were.

I suggested he approach her with an open mind during supervision: As Bert Karon used to say, we can learn as much from what our supervisors do poorly as from what they do well. The following evening, rather late, George called again. He had taken my advice and been friendly. Now she had just called him at home, well into the evening, and asked him to join her at her apartment. George was petrified. He had said he would get back to her in a minute and called me so I might tell him what to do. I pointed out that he already knew what to do. And of course he then did: If he was uncomfortable with these loose boundaries, as most would be, he should just call with his apologies and re-confirm his regular supervision daytime meeting at the prison.

"All right," he said, *"Thanks for confirming that I knew the right answer and that it was the best thing to do. But what would you have advised me to do if I had decided that the best thing for me was to go to her apartment?"* That one I knew: **"I would have said don't drink the coffee."**

Chapter 14. Turtles, Dogs, and Eagles

Some years ago, my graduate psychology classroom in Nova Scotia, Canada was fully decorated with the art of second graders.

The young artists had been separated two years earlier into 3 class groups. This division was primarily based on IQ test scores. Although the children were not told their own scores or which group was high or low, they could guess. The groups were named after animals: Eagles, Dogs, and Turtles.

There were a few exceptions to the IQ as a basis for this assignment: some of the children from wealthier or more influential families, despite modest IQ scores, were assigned to the Eagles, while some of the High IQ core children who had challenging behavior were assigned to the Turtles.

Two years later, a new Grade 2 art teacher was working with these children. She saw herself as quite progressive in that past art teachers had taught all children from the same formula while she had adapted her methods to the perceived differences of the ability of the three groups.

She was eager to share her results with my university students and the results sat on our wall.

The Eagles had been given a wide variety of art supplies and had been asked to do a winter scene. She then consulted with each child artist as requested until all the young artists had finished their work.

The wall in my classroom set aside for the resulting artwork of the Eagles was ablaze with color and talent, reflecting the creative atmosphere the artist had enjoyed.

The Dogs on the other hand, were not asked to create a winter scene, but more specifically to copy a snowman the teacher drew for them on the board. Each young artist was given a piece of black paper and white chalk. The teacher circulated while this art was done to assist the Dogs in making the most accurate copies possible.

The resulting artwork occupied another wall in my classroom: row after row of identical white chalk snowmen on black paper differing only by the name of the child artist at the bottom.

The Turtles were given the same assignment as the Dogs but the art teacher didn't expect much of them and just patrolled to keep order. Many of their pieces of black paper became thrown airplanes while many pieces of chalk became missiles to shoot them down.

The wall in my classroom set aside for the Turtles had a variety of crumbled pieces of black paper with varying chalk scribbles; few looked much like snowmen. The teacher was accepting of this for the Turtles as she assumed their abilities were limited, eschewing a "one size fits all" mainstream approach to teaching art.

She was of course badly mistaken. We knew by the 1960s that IQ scores assessed a very narrow range of ability and were often biased. We knew by then that IQ test scores were not independent of education but rather reflected its quality.

I had been fortunate to work with Robert L. Green and colleagues on testing the thousands of children displaced from Virginia schools for 4 years to avoid desegregation: intelligence and its measures clearly depended on schooling (Green & Morgan 1969).

We shared this perspective with our friendly art teacher but she was not convinced.

She pointed out that these three groups were treated differently in *all* their subject areas by the teachers and did not feel it was her place to make policy changes. She shared that her Principal was very firm about this.

The graduate students and I made a private prediction. This was the only public school in a very small rural university town. It seemed to us that these children were being socialized for community roles as adults.

The Eagles were trained to think for themselves and would become adaptive business or professional leaders. The Dogs were being trained to conform and follow orders exactly and would become the uninspiring but reliable employees of the Eagles. The Turtles were being trained to fail and would become the clients of the various community institutions serving misfits, including the jail.

We predicted that as adults they will fill the roles the school had prepared them for.

Twenty-five years later I participated in an international psychology congress in Halifax, Nova Scotia, and took some travel time to revisit this rural university town.

Many of my former graduate students still lived there. Sadly, our predictions for the Eagles, Dogs, and Turtles had come true. (Morgan 2005).

How about educating *all* our children as the Eagles were? Don't they deserve to fly as high as they can?

That is both a global opportunity and an uncompleted responsibility.

Chapter 15. Elders with Anticipatory Trauma

"The death of an elder is like the burning of a library."
— Alex Haley

"Inside every old person is a young person wondering what happened."
(Observed refrigerator magnet, San Francisco, 2008)

In my postdoctoral internship year, I worked with a group of chronic and institutionalized elder patients in a state hospital in Hawaii. We met every day for 90 minutes, Monday through Friday. All ten patients were experiencing severe memory loss to the point where recognizing the other patients, much less their own names, was challenging.

None had been diagnosed with Alzheimers or stroke but all had been erroneously labeled as psychotic. Achieving this unwelcome identity, they had settled into years of hospital routine and care.

Luckily, none had been electroshocked or lobotomized, possibly because they were peaceful and had never attacked a staff member. In one study, assaulting a staff member had a 1.00 correlation or 100% incidence of patients receiving ECT (Morgan, 2005a).

After a month of intense group work, we were getting nowhere. They managed to speak of remote past events in their life but both present and future remained blurred or invisible.

Empathy for Institutionalized Elders

Those we love will always be vibrantly alive in their own time and place. Those moments—or as we call them, "time statues"—we shared can be revisited as we wish, at least in our mind. As we live our life, scene by scene, we are all creative artists in this temporal theater. Some of these dramas glow. Some are just fun. Some may highlight a new path forward.

This complete life sequence of moments does of course include temporal vignettes that would not be happily visited by any time tourist. Then again, we can be very proud of other scenes that we have created, particularly if we become aware that, as we shape each moment of our existence, the results endure (Morgan 2005b, 2017). Therefore memory is an elder's most valuable asset.

For those experiencing senile and dysfunctional memory loss, not all time statues endure. Recent memory becomes far too transient, walled off from the view of normal cognitive functioning. Ruled out first must be neurological dysfunction, including strokes from cerebrovascular causes, accidents causing subdural hematoma, and, of course, Alzheimer's disease. (Alzheimer's, suggested by psychological tests, has in the past been validated with confidence by autopsy, a procedure living patients understandably avoided. Modern technology may yet do this better.)

For inpatients currently found in prisons and hospitals housing geriatric patients, manifesting none of these medical explanations for their mental fog, their condition has been at times erroneously termed "senile psychosis," a pseudo-psychosis. A fundamental misunderstanding of diagnosis can easily lead to harmful treatments, a classic example of patients being hurt despite the hopefully positive intentions of those trying to help, a classic iatrogenic mistake (Morgan, 2005c). Despite the mislabeling, such psychogenic dementia may still respond to psychological intervention. And has.

Beginning the Group Process

My supervisor, neuropsychologist Dr. Howard Gudeman, was an adept at existential psychology (confirmed by Rollo May 1986). A wise and patient professional, he eventually sat in with us and helped the group begin. Still, we had hit a progress plateau.

As interns do, I annoyed him by suggesting psychoanalytic interventions. How about addressing their "oral needs?" To my surprise, he agreed.

I brought in comfort food each day and this was received gladly. A breakthrough. Then in each session we began doing spontaneous and interesting things—going for a walk to the ocean, painting graffiti on the walls, telling jokes or stories. We had "remembering the years I was in High School" days where the dress/music/events of an era were relived.

In a month, the "here and now" group process of my existential supervisor began to work. All group participant names were remembered. Perceptive discussion of everyday hospital life was shared freely. We had made the present fun and safe, so they had carefully ventured into it.

Patient T, a Portuguese-American man and the youngest at age 69, shared his frustration with his 92-year-old mother's daily calls, trying not to continue his lifetime of being over-controlled by her. Patient V, a Japanese-American woman of 77, had the habit of putting out cigarettes on her arm and wanted help to stop. She got it.

Understanding the Progress Transfer Gap

But none of these newly restored communication abilities transferred to their home hospital wards the rest of their day. No progress was seen there by ward staff. One patient said in a session that once they stepped outside the group room, confusion rolled back in like a fog. I understood that their normal routine was boring to unpleasant but that didn't seem enough to explain the functional return of such pervasive pathology.

Howard Gudeman in his role as my supervisor suggested an existential perspective. What if they were each being immobilized by a traumatic fear of death? (Based on later experience, I would add the fear of physical disability.) Dr. Gudeman's innovative neuropsychology rehabilitation techniques were eventually published somewhat later (Craine & Gudeman 1981; Gudeman 1982, 1984.)

Given their age and environment, this was not an irrational fear. Most of their friends had died. A season rarely ended without a funeral for somebody they knew and cared for. They grieved then also for themselves. They lived daily in a world that, despite its beauty, had constrained and diminishing possibilities and, for now, an unthinkable (suppressed) future. This was a traumatic grief that they had never confronted. Hiding from it in their remote past memory was the dysfunctional answer.

The Group Treatment Approach Reaches a New Level

By this time, months had passed. Patient T's mother had died. He had worked through his embarrassing relief as well as the expected grief. They trusted me. So when patient T finally reached closure about his mother's death, I began to talk about confronting our own death. They tolerated this, identifying it as my own late-blooming craziness. It was a delicate intervention since I was at least a half century younger than they were and therefore much safer from death temporally.

It took another month, but now all were discussing their own mortality, generating individual plans. Some decided to postpone the inevitable by exercise and nutrition. Some became more religious, seeking a joyous afterlife. Some became more spiritual, identifying with the tropical beauty and traditions of our Hawaiian surroundings. Some, including me, took an interest in life extension, life span, and applied gerontology. These became my eventual career.

This new level's approach took several months more before all group participants were at peace with their own mortality, even drafting their own epitaph, obituary, and will.

Diagnostic Correction and Group Closure

With the fear of death trauma reduced, all developed restored memory, both at our meetings and throughout the rest of their day in the ward. After our year together, they had earned a fresh diagnosis or, as was the case, discharge planning.

This outcome of the entire group's success opens a new challenge, even beyond termination anxiety, as chronic patients anticipate a return to an unknown community. The curtain calls of symptoms might be expected as usual but could require additional planning led by social work expertise.

It may be useful here to continue the group process a little longer. These discharge transitions need to proceed gradually, at their own speed, in a way so as to maintain safety from trauma. Elders typically experience a slower time experience than younger staff. Even after that, follow-up post-discharge may well be aided by a continuation of the group at regular outpatient intervals.

Re-entering the contemporary outside world after spending decades as in-patients was daunting at best for every group member. Some fresh trauma had to be confronted there, but that is another story. Ultimately they made a safe transition.

Shining a light on the fear of death can help any community seek a better future. Neuropsychologist Howard Gudeman's existentialism had great value after all.

The Dysfunction and Treatment of Anticipatory Trauma Then, Now, and Next

Although this clinical group approach for the too often neglected inpatient chronic elders having pseudo-psychotic diagnoses was published following my internship (Morgan 1965, 1967, 1981), decades went by before the therapeutic viability of this approach gained more visibility for practicing clinical psychologists. The pioneering work of Drs. Bert Karon and Gary Vandenbos in their breakthrough 1981 book *Psychotherapy of Schizophrenia: the treatment of choice* brought professional attention once again to try more psychological interventions, including for this population of institutionalized elders.

My longtime colleague and friend Bert Karon maintained this valuable perspective throughout subsequent decades in a series of journal articles (Karon & Widener 1999) up to the end of the 20th century and into the 21st. Not to be left behind, the American Psychological Association (APA) has formally developed a new post-doctoral specialization in treating serious mental illness (SMI) (APA 2019) as reflected in Mary Jansen's earlier collaboration with the APA on a Practice Initiative Curriculum meant to reframe psychology for the emerging health care environment (APA & M.A. Jansen 2014). A recent study of more than 40,000 lifetime SMI adults in the USA found a full third of them in remission for a year or more (Salzer *et al* 2018) and that with mostly longstanding traditional treatment or its absence.

Psychological treatment of patients erroneously labeled with psychosis can no longer reasonably be seen as solely a medical concern, with treatment restricted to medical personnel. Adding psychological treatment options adds essential hope for the oft neglected institutionalized elders discussed here.

Building on his important work with decades of his own contributions to understanding the psychology of death anxiety (Neimeyer

1994), Robert Neimeyer (2012) more recently incorporated this clinical approach in his Grief Therapy book with a few of my own invited chapters on what I have termed "anticipatory grief." This is still a dysfunctional defense against a personal world of aging with narrowing possibilities, disability, and an overpowering fear of death.

Confronting this in a group setting can lead to recovered and enhanced memory, particularly for recent events. It can also improve functionality, reduce depression, facilitate realistic 5-year future plans (an important intervention), and discard erroneous diagnostic labels of psychosis or physical senility. The valuable life experience of elders, key statues in time, is well worth it.

Review of Practice Points

- Institutionalized elders may be erroneously labeled as psychotic when unable to correctly answer the person/place/time screening questions.

- If physical dysfunctions can be ruled out and questions about the past are answered more effectively, the probability is higher that the patient's senile behavior is psychogenic.

- A group process approach may well be a good intervention, especially if it makes the meetings varied and interesting, thereby making them trauma-safe.

- Transfer of progress to the patient's life outside the group meetings can be enhanced if fear of the future is resolved and planned for, especially fear of death or disability. Fear of the future and unhappiness with the present may have triggered a memory withdrawal to the safer temporal statues of the patient's past. This would be escape from anticipatory trauma or grief.

- This group process, especially with chronic patients, might best be done daily and continue for months until the dysfunctional behavior ends and effective memory returns.

- The outcome of success will open a new challenge as chronic patients anticipate a return to an unknown community. Curtain calls of symptoms might be expected but could be brief with effective social work collaboration and planning.

- Success will be followed by careful discharge planning with post-discharge support and followup. The group process may be useful here as well while these discharge transitions proceed gradually in a way to maintain safety from trauma.

- Research and replication on the re-introduction of this intervention holds promise for current 21st century practice, particularly for these elder patients and their valuable memories. They have much of post-trauma value to contribute.

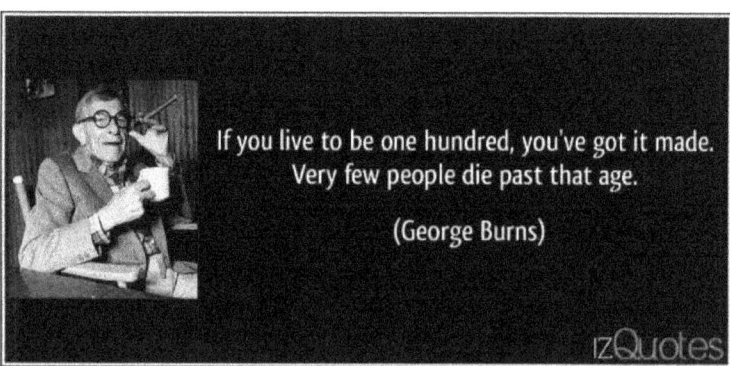

Chapter 16. Close Encounters of the Anomalous Kind

Master hypnotist David Cheek's approach to problem solving: "Go to bed with the question, wake up with the answer. Your unconscious does all the work while you rest."

Definition of anomalous

*https://**www.merriam-webster.com/dictionary/anomalous**:*

1: *inconsistent with or deviating from what is usual, normal, or expected:* <u>irregular,</u> <u>unusual, as in r</u>*esearchers could not explain the anomalous test results.*

2a: *of uncertain nature or classification, as an anomalous figure in the world of politics.*

2b: *marked by incongruity or contradiction,* **paradoxical**

Some Anomalous Experience Vignettes for Basic and Applied Psychologists

At a university in southern Colorado, a psychology student of mine set as his class project a test of whether or not pyramid shapes preserved food. Some anecdotal evidence for this existed but he wanted something more scientifically rigorous. I agreed.

Drawing on his early expertise as a biology major, he cut cross-sections of onion slices and placed them on nine plates. He covered three of the plates with pyramid shaped cardboard containers. Three other plates were covered with normal square shaped cardboard boxes of equal volume. The final three plates remained uncovered. At the end of each day, he counted the enucleated cells in each onion slice, a measure of decay. At the end of the week, only the onion slices in the pyramid containers were mostly preserved. The other online slices were fully decayed and our noses concurred.

Why? I hypothesized certain container shapes can create a very small (magnetic?) force deadly to bacteria but not anything much larger.

Well, that was in the late 1970s.

In the 1980s at a Canadian university in Ontario, I began a replication of this study so I might add this unusual research to my otherwise more traditionally written gerontology books (Morgan, 1981a, 1981b, 2005). There an academic colleague visited me with great enthusiasm, in the interim before I learned that the replication worked and the anomalous effect was the same.

He said: *"You are right to scientifically debunk this pyramid nonsense! Publishing the results will prove our department has a solid science faculty."*

I asked him: *"What if the results do replicate the original study? What if there is something important to learn about pyramid shaped containers?"*

Without hesitation he responded *"Burn the data and don't tell anybody!"*

I published the results. More than once.

Little has changed in our present century. Yet I have been so lucky as to know some colleagues who are exceptions, and their pioneering work in what might be called (erroneously) "parapsychology" is exceptional. The subject matter may be unusual and the results untraditional, but if the science is sound, it is not "beyond" (para) psychology.

Early research of this kind was primarily defensive in nature. The first pioneer, Duke University's J.B. Rhine (1934, 1957), typically put participants through thousands of trials over many hours so as to produce overwhelming mathematical proof of anomalous abilities. Naturally fatigue set in and the research could be inconclusive or frustrating. Another common research approach used random or nonsense syllables. It turned out that meaning, emotional as well as cognitive, was important to take into account (Teague, 1973).

Yet, for first addressing this area of psychology in a systematic way, even inventing the field despite scorn throughout the scientific community, Rhine should be honored. For applied psychology and clear replicable demonstrations, I would of necessity also honor Gertrude Schmeidler (1945, 1946). More about her work below.

In my early gerontology books, I wrote that transpersonal psychology for me was primarily defined as learning about human potentials. In a later discussion this century, Bob Frager described transpersonal psychology as "all of psychology" compared with a narrow traditional textbook psychology definition covering only those events that are seen as worthy by society. Topics that don't frighten anybody. This constricted view of psychology was labeled by Charles Tart in 2009 and other of his works as "scientism," a pursuit opposed to actual open-minded valid scientific inquiry.

The broader more complete view of psychological inquiry has valuable implications for both the future of basic psychological research and important contemporary psychological applications. I introduce a few key pioneers here, meriting great respect in our field, as I knew or know them.

These three are no longer with us: William Braud, David Cheek, Arthur Hastings.

William Braud, Ph.D. began his career as a rigorous research psychologist from the University of Iowa. He never lost this. Instead, as his career advanced, he applied his methodological rigor to understanding anomalous issues, often ones impacting our daily experience (Braud & Dossey 2003). These might address such concerns as:

- How does a parent know that their child is in trouble before anybody else does?

- How do you know if somebody is watching you when you walk down the street?

- How did you know who was calling you on the phone before you answered it?

- Why do many dogs know their human is coming home even an hour before they arrive, go to the door, and wait as though on cue (noticed often at residential group homes)?

- Can successful therapy for an adult relieving childhood trauma flow backward in time to comfort the actual child that became the adult?

William kept his friendly scientific skepticism while fearlessly exploring events like these, gathering the formal evidence in controlled and publishable form. He, with colleague Rosemary Anderson, developed innovative research approaches for this form of investigation (Braud & Anderson 1998, Anderson & Braud 2011). William was a brilliant colleague with the imaginative vision of an Einstein. We miss him.

David Cheek, M.D. began his career as an archeologist, then a physician specializing in obstetrics and gynecology. While maintaining his practice for most of his life, he also pioneered a very client-centered respectful form of hypnosis, one still largely practiced in modern hypnosis (Cheek & LeCron, 1968, Cheek 1993). His clinical hypnosis texts defined the field, leading many to refer to him as the Dean of Clinical Hypnosis and, with Ernest Rossi, a major modern pioneer in the psychological and medical applications of hypnosis (Rossi & Cheek 1994). David was the one who discovered that unconscious surgery patients were in a very suggestible trance state such that what was said in their presence could help or harm them. Modern trauma psychology is beginning to be aware of this.

David did have an interest in case-centered anomalous experience. We debated our separate explanations a lot. Here is an example:

A seven-year-old boy was brought to David for care. He was in a catatonic state, speaking to no one and not moving. The boy's mother had been a patient of David's but was the day before murdered in the parking lot of San Francisco's Presidio. She had been knifed and bled to death over a period of time. The mother was the boy's only parent and he was her only child. Police found him frozen in position at home. The next day David sat with the quiet boy in his office. David recognized that his young client was already in a trance state. He asked the boy if there was somebody inside him that wanted to speak. The boy moved for the first time, long enough to nod yes. David said it was safe to do so. Suddenly the boy spoke in a voice not much like his own, older and more female sounding. In that voice he described, as his mother, what had happened in that parking lot, who had done it, and finally her dying wishes for her son's care without her. Following this. Dr. Cheek shared all this information with the police, learning it was all accurate, eventually capturing the killer. The boy was cared for much as the mother had wanted. Or had requested?

David called me on the phone to share all this, ending with his satisfaction that this to him was clear evidence for life after death. (I do recommend a reading of Cochran's 2004 research on the psychology of such reported experience.)

As many had argued before us, I suggested an alternative hypothesis. Since the bond between mother and child was so powerful, it would be reasonable to assume that in her final minutes of life her thoughts would be powerfully directed to her son, her only child. We did not require the Jungian Collective Unconscious to hypothesize that at least under such severe circumstances, mental communication between two people so closely bonded could take place at a distance. Much less unreasonable today when quantum physics is exploring and applying this phenomenon.

So David chose a life after death explanation and I went for transfer of thoughts at a distance under emotional pre-death conditions.

As I got older, my multiple causality perspective would welcome his hypothesis to also be correct. At least under some circumstances and in some way. I like to think of this fine unselfish pioneer as still around somewhere. Of course he will always exist in the temporal geography he inhabited, a welcoming statue in time (Morgan 2017).

Arthur Hastings, Ph.D. was a former Stanford University and Institute of Transpersonal Psychology research psychologist, and part-time magician. Arthur was the colleague who organized anomalous research into logical sequence, into holistic description. He consulted at the Stanford Research Institute International (SRI) on remote viewing projects and published articles on these successful studies. He investigated poltergeist phenomena using his knowledge of conjuring techniques to identify several cases of deception or misinterpretation. He wrote critiques of Israeli psychic Uri Geller and of deceptive psychic practitioners.

In 1980 Arthur edited *Health for the Whole Person*, one of the first books on holistic medicine. In more recent years, he was annoyed with the political eclipse of medical science in the USA exemplified by putting potentially useful pharmaceuticals on schedule one to prohibit research. This was, for Arthur, particularly true for MDMA, a drug that used therapeutically seemed to open effective new trauma healing avenues.

So, as already discussed, he published a study demonstrating that hypnotic recall could reproduce the effects of MDMA, even if only taken once (Hastings 1994) with replications in subsequent years (Hastings *et al* 2000, Hastings 2006). As was described in an earlier chapter, long before we worked together, I contacted Arthur about his first MDMA paper. Although Arthur was fully focused on MDMA therapy applications, I thought and still think that maybe we could mimic the effects of a whole range of prescription drugs, making the best effects available without cost or without windfall profits for the pharmaceutical industry, a very attractive future possibility.

Doing teaching or research with Arthur was always a pleasure. Like our colleague William, he was a real adept with scientific method, but one with a heart. And as a magician, he was insightful at seeing past illusion to find the truth. By viewing from fresh angles, he would locate the needed formal evidence.

More on Arthur later. We miss him too.

Still sharing the planet with us

As I write this, I am pleased to report that these three researchers into understanding the psychology and applications for anomalous experience are still with us:

Etzel Cardeña, Ph.D. is Thorsen Professor of Psychology at Sweden's Lund University where he is currently the Director of the Centre for Research on Consciousness and Anomalous Psychology (CERCAP). He has served as President of the Society of Psychological Hypnosis (APA Division 30), and the Society for Clinical and Experimental Hypnosis. Professor Cardeña has written more than 300 publications including the books *Altering Consciousness* (Cardeña *et al* 2011a, 2011b) and *Varieties of Anomalous Experience* (Cardeña *et al* 2014) and another on trauma psychology (Cardeña & Croyle 2005). Originally from Mexico, Cardeña studied at the Universidad Iberoamericana in México and completed an MA in clinical psychology at York University in Toronto, Canada and an MA and PhD in Personality Psychology at the University of California, Davis. His doctoral thesis under the supervision of Charles Tart was on the phenomenology of deep states of hypnosis. He subsequently went on to do post-doctoral work in the areas of dissociation and hypnosis at Stanford University under David Spiegel. But wait, there's more: he is also the Artistic Director of the International Theatre of Malmö and has worked in theatre as a director, actor and playwright in Mexico, the USA and Sweden. He did graduate studies in theatre directing at the University of California, Davis, after having worked professionally in theatre in México and been offered scholarships from the Polish and Canadian governments to do graduate work in acting. But our work together goes back to our faculty labors in Palo Alto, California at what was then the Pacific Graduate School of Psychology 1986-1990. In addition to all the preceding description and contemporary leadership in the study of anomalous experience (Cardeña 2014), Etzel left an indelible impression on me, in those years and now, as a fundamentally ethical scientist with strong character and integrity. These qualities describe the others I note here as well, but on Cardeña it glows.

Stanley C. Krippner Ph.D., shown here with his colleague and former student Angel Morgan, is an executive faculty member and Professor of Psychology at Saybrook University in Oakland, California. He was previously director of the Kent State University

Child Study Center, and director of the Maimonides Medical Center Dream Research Laboratory in Brooklyn, New York. He has written extensively on altered states of consciousness, dream telepathy, and parapsychological subjects. His research and theory fit well into the current physics explorations and applications of quantum theory.

Of his voluminous publications, one might begin with his east-west psychology contributions (1980) or the more recent comparison of human potentials with human illusion (2010), or the contemporary application of his work for addressing the current PTSD epidemic (2018).

He has taught this latter PTSD prevention and treatment in a course with my daughter, Angel K. Morgan, Ph.D., who was once his graduate student at the Saybrook Institute in San Francisco. That's them in the photo above. Angel was often the sender in Stan's dream reception demonstrations at the annual International Association for the Study of Dreams (IASD) convention. Today she is an expert on the psychology of dreams, including PTSD reduction approaches utilizing Senoi nightmare resolution techniques (A. K. Morgan, 2011, 2014, 2016) and is President of the IASD.

Stan's professional career has also intersected with another of my daughters, Cinnamon Camo, when she was caring for the shaman Rolling Thunder (RT) while at UC Santa Cruz. Stan and I visited RT there during his recuperation from an operation. From Stan's shamanic studies, he published several books on this topic, including a very recent one in 2018.

Charles Tart, PhD. is internationally known for his psychological work on the nature of consciousness, as one of the founders of the field of transpersonal psychology, and for his research in scientific parapsychology. His two classic books, Altered States of Consciousness (1969) and Transpersonal Psychologies (1975), became widely used texts that were instrumental in allowing these areas to become part of modern psychology.

He received his doctoral degree in psychology from the University of North Carolina at Chapel Hill in 1963, and then received postdoctoral training in hypnosis research with Professor Ernest R. Hilgard at Stanford University. He was long a Core Faculty Member at the Institute of Transpersonal Psychology (Palo Alto, California) and a Senior Research Fellow of the Institute of Noetic Sciences (Sausalito, California), as well as continuing as Professor Emeritus of Psychology at the Davis campus of the University of California, where he served for 28 years. He was the first holder of the Bigelow Chair of Consciousness Studies at the University of Nevada in Las Vegas and has served as a Visiting Professor in East-West Psychology at the California Institute of Integral Studies, as an Instructor in Psychiatry at the School of Medicine of the University of Virginia, and a consultant on government funded parapsychological research at the Stanford Research Institute International.

Some of his other many books include *Learning to Use Extrasensory Perception* (1976), *Psi: Scientific Studies of the Psychic Realm* (1977), *Mind at Large: Institute of Electrical and Electronic Engineers Symposia on the Nature of Extrasensory Perception* (1979, with H. Puthoff & R. Targ), *Waking Up: Overcoming the Obstacles to Human Potential* (1986), *Open Mind, Discriminating Mind: Reflections on Human Possibilities* (1989), and *Mind Science: Meditation Training for Practical People* (2001). He has had more than 250 articles published in professional journals and books, including lead articles in such prestigious scientific journals as *Science* and *Nature*.

As well as a laboratory researcher, Professor Tart has been a student of the Japanese martial art of Aikido (in which he holds a black belt), of meditation, of Gurdjieff's work, of Buddhism, and of other psychological and spiritual growth disciplines. His primary stated goal is to build bridges between the scientific and spiritual communities and to help bring about a refinement and integration of Western and Eastern approaches for knowing the world with applications for personal and social growth.

Once the 21st century began, we were colleagues in Palo Alto for a few years. Behind his open and quietly humorous demeanor was a very fine scientist, one still today exploring the outer reaches of psychological application with rigor and care. My letter to him on reading, finally, his book *The End of Materialism: How Evidence of the Paranormal is Bringing Science and Spirit Together* (2009), follows.

Brushes with Experiential Parapsychology: A Letter to Charles Tart

Hello Compadre-

I finally got around to reading your 2009 book "The End of Materialism," which of course is more about escaping the limitations of what is called materialism, since materialism is still with us. Maybe what was meant is more like leaving the city limits, the place where it ends for others. The city still remains, but the wide world(s) beyond hold much more to explore for those still curious. To do this, you gather evidence and anecdote, expressed in the good-natured clarity of Charles Tart.

In any case, I very much enjoyed the book so live with it, my friend, this is a fan letter.

It brought to mind a few passing memories of my own, consistent with the anomalous ones that you explore consistently, at least one of these being an important one engendered by a chapter in your first most famous book, Altered States of Consciousness, *from a half century ago.*

San Francisco 1973

The Camel Races were being held at Bay Meadows Race Track. I took Dianne and her girlfriend Vicki since none of us had ever seen camels race. Nor would we that day. Camels only were in the first race but they turned out to be indifferent to human expectation. Few if any ever reached the finish line. It was funny and fun though. Now, having seen camels meander, we were ready for the regularly scheduled horse races, another first for us. Dianne handed me the day's listing where the names of all horses were listed. She challenged me to pick the winner of race number one. It wasn't a friendly challenge. Dianne was very skeptical of parapsychology explorations my students and I were doing by hypnosis at psychology's first professional school in its earliest years.

I really wanted to meet this challenge somehow, so I studied the racing sheet very intensely, wondering what to say. I noticed what seemed to be a glow around one horse's name. I confidently said the name out loud and suggested they bet on it. Dianne laughed and declined to bet. The horse came in first. Now both women were excited about my apparent ability to pick a winner. I was challenged to do the same for the second race. I suppressed my own surprise and with seeming confidence reached for the racing sheet. The desire to show off was strong in me. But this time there was no glow to be seen. Just a faint discoloration around one of the names. Hoping for the best, I chose that horse to win. They ran to invest all the funds they had with them on this horse. To my relief, that horse came in first.

Now both Dianne and Vicki were true believers. They had visions of buying us a mansion, their own complete new wardrobes, maybe a cruise around the world. What was the Riviera like this time of year? I calmly accepted the racing sheet for a third try. This time I could see no glow or discoloration of any kind. Whatever ability I had experienced before was not to be found now. As had been my expectation. I tried to tell them this but they were having none of it. An exchange of that era was "Whatever happened to your get up and go?" with the answer: "It got up and went." Following this thought, I yawned, stretched, and said I was going home. Which I did. The indignation of my two companions lasted for as long as I knew them.

St. Bonaventure University (SBU), Olean New York 1967-1969

The low self-fulfilling prophecy or resistance to anomalous experience was called "psi missing" by Gertrude Schmeidler (1945, 1946). (I note she died the year your book came out but infer no causation in either direction.) I didn't like her "psi-missing" term as it seemed more like "psi negative" to me, an example of self-programmed failure.

I did love her experiments though and set out to replicate them with the huge audiences beginning faculty like me got in their mandatory introductory classes. Out of hundreds of students sitting in the auditorium, it was not hard to find a few volunteers who either believed telepathy impossible or actual. Most were agnostics on this point or at least too inhibited to take any stand. A coin was tossed by me 20 times out of the sight of all students in the class. The believers that volunteered in my classes never scored beyond chance level. The fervent disbelievers often (the majority of them) scored well beyond chance: with all or almost all guesses wrong.

This made sense to me. We are much better at sabotaging ourselves so as to meet low expectations, than accepting the success that can come by meeting high expectations. Key football players betting on their own team may just be expressing confidence but if they are already playing at their best, then no enhanced performance can be guaranteed. Yet if those key football players bet against their team, then the probability of impaired success is highly likely. It is just easier to fail. Best to keep expectations high, even against all odds. (At one for-profit university owned by Goldman-Sachs, I advised the under-resourced faculty to think of their glass as 10% full).

This I replicated in class after class for two years at SBU, two years next in Nova Scotia at Acadia University, and four years finally at San Francisco State University. But 1975 was the last time I did this. For one, I had moved up the ladder to small graduate seminars and no more abundant supplies of non-psychology students. But there was another more personal reason.

My father had very firm opinions. He was absolutely certain that my interest in parapsychology was a waste of time. So at a family gathering I challenged him to participate in a Schmeidler coin tossing experiment. You see where this is going. As my children watched, their grandpa guessed every coin toss wrong. As he turned around to learn his score, he noticed the amazement on their faces and, I think, for a second he allowed himself some pride at thinking he got them all right. The results of course were announced as the opposite. Not only did he miss every guess, but this failure, as he saw it, was being used to disprove his previously stated emphatic belief. He was not convinced that this demonstrated strong ability on his part, even if he used this ability against himself.

Let's just say he wasn't particularly happy. I regretted embarrassing him that way. From that point on, I realized that most students seen in class, disproving their own disbelief by outstanding failure, would be made to feel miserable. There might be a few who understood this revealing of unexpected ability as an opportunity to revise their understanding of themselves and the universe they inhabit. Such people are hard to find in a population of skeptics usually impervious to divergent information.

Wolfville, Nova Scotia 1969

At Michigan State University in 1965, Paul Bakan and I explored fast ways of applying sensory deprivation to experience hallucinations without drugs. The three key elements were lying down, restricted vision (papered over swim goggles), and restricted head movement. Within an hour, sometimes in minutes, people experienced visions not in voluntary control (something Arthur Hastings explored years later in another setting with his 2002 Psychomanteum research).

In a western Nova Scotia university I set up a lab to continue this work. One student who participated wanted to see if she could use our apparatus to see playing cards that I held while her vision was restricted. I agreed. I went through an entire deck of cards one at a time. Each time she visualized a card and reported what she was seeing. Often she excused herself because she was anxious about her performance. When we were done, I had the sad task of telling her that she had not been correct about a single card. Which met her catastrophic expectation squarely. Yet I noticed that she had picked the color of the card, red or black, correctly every time, something highly unlikely due to chance.

A few years later in San Francisco, where the 1960s were still alive and well throughout the 1970s, I noticed my daughters' primary school friends liked to play a card game where the winner was the one who wound up with all the cards. In each round a child had to guess the card every other player was holding, one at a time. The guessing got better and better over the summer, an actual learning curve.

No experiment here, just children playing a game. And even improving with practice.

San Francisco 1971-1975

The California School of Professional Psychology was our first American professional school, originally with just two campuses in San Francisco and Los Angeles.

The first generation students were generally as experienced (and as old) as the faculty. These pioneering students included Frances Vaughn, Benjamin Tong, Nathan Hare, Reiko True, Leonard Elkind, and many others eventually well known to psychology.

They lacked only the doctorate. Without a core curriculum, we 13 founding faculty had the opportunity to fit the classroom training to the actual needs and interests of these very capable students. There would be dissertations with freedom as to focus and the innovation of a proposal that would be binding on the school once the proposal was approved. With such a free hand we generated innovative curriculum.

Founding faculty member Andrew Curry, MSW, an African American world-class expert on group process, created a liberal arts cluster. This included the Tantric Feets Dance Ensemble, the Freedom from Disabling Pathology Gazette, growth groups including psychodrama, alternative healing techniques, martial arts, and even a course labeled Psychic Intuition. This last course offering troubled the school president, Nicholas Cummings, but Andy told him it was a philosophical discourse on "ways of knowing."

Nick was already troubled with the San Francisco campus and what he called its "curriculum buffet." He also wondered why mail from the Los Angeles campus was delivered to his San Francisco office in a day, while our San Francisco campus took a week to get to the same office. (This time distortion turned out to be only a turning back of the postage meter so late submissions still seemed to have been mailed within their deadline.)

Some of the innovations were brilliant successes and some fell flat. Possibly the best decision I made as Dean at the time was to bring hypnosis into the curriculum for the first year students. Eric Greenleaf did a visualization class and David Cheek did a gratis hypnosis training workshop. The students applied this learning very effectively to reduce test anxiety, enhance speed reading comprehension, and even pursue personal experiments in parapsychology.

Many of these innovations last to this day in very traditional graduate schools of psychology. Some of the more specialized additions given to first year graduate students carried on in uniquely progressive programs like the Institute of Transpersonal Psychology where Robert Frager built Aikido and other martial arts into the required curriculum.

The early hypnosis training is still a goal I would like to see programs provide to their students as a core course.

Virginia 1979

I had read Robert Monroe's Journeys Out of the Body *while still working in Southern Colorado 1975-1978. I knew somebody who was working with maximum security patients, including some rapists and serial killers, locked up there. I had already convinced the administration to stop providing weekend passes to town for these dangerous patients as behavioral incentives.*

In all fairness, I suggested to staff that those patients likely to be locked up for the rest of their life there without passes might benefit by learning out-of-body experience, so as to at least journey out of their imprisoned bodies. Obviously I hadn't thought it through. I was told they already did that all the time. Not a comforting thought.

Monroe's book also helped me understand the nature of a Nova Scotia ghost in 1970. At that time in this Canadian western Nova Scotian university town of Wolfville, the Scottish sense of frugality prevailed. You were not expected to buy a house until you had saved enough to pay cash for it.

Being a new young faculty member from the United States and with a *large family, I took out a mortgage for $40,000 on arrival. This bought us a 30 room-furnished mansion up on a hill facing the Bay of Fundy, plus acres of woods. The ten bedrooms were far more than we needed, so we took in students that the university dean found to be unsatisfactory for dormitory living. Bright, joyful, and creative without exception.*

The home was called Morgan House. It would have its own broomball team.

Once we had all settled into our new home, it was soon reported that every Saturday night, sometime after midnight, an old woman would walk through the wall and observe the partying going on in various rooms, shake her head in disapproval, and walk out through another wall. Almost every adult in the house saw this specter but me.

The ghost of Morgan House was accepted gladly by all as key atmosphere. The fact that the mansion had once been a nursing home was a ready explanation for the visitations.

Then one sunny afternoon, I was walking down the main street when the resident students with me got excited, pointing across the street: "That's her! Our ghost!"

The elderly woman responded to this attention by running around the corner out of our sight and was not to be seen again. Now that we know she was not a ghost, what explained her visits?

Robert Monroe's work suggested a possibility. After all, Morgan House with its high concentration of youthful freedom in a fundamentalist town where dancing and movies were considered sinful, well, it definitely triggered curiosity.

My own experience with Robert Monroe in 1979 was funded by the state of Nevada's training funds. It seemed to me even then that what is now called Hemi-Sync had promise for treating chronic patterns of substance or alcohol abuse by teaching new tools of self-discovery.

I was in the second training session Monroe put on, closely following the close of the first one (Elisabeth Kubler-Ross was in that primary group- she thought my life extension work demonstrated being stuck in a stage of denial.)

The first group had celebrities like John Voight wanting to learn how to travel outside their body. My group instead had more than a few military and intelligence specialists wanting the same thing.

We were nightly awakened at random times, rolled out of our sleeping bags, and went through the procedure until we managed to maintain lucidity at deep delta wave relaxation.

I could see the opportunity for clients and patients to use these skills to make breakthroughs in self-defeating patterns such as addictions.

I experienced the dual earphone input of induction-like directions to one ear and repeated slow wave forms in the other, as a form of tech-savvy hypnosis.

Bob Monroe rejected this H word completely, probably thinking of exploitive stage hypnosis. I knew altered states used in professional or even self-hypnosis can be helpful and healing if done well, particularly with the respectful methods of David Cheek. I still think the Monroe process utilizes a benign form of hypnosis.

In our workshop, we eventually traveled to deeper levels of involvement from focus 10 to focus 15 to focus 45. The highest level we reached often led participants to contacts they experienced as spiritual or, in some cases, an emotional break through.

For me, I found that some trauma I had been carrying for about a year turned into a release of laughter. I had been stoically suppressing joy. While I had not journeyed outside my body, it had been well worth the journey outside Nevada.

Cinnamon 1968-Today

That 30 room mansion called "Morgan House" in Nova Scotia, Canada, had my daughter Cinnamon at its center. Of pre-school age, she was the youngest child in the midst of 30, mostly adults,

and got tremendous attention from all of them. This was in large part because of her character. Even before she was two, she would refuse to taste an ice cream cone until she knew everybody else had one. One Christmas in Morgan House, I was overheard telling her and her much older siblings that funds were low, so each would get just one present that year.

Cinnamon, age 3, stepped forward, saying "Don't give me any presents then. They can have mine." Her older brothers and sister thought that was a great idea (I didn't). The people of the house all soon knew of this. Naturally she was swamped with presents from all of them on Christmas. Altruism can be very rewarding.

Cinnamon was born in 1968 at a very traditional hospital in the Allegheny Mountains. Once the baby was incubated with her pink blanket, I came to the window for observing the newborn prisoners. Cinnamon was crying.

I asked the nurse to take her to her mother. Nope: not the right scheduled time. I pointed out that she was crying. Nope, said the nurse, the cortex is nonfunctional for the first five years of life, so what I was seeing was only reflex. No feelings or self-awareness until her fifth birthday? We got out of that place as soon as we could.

Our karmic opportunity happened about 18 months later.

My students alerted me. The Saint Bonaventure University faculty member teaching child development, in a classroom I used after her, was a source of the same nonsense: no cognitive functioning before five years of age. Learning this, I carried Cinnamon into her classroom just as the instructor was finishing her lecture. As I went up front to introduce her to the baby, I slipped Cinnamon some chalk and as I *was holding her she began to draw a snowman on the blackboard. "Why, that's very good!" Dr. Simrall exclaimed. "Thank you" said Cinnamon. "Well, she's 18 months old now. Why not?" I said. The instructor turned to the class: "Oh no, that's not normal. She's just very precocious by many years. Some genetic mutation, maybe." Me: "Not at all. We just have always given her a lot of attention and she has responded as any child would." The class applauded and Cinnamon smiled.*

At age 8 she had a problem on the rural Colorado school bus. The driver warned her passengers that she would paddle anybody that made a fuss, no matter who started it. Some boys took advantage of this by pulling the hair of the girls and pinching them. Their victims were afraid to complain for fear of being paddled.

Now a single parent, that summer I enrolled Cinnamon in an adult Aikido class at Aspen. By the second week she had learned to fall and roll (saving her grief in a bicycle accident years later). She did something painless to my wrist that made it difficult to move my hand for a few minutes. She proudly challenged me to pick her up which I did easily. Then she shut her eyes and concentrated. "Pick me up now" she said. This time when I tried she seemed stuck to the ground (an Aikido exercise called anchoring). She proudly stated that "four grown men couldn't pick me up today."

Her Aikido instructor was not much taller than Cinnamon and chose her as his demonstration partner. He had set aside his prohibition against training children because of her very sunny disposition and eagerness to learn. Clearly she was ready for the boys on the bus.

Not long after this, both Cinnamon and her younger sister Angel gained Rollo May as a godfather. In his "Days of the Giants" lecture to a very large California audience, Rollo outlined how the fundamental character flaws that challenged the original greats of psychotherapy led to their contributions. Prior to beginning, he complimented me as "one of the finest psychotherapists he knew."

I was stunned by the compliment and very puzzled. I had never been in therapy with Rollo nor had he ever seen me work. I told him afterwards: "Based on your lecture, I must have overwhelming character flaws."

He replied with a smile, "I was just judging you by your children."

Cinnamon went on to get a degree at the University of California Santa Cruz, helped native healer Rolling Thunder recover from a diabetic leg amputation, and helped run a university preschool program.

She settled in that Santa Cruz region, with her own daughter Ava.

Cinnamon writes and performs music. She still knows how to fall and land on her feet.

Angel Kwan-Yin 1971-Today:

Angel is my youngest daughter, born in Nova Scotia, Canada, during our final days in Morgan House. Before she was a year old we had moved to a home in San Francisco, albeit with some challenge from US immigration. Although she was a newborn with blonde hair and blue eyes, her middle name of Kwan-Yin convinced some bureaucratic cretin that we were trying to smuggle a Chinese baby in from Canada for sale in San Francisco. With substantial time and affidavits, we finally achieved dual citizenship and the right to keep her. The naturalization paper was stamped with her infant photo and baby footprint.

Angel as a toddler was called "Superbaby." She had immense strength. We might be sitting on a substantial living room chair or couch when suddenly it would start moving. A little giggle behind it would let us know that Angel was there. That continued up to about age two. One day I asked her to move my chair while I was sitting there to demonstrate her powers to some guests. She declined: "Little girls aren't strong enough to move big chairs with people in them" she explained, and so an older brother had convinced her. I asked her to show us what she used to be able to do and she complied one more time. But that was the last. Psi negative again.

She did come to us when I, and even some other family or friends wanted her to join us, even if it was not out loud. She would come running down the stairs from her bedroom at any random time we did this, usually with a special welcome or other fun thing waiting. This lasted until age five. When some would say erroneously that her cognitive abilities would have just begun.

At this age five she had some nightmares, visualizing people she had never met who were prisoners in maximum security not far away. I had read the Charles Tart's famous Altered States of Consciousness *and decided to apply the Kilton Stewart chapter on Senoi dream technique. She found this to be very helpful. So much so that when she began college at UCLA's Film and Theater program, she also began attending a dream group and having private dream sessions with Kilton's widow Clara Stewart Flagg.*

A few careers later, she went back to Saybrook University in San Francisco to get her psychology PhD with Stanley Krippner. Her dissertation was on the psychology of dreams, inventing a blueprint for a future research site on this topic called DreamBridge www.

thedreambridge.com. *Now an expert on the psychology of dreams, including Senoi method, especially nightmares, she writes for the Huffington Post. She continues with this work on film, publications, and books in Ashland, Oregon (A.K. Morgan, 2011, 2014, 2016, 2018).*

A small thing- In your book, you refer to only five basic senses as most psychologists still do. From our colloquium discussion at ITP a decade ago, the basic ones acknowledged for some time now number 10. The five senses most people think of are touch, taste, smell, sight, and hearing. This misses the next five which include the sense of hot and cold temperature (separate receptors as one can feel both heat and cold at the same time), pain, balance, and body position or kinesthesis. To be basic, each has its own specialized receptors and sensations. I learned this in Howard Bartley's class at Michigan State University in 1961, using his 1958 perception textbook. That leaves parapsychology pioneers not the 6th sense but the opportunity to find the 11th and on, many more than these basic ten.

Your definition of "spirituality" as different from religion is very sensible. On the other hand, the word allows hostile skeptics to conflate your perception of spirituality with the fraudulent spiritualists that Eric Weiss (Houdini) loved to expose or the Lillydale ones so embarrassing Elisabeth Kubler Ross in her senior days. (Or the Father Divine and other cults insisting that the death of their immortal leader was only a "dirt nap.") Ah well, a rose by any other name won't know the difference. Whatever we label your journeys of understanding, your good-natured clarity in sharing them with us, this book and all that came before remain well worth reading. By now quite a few generations are the better for them. Much of this valuable information and insight is enhanced by the example of a scientist unafraid of genuine science. I appreciate even more having

had an opportunity to work with you as a colleague and friend."
— Robert Morgan, 2013

Some last thoughts

A sense of humor can be a great antidote. Anomalous contrast is the spice of life. And that means time for a sidebar on existential anomalies for other species.

Sidebar: Do Hamsters have Ghosts?

Timmy was only four so he relied on family giants, compared to him, to explain the why and what of the world he found himself in, one he was trying very hard to understand. The only giant at home this morning was a shorter one, his 15-year-old sister Grace. So when he knocked on her bedroom door, he ignored her loud "GO AWAY!" and kept knocking.

Finally her door opened and, looking down, she said "WHAT?!"

Timmy stepped firmly into her doorway, asking "Do hamsters have ghosts?"

Grace was intrigued by this strange question and, deciding this might be fun after all, invited him in. They each sat down on a chair in front of her bed. She began with "What makes you think hamsters have ghosts?"

"Well on Halloween you said people have ghosts that come out when they die. Why not animals?"

Grace was not to be digressed into abstractions: "What's this about hamsters?"

"Umm last night I kept hearing little noises in my bedroom. Could *have been little hamster feet. But when I turned on my light there was nothing there."*

"Hmm. Like the baby hamster you flushed down the toilet last Saturday? Feeling guilty maybe?" Grace smiling here but not really a nice smile.

Timmy turned a little red in the face but put forth the same defense that had worked with their mother: "I was just giving him a bath or shower or both. I thought he was too big to get flushed away!"

Grace was not buying it: "Like the gold fish and turtles you flushed away in that same toilet?"

"That was a long time ago!"

"That was last week."

"That's a really long time. Anyway I was helping them escape to the ocean. They were homesick. Like 'Free Willie' escaped on Disney TV."

"The ocean is a thousand miles from here. I think if they were hoping for ocean, once they got to where they got to, that place where all the poop and pee go, they would not have thanked you very much. Probably hate you now."

This time it was Timmy's turn to refuse to be digressed, particularly on something he didn't want to think about. So he said "Just tell me. Do hamsters have ghosts?"

Grace thoughtful here. Even ants and mosquitoes? Tiny pinpoint apparitions haunting those humans who dispatched them? Even the bacterial animals she killed with her mouth wash? Well, hope not. But back to Timmy. After a pause: "I suppose all animals can turn into ghosts. Why not? I hadn't thought about that before but it makes sense. Maybe that WAS your hamster's ghost. I'd want to haunt you too after being flushed down a toilet."

Timmy considered this. Then: "Why aren't we haunted then by the chickens or cows or fish we eat? Wouldn't they have ghosts too?"

"I suppose they would or could. Each one is a person in their own way. Maybe you should not eat ANY of them anymore. If you don't want to be haunted." Grace smiled a wider smile. This WAS fun.

Timmy considered this too. Finally: "Then I guess I will just only eat fruits and vegetables. Don't think THEY Have ghosts."

"The fruits and vegetables we eat are the babies of the mother fruits and vegetables they come from. We eat them anyway because we pretend they are not alive."

"Pretend?"

"Okay Timmy, I'm going to read to you from a book I have and it's all about this. It explains everything." Grace was imagining the fun that will come at the family supper that evening. "It's called **The Secret Life of Plants***."*

II. LANGUAGE & INFLUENCE

David Cheek, MD

Chapter 17. Language Malfunction

"I am so worried for you! I do NOT want my husband to kill you!"

I was on the boarding line for my plane. She grabbed my arm.

International psychologists navigate many cultures. The trip is always worthwhile. True though, lots of surprises. This was one of them.

San Francisco psychologist and actor Benjamin Tong gave me many valuable insights on language. One of my favorites was the delicate way in which reviewing an unpleasantly jarring performance might be politely expressed: *"It had its moments."* This was one of those moments.

I met her at an international psychology congress, one in my final years of unmarried life. She was from a country where the two languages of our association, English and French, were rarely spoken or understood by most of its inhabitants. Nor did the ones I met feel they were missing anything. Not her though. She struggled to master fairly competent English conversation, possibly overestimating her success. But I admired her effort. Besides, other than a few words learned from movies, I had no command whatsoever of her own language.

Her goal was to get an adanced psychology doctoral degree. I doubted her language progress would be equal to the reading or lecture of any graduate program in the English language. Still, that was exactly what she wanted to do. What she wanted my guidance to accomplish. On the other hand, I was impressed by her as a person. She had wit, poise, beauty, intelligence, and the confidence of somebody with infinite resources. I told her what I could of best seeking the path she wanted to be on. Including acquiring more language proficiency for that choice.

She sat next to me when I saw her again two years later. The international congress this time was hosted in her own country. This was the Opening Ceremony. Like the Olympics, countries vied to host these international meetings. For participants in her country, this would likely be the only conference of its kind in their lifetime. As such it was grandest and spectacular. Plus, through her eyes, her lifelong cultural perspective. The entire event took on fresh color and intensity. Full of meaning that I otherwise might have missed completely.

After the ceremony, over dinner, she shared her life story. Married young to the globe trotting son of the founder of a powerful international corporation, she was often alone in their home. She spent each day writing him a letter about her own observations, ideas, and experiences. At the end of that first year, he published her letters as a book. One that was well received. As years went by, the annual book of her comments on that year become ever more popular. She became a celebrity in her own country. Although no translations to other languages made the books available elsewhere. Still, each year loyal readers looked forward to tales of this favorite couple, both traveling now but rarely together.

In fact, this very conference, even our dinner together, might appear in her next book. Although I would not be able to read it without a translator, I was promised a copy. We did not meet again after that evening until another international congress four years later.

Once again we sat together at an Opening Ceremony in a country she knew very well.

Just before this conference, she had flown all the way from her own country to Los Angeles just so as to have lunch at a top restaurant with my youngest daughter, a theater student at UCLA. She asked my daughter to tell me that she would be at the next World Congress and hoped I could meet her there.

I had already intended to go. So I did. Now, as we sat through the opening music, tears began streaming down her cheeks. I asked her what was wrong. She responded with *"My husband and I. We now separated."*

How sad. Her entire public face in her home country had been invested in this marriage.

Mortality statistics suggest that a divorce from a longtime partner can be more stressful than losing one through death. Worse yet, for such a highly visible couple, to be entering a divorce through the door of a legal separation. And she definitely appeared devastated.

I was not married yet that year. So I spent the next week with her, resolved to cheer her up. We toured the host country together. A very intense and satisfying set of days. Happy statues in time.

Her tears were gone now. She thanked me for her better sleep at night. She promised that now we were a couple, our time together would be highlighted in her next annual book, a central chapter. Untranslated though. Not sure I wanted that particularly. But the gift made her happy.

By our last day together, she had become extremely anxious. But she would not say why.

Finally, it was time for me to go to the airport. She came along to say goodbye.

As I stood in the boarding line, that was when she told me: ""*I am so worried for you! I do not want my husband to kill you!*"

I asked her why she thought that. Wasn't she and her husband separated?

"Yes. It is as I said. Separated. He in London. Me here with you."

–

Note: The next year I met and then married the woman I have been with all these decades since. My billionaire separated friend sent us a $5 cashier's check as a wedding present. At her level of income, this was meant to be received as an insult.

We cashed it anyway. She did send me the book detailing our adventure together. Someday I mean to have it translated.

More.

Sometimes though language malfunction can be set to music. This example is a modern more diverse take on a century old song. One our greatgrandparents kept popular for lifetimes, even to be found here and there today. We can keep the melody as it was.

FIVE FOOT TWO AND MIGUEL

Five foot two, eyes not blue,
But, oh, what those five feet could do!

Has anybody seen muh gal?
Gravel voice: Miguel's not here!
Turned up nose, painted toes,
Funky, yes sir, one of those!
Has anybody seen muh gal?
Gravel voice: I tole you! Miguel's not here! Vamoose! Ondalay!
Now if you see a five foot two, eyes not blue,
No need to fear,
We got the diamond rings, and all those things,
But muh gal isn't here?
Cause we have the loot, muh gal cute,
So there's no need for any shoot!
Has anybody seen muh gal?
Gravel voice: Okay! All right! I'm Miguel!

Language and the Unequal Narrowing of Resources

They have been at a great feast of languages and stolen the scraps.
  — William Shakespeare (Slattery, 2005)

Almost 150 years ago, after a long and puffy speech by Stephen Douglas, Abraham Lincoln asked the audience "How many legs would a horse have if you called his tail a leg?" "Five," called out some of the onlookers. "Four," replied Lincoln. "Calling a tail a leg doesn't make it true." (Lederer, 2005)

The Russian word for "No" is pronounced "Nyet." One can think of this from an English-speaking point of view as cultural optimism: sounds like "Not yet," a cautious hope that no may still become a yes. Others would say that "no means no." So: is the Russian negative like a glass half full or a glass half empty? I would say that "Nyet" means the Russian glass can be considered 10% full. Rollo May often said that both optimism and pessimism are "classic mistakes" (May 1986). Hope is the best we can aspire to. Ten per cent hope then.

Some politicians today, even at the national top, share much context with language. The phrase that begins a relatively candid comment is sometimes *"To be honest ..."* suggesting that what else they say may not be honest.

One national figure, known for thousands of untrue statements, liked to preface some of the most outrageous distortions and boasting with *"Incredible results"* (to me: not credible) or *"Fantastic results"* (to me: pure fantasy) or *"Unbelievable results"* (just as it says—don't believe it).

Especially hard for the new English speaker are the colloquialisms, varying in meaning with context. What a difference in consequence between, say, a pheasant hunter telling his friend *"Get ready to shoot the bird!"* and a teenager on a church camp bus seeing law enforcement driving by their open window saying to his friends on the bus *"Get ready to shoot the bird!"*

In Albuquerque, one of the three main hospitals is named *"Lovelace"* after its founder. But it is pronounced *"Loveless."* Their hospital for women, pronounced the *"Loveless Women's Hospital,"* may not be as enticing as it deserves. Still lots of potential patients though.

I also remember from my early years in Buffalo that the *"Amigone Funeral Home"* made it to Ripley's believe it or not. Its rival funeral home had a huge welcome billboard for those entering the city: *"From the Beginning to the End with a friend, Dan Montgomery Funeral Home."*

Language is always changing, incorporating words and concepts from other languages, ever moving to lazier shorter spellings or pronunciations. In Reno, Nevada, I witnessed the sexualization of language as it evolved there.

As a solo parent then of two young daughters, I took note when they each came home from school with a dubious contest form. Reno had a major morning newspaper and another evening newspaper, both engaged in a heavy competition for subscribers.

The public school had been promised a reward by the winning newspaper. Each child brought a form home for the parent to choose. This choice would be reflected in the child carrying around an advertising sign for a week saying either: "*I like it in the morning*" or "*I like it at night*" depending on which newspaper the parent chose.

Well, whenever forced to choose between two alternatives that both look questionable, psychologists are very able to find a third. I declined to check either "*I like it in the morning*" *or* "*I like it at night*." I just wrote in my own approach to newspapers in those lean times: "*I like it when I can afford it*." My daughters were excused from carrying any advertising signs.

The illusion that naming something fully explains it is called a *nominal fallacy*. In early childhood education, much less education at all ages, this is often a temporary palliative for ignorance. In psychiatric diagnoses this can also be a classic mistake (Morgan, 1982). Does the labeling truly define a condition or merely create pervasive linear pseudo categories so all-inclusive and vague that they can be exploited commercially? (Morgan 1982, 1983; Breggin, 1994; Breggin & Cohen, 2000). Here as always, reality is found in the space between the things we name.

Hypnotists know the power of language well and use it carefully (**"pain"** becomes **"discomfort"**) to influence expectation (Cheek 1968, 1993; Rossi & Cheek 1988; Battino 2006).

Note: David Cheek, in his many years as a gynecologist, was told by a teenage patient that she was having nightmares about people laughing at her and she had no explanation. David had taught her autohypnosis, as he did all his patients, and she willingly went into a light trance. With David's guidance she recalled a conversation from her recent appendectomy. She was under general anesthetic and unconscious but the memory was clear: she had a weight problem and the surgeon was joking about her appearance to his operating room nurses. The operation went well but the patient left with unconscious trauma.

It was one of David's greatest contributions to us all: we can remember what is said while we are under general anesthetic. More than that, we are in an emergency state of crisis which means we are in a highly suggestible level of hypnosis. Helpful words can aid a patient's healing and the wrongs ones could kill (Cheek 1968; Rossi & Cheek 1994).

In the case of David's teenaged patient, she now knew the origin of her nightmares and could confront them. She scheduled and held an appointment with her surgeon. He was stunned that she was aware of his misplaced sense of humor, and confirming her memory, he apologized. No more nightmares.

Existential psychologists discourage the use of "**I had to**," "**I need**," "**I must**" in favor of "**I choose" or "I want**" as more authentic and a way to reprogram from passivity in the face of challenge.

Then too, I will always cherish memory of the indignant Appalachian principal that wanted this sign removed from the street in front of his school:

"No slower than most" he insisted.

Life Transition Specialists

Fresno, California, 1983. As an aside to my professional school job, I set up a part-time clinical psychology practice with two of my faculty.

We did our business cards on wood grain stock. This allowed each card to have the same contact information but the wood grain pattern on each card was unique, illustrating our regard for each client as an individual.

We found a great but inexpensive downtown location for a large office building in the middle of the city, opposite the park.*

We recognized that a main source of client dysfunction could be challenging transitions. These might include adjusting to a new geography, a new marital status, a new job, a new school, a new culture, the loss of a loved one or an old job, unexpected physical or emotional trauma. Situations where counseling interventions might make a crucial difference in navigating the transition safely. Destigmatizing psychotherapy is a smart thing to do, analogous to tuning up the car. Helping those who fall to land higher.

Capturing all this in the title of our practice, our wood grain business cards declared us to be the *"Life Transition Specialists."*

Taking advantage of our location in a building with floor after floor full of office staff, we advertised an Open House, inviting the hundreds of neighboring workers to a grand opening.

The first few hours had passed and very few people had shown up. Why?

Finally a visiting secretary shed some light on this. Pointing to one of our unique wood grain *Life Transition Specialists* business cards, she said: *"You people are morticians, right?"*

Dr. Len Elkind was one of the faculty working in that practice, there that fateful day. He had his own earlier transitional time statue to add:

"I wanted to do my Master's Thesis on Hypnosis while at The University of Hawaii. It was a VERY small department (12 of us, I think, 3 of whom had experience with hypnosis). This freaked out the clinical professors and I wound up creating a Likert scale to measure Attitudes Toward Pornography, at my advisor's insistence.

This publication led to my being on a live TV show with the State Librarian, the head of Citizens for Decent Literature, and a Hawaii State Senator. At one point, the Senator spread a number of "lurid" paperbacks across the table and, when the camera focused on them, emphatically renounced them as leading to sexual excess and violence. So I asked him if he had read all those books and he emphatically replied, "Absolutely!" stamping his fist on the table. (wait for the drumroll…) So I asked him if he had raped anyone lately.

Some years later, this study led to my being hired at a new treatment center in London, England. I was hired over the 8 English applicants and I assumed it was because of my unique skills, only to discover that the psychiatric director assumed I had a large library of pornography that I used to test the subjects. He was obviously quite disappointed to discover that that was not the case."–Elkind (2017)

–

* That first night in downtown Fresno, I sat on a bench in the park opposite our new office building. Enjoying the warm California weather, best there in the evening, I noticed what seemed like waves moving across the grass. Soon the park was covered with these moving ripples. Looking closer, I realized they were multitudes of cockroaches. Not in the tourist brochures.

In Canada

It was my first day teaching clinical psychology to Canadian students at Wilfrid Laurier University. I was writing some schedule material on the Board when I was corrected.

I had pronounced the word "schedule" in an American way and not the proper Canadian or British way. The first syllable I had pronounced as 'sked' while they pronounced it as "shed." A "*schedule?*" Several patiently explained to me that the *true* English pronunciation of any word beginning with "sch" is a soft "sh." The c or k that follows the s is *always* silent. Well, I already knew that the last letter of the alphabet was called "zed" there and not "zee." The word "shone" is pronounced "shawn."

But this new rule was puzzling. In *any* word beginning with "Sch," the "c" is *not* to be pronounced. Okay then. I repeated the correct pronunciation of schedule, "shedule," to the group's satisfaction. Then, returning to the course content, I wrote "Schizophrenia" on the board in large letters. I asked the class: *"Please pronounce this in the proper Canadian way."*

Time release but it worked. Point made. Sure wish the British and Canadians knew how to speak English.

Language Malfunction Today

By the 21st century our language had become increasingly conditional and hesitant: "**Let me tell you**" and "It **may be that our team won tonight but**..." (even though our team *definitely* had won). Some regional communities retain some directness. In my city of origin, Buffalo, New York, a typical response when somebody wishes you well is **"The same to you."**

If you've relocated from one of these "old country" communities (i.e. people from the East Coast now settled farther West in warmer and gentler parts) you are expected to modify your language, particularly at gatherings of friends and family. Accordingly, I tried substituting **"May we all get what we deserve"** but my wife tells me that it's no improvement.

And there is a shadow side of course. Whether the effect is purposive or not, a name can shape a person's entire identity. Uncas Slattery's pioneering book of more than 10,000 "**unfortunate baby names**" has many such illustrations (Slattery, 2005). My own favorites are Culprit, Debris, Ennui, Façade, Fiasco, Genitalia, Inertia, Innuendo, Kujo, Lethargy, MagnumBolus, Malady, MeaCulpa, Malice, Morsel, Nightshade, Oblivia, Onan, Orca, Paparazzi, Parody, Quagmire, Rotunda, RubyRidge, Stigmata, Trauma, Travesty, Umbrage, Varlet, and Verruca.

This collection began when Lonnie Alexander, a friend of my father's, told us a story about a soldier he knew when serving in World War Two. Their all-Black unit was stationed in Italy. It was this soldier that had married an Italian woman even though she knew no English and his Italian was negligible. Somehow they still communicated well enough so that she soon was pregnant with their first child. By the time it was born in an American military hospital, her husband was away at a major battle. Pressured to name the baby immediately, she spotted a word in her medical chart that sounded quite beautiful. In this way her baby daughter was named "Genitalia."

The unfortunate baby name collection grew from there.

We know that words have power. The Sapir-Whorf hypothesis (LaBarre 1961; Kay & Kempton, 1984), that language shapes our culture as much as the other way around, has led to language usage less destructive to women or minorities within many communities.

And, of course language currently can be more contradictory than it ever was. Politically this is called "Opposite Land." Corporations have their own contradictions:

Business too is consolidating.

Outsourcing, a way for governments to shift responsibility to distant relatives, has been one aspect of global economic narrowing.

Family farms are becoming monopoly agribusinesses. Acquisitions and consolidations have narrowed ownership to a very small number.

There are about seven billion of our family now walking the earth.

Of these, less than a hundred people now own half the world's resources (Wearden, 2014).

In this accelerating economic inequality, *has* the word "owner" become "onerous"?

Or is this yet another aspect of the globalization of our human family?

Chapter 18. The Discovery of Poison Ivy and Quicksand

*Two roads diverged in a wood and I—
I took the one less traveled by,
and that has made all the difference.*
   — Robert Frost

Chapter 19. Existential Exceptions to the Truth

By the age of four I had a reputation for telling the truth. This seemed to impress the friendly giants called parents and neighbors. I saw no difference between honesty (no lying) and candor (no diplomacy). If a new mother's baby was beautiful, I said so. If it smelled bad, I would say that too. In time I enjoyed the strong belief that I was the rare child that would, as we now say, always keep it 100 (100% true).

Stronger than this satisfaction though was an abiding curiosity about this strange world I found myself in as a child. So I planned my very first psychological experiment. I would test the strength of their belief in me. I told my parents something obviously untrue. Their response was unexpected. They decided I was just another normal child and their complete trust in my honesty was instantly gone. Even explaining that this was just a test made no difference. They didn't believe that either. Later I would realize that without the informed consent of participants in an experiment, things will go awry very quickly.

Fast forward thirty years. At the end of our marriage in 1977, my soon-to-be ex-wife and I sat down for a few final borderline friendly words. What were the very best and worst aspects of our time together? She told me that my worst quality was my "obsession with honesty." Grateful that this was the worst, I wondered if she meant too much candor. Still, telling the truth seemed central to who I was, for better or worse. Then I remembered the exceptions.

Let's go back five decades. It was my last year in graduate school at Michigan State University. I was one academic quarter away from earning my PhD in Psychology. A Doctor of Philosophy degree without a single course in philosophy. At the age of 24, I considered this whimsical, amusing.

Moreso because one of my favorite uncles, Marvin Farber, was a celebrated philosopher. A former student of Husserl, he had been instrumental in saving the European phenomenologists from Hitler's holocaust and in doing so was credited with keeping this branch of philosophy alive. He founded the journal *Philosophy and Phenomenological Research* in 1940, and served as its editor until his death in 1980.

I had yet to read his work then but I had learned from his children, my cousins, about his dinner paradoxes: "Finish everything on your plate that you possibly can, but not a bite more." His critique of political sophistry included the widely quoted "Dirt is earth matter in the wrong place." Yet, despite this encouraging preface to philosophy, I was well on my way to a PhD, much as today's psychology graduates, without a course in philosophy. Until Professor Walsh.

The most popular course in the university that quarter was one on Existentialism. No pre-requisites and no class enrollment limit. The class grew to be so successful that the professor had to teach in an auditorium. Some said this popularity was because of the existential emphasis on situation ethics. Many students interpreted this as an enhanced opportunity for persuading sexual liaisons, a being in the moment as an applied existentialism. Being newly married and not in need of such techniques, I still was attracted to the existential perspective. It just seemed to fit my own growing psychological perspective.

So I enrolled. On day one, Professor Walsh sat cross-legged on top of a desk facing his multitudes of students. In a strong calm voice he asked *"Please raise your hand if you have ever had a philosophy course before now."* Only a very few hands went up.

"As I thought. All right. To understand existential philosophy you first will hear about philosophy. For these first four classes. Then we will get to the existential branch. Today I will begin with logic." Interesting. I would learn about the roots of my discipline after all.

He went on with a practical demonstration: *"In today's America, university faculty are being told to sign a loyalty oath to our country if we want to keep our jobs. This of course is controversial as it should be. In our own university, quite a large number of faculty are from other countries, making this strange right wing requirement even more absurd. Our own university president has come up with what he considers a solution. We are only required to sign an oath that as faculty we will always seek and tell the truth. Many have signed. I will not."*

Rebellion on the campus? Always fascinating. Do go on. He did.

"Here is why I have made an existential decision to not sign this oath:

- *I may think I am telling the truth but it turns out that I was wrong.*

- *I may tell a joke which usually means distorting the truth.*

- *I read and write fiction which obviously need not be truthful.*

- *I might just test your attention in class by saying something wildly untrue."*

I knew from early experience that that last one might backfire. Still, I have always been grateful for the clarity and precision of applied logic, not to mention his demonstration of courageous integrity. And of course he had already begun teaching us the logical semantics of existentialism. Nor was he fired. The search for truth is still the basis of all scientific inquiry. Add logic, intuitive insight, and a conscience—honesty, despite the noted exceptions, still stands as the best path forward. Our survival as a human family likely depends on it.

An Existential Chorus

Anytime you're feeling lonely
Anytime you're feeling blue
That's the time to remember
That your troubles come from you.

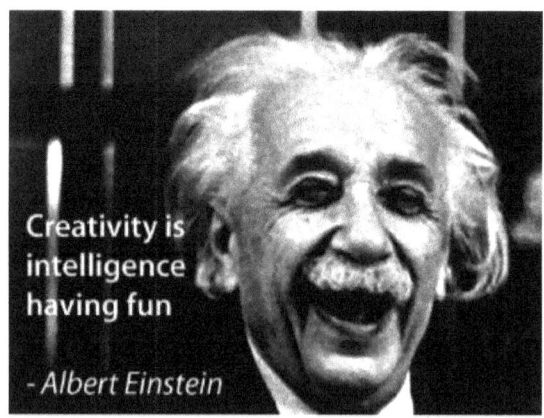

Chapter 20. Fresh Breath Top to Bottom

In 1865 **Joseph Lister** *successfully introduced carbolic acid to sterilise surgical instruments and to clean wounds. Applying Louis Pasteur's advances in microbiology,* **Lister** *championed the use of carbolic acid as an antiseptic, so that it became the first widely used antiseptic in surgery.*

In 1914 a company named their furniture polish after Joe, calling it "Listerine." They sold it to hospitals, promising it would rid them of bacteria to protect their patients and staff.

But it did not sell well until somebody put it in their mouth to kill bacteria there, finding it made their breath smell better. This seemed like a good bet for hawking the product.

Still, even this use barely covered their production costs.

So* they tried the fresh field of advertising to sell their own breath-freshener as a cure for a phony disease. The loudly whispered radio jingle:

**"He said that she said that he had Halitosis.
She said that he said that she had it too.
What can they do?
Buy Listerine Mouthwash, for *both* of you."**

Then Listerine sales took off. Inventing a disease label like "Halitosis" for simple bad breath made buyers rush for over-the-counter bottles, later in many other forms.

Almost. Today again antiseptic protection against disease is essential.

*So: We have here a new sales pathway for Listerine. Bad breath or its pungent equivalent can come from other body passageways.

A new jingle might complete coverage by introducing a nether disease label, one complementing Halitosis:

"He said that she said that he had Buttitosis.
She said that he said that she had it too.
What can they do?
Buy Listerine Suppositories, for *both* of you."

*Note: Every era has its own special words. In the 1940s one such was "Evidently."

By the 1960s this was replaced by "Apparently." Movies, TV, newspapers all loved this word.

In 2021, the new word was "So" which in media preceded interview responses, especially by august authorities on TV. It has a sense of anticipation and thoughtfulness.

So: its use fits here. Evidently.

Chapter 21. Insulting Introduction Equity

A recent radio interview with an international topic expert, a woman well known to me, was introduced by the female moderator stating that her visiting female expert was "drop dead gorgeous."

This focus on her looks ignored an earned doctorate, years of publications and accomplishment, organizational achievement, and impressive global experience.

A male saying this would be in deep trouble, but the female moderator had some gender protection.

Still, one might then expect the moderator, if she wanted to be seen as even-handed in her praise, to demonstrate equity in her comment on the appearance of those invited experts that she will rate as less impressive.

Here then are some equity examples of how she might introduce other female guests.

Example 1: *"Our lovely cat this morning once again brought me a dead mouse. When our next guest arrived here in person for the interview, our cat fainted. Possibly the poor kitten thought our guest's appearance was like a REVENGE OF THE GIANT MOUSE movie. Anyway, here is…"*

Example 2: *"Our next guest is sought out by other women and myself to be seen with us as often as possible. The boost by contrast to my own attractiveness is substantial. Welcome ..."

Example 3: "*All the way from Louisiana, our next guest is well known for her cooking and for her unique appearance. It is said one look at her on the tracks would force a freight train to take a detour on a dirt road. Since this is radio we can protect your eyes and just concentrate on the cooking.*"

Example 4: "*Our upcoming expert has been around for many years now. It has been said she was the inspiration for Oscar Wilde's novel THE PICTURE OF DORIAN GRAY. Not Dorian but rather the aging portrait. Still, while we have time, it's not too late to introduce..*"

Example 5: "*The healthy practice these days of wearing a mask over her face has been universally applauded for our next guest. And universally recommended that, once the pandemic is over, she continue the practice indefinitely, especially where others are eating. It is my pleasure to introduce...*"

Try this at home. For guests of all genders. Therapeutic. Prepare to be surprised.

Chickens appalled at seeing their favored neighbor Had moved to a warmer climate, leaving them behind.

Chapter 22. Musical Contest

Man singing: *I can do anything you can do better. I can do anything better than you.*

Woman singing: *Ovulate?*

Man singing: *Well then, here is the end of the song.*

Woman singing: *Lactate?*

Man not singing: *Hey! I said the song is over!*

Woman Singing: *Capitulate?*

Man not singing: *Jeez!*

Done best as a duet. My own partner has always been game for this.

Or then this for the progeny:

SONG FOR FIRST GRADE CHILDREN (ALWAYS NUMBER ONE): PIRATE GOLD

<u>GIRLS</u>

Yo Ho Yo Ho, a pirate's wife you'll be!

And most of your life, he'll be gone to sea.

Well, when he comes back, it never gets old…

Cause you get to spend his gold.

BOYS

Yo Ho Yo Ho, a pirate's life you'll see!

Away from your wife, you're mostly gone to sea.

Well, when you get back, it never gets old…

Cause you buried most of the gold.

CHORUS FOR BOTH GIRLS AND BOYS

Yo Ho Yo Ho, the Pirate life it will be

And when you grow up

You'll remember this song

And send some gold to me.

Chapter 23. Surfing the Tsunami

Paul was an immigrant. In his home country he had gained some respect as a reporter for a major paper. Based on that he had managed a transfer to a San Francisco newspaper. Although his mastery of English as a second language was incomplete, based as it was on a childhood of TV crime reruns like *Columbo*, *Perry Mason*, *CSI*, and the endless episodes of *Law and Order* shows. He did best with written English and so had high hopes for his new career. They placed him where no other reporters wanted to be: holiday features.

He was soon noticed when, for Thanksgiving, he referred to "leftovers" as "the remains" and the carving of the Turkey as a "kitchen autopsy." Introducing Easter and Christmas miracle paragraphs with the word "allegedly" gained notoriety as well. San Franciscans are known for their sense of humor and their tolerance for diversity. His editor was an exception. Paul's job at the paper ended. He was now considering his options. Clearly the best was advertising.

*

Watson was Sherlock's fictitious companion and physician. But here I will write of a very real and different Watson.

John B. Watson was an early founder and principal leader of the field of behavioral psychology, new a century ago when he first appeared as an academic celebrity (Watson 1913, 1930), due to his ahead-of-its-time experimental research on emotions (Watson & Raynor, 1920).

This included human sexuality, performed personally, frequently, and carefully tabulated with his lab assistant, Rosalie Raynor—which, when discovered, led to the end of his marriage and his banning from academia (Buckley, 1994).

Newly married now to Rosalie, Watson then took a position with Madison Avenue advertising in New York, where he remained for the rest of his professional career (Coon, 1994). He was only redeemed at age 79 in his last year of life with a gold medal awarded by the American Psychological Association for his pioneering contributions to psychology (Kimble *et al,* 2013). He was also the first psychologist to lend his considerable skills to that field of advertising, a ripple for the profit motive then, but a tsunami today.

Words to Sell: The Invasion of Commercials

Our current era may be remembered for many things. For one, 21st century reactionary pressures to reverse our great potential for scientific progress and retreat to 19th century levels. For another, ever more powerful monopolies led by those seeking exponentially expanding profits at all costs. From this, we now see the ubiquitous commercials invading more and more of our experience, dominating radio and television, appearing online, on the telephone, in movies, and in print. This is the era of swarming commercials.

Some of these assume profoundly uneducated customers. One television ad, regularly aired for months now, promises results six times better than a competing brand. To be sure their point is understood, the commercial ends with a voice-over explaining *"And six is greater than one."* Another one, soliciting complainants for a class action lawsuit, based on the iatrogenic insertion of surgical mesh, confirms that you are eligible to contact them and sue if you have been damaged *"or even died."* Not sure how many of the latter responded.

Surrounded by the temporal epidemic of these commercials, our life experience is being drowned by these pleas of unlimited greed. What can be done? "Do not call" lists for telemarketers? Government intervention? Consumer organization? Income inequities reaching a level so great that we no longer have the income to attract any commercials? Restoration and expansion of actual democracy?

Maybe something focused on the prime movers of this problem. Hmm. How about this? Well trained and highly intelligent service dogs assist the visually impaired and otherwise handicapped people these days. Some are there to help their humans recover from diagnosed trauma. These service animals are welcomed into restaurants, meetings, hotels, and other venues alongside the persons that they are assigned to assist. They do this well. How about this: service dogs especially trained and assigned by law to accompany those influential and privileged leaders among us who happen to demonstrate behavior consistent with ethical impairment. In this case, the dogs would be trained to growl at any dishonest vocalization by their human. Dogs might be trained to sniff out dishonesty as they have already been trained to locate smells of drugs, weapons, or disease.

Further, should their person commit a clearly unethical action, one promising to damage another person, a canine bite would take place. Such valuable dogs, fully ready to accompany the ethically impaired, might immediately be delivered to heads of state, CEOs of major corporate monopolies, and those many other generators of the ubiquitous commercial swarm that we know full well are so obviously in need of this service.

Words to Remember

I was at Saint Bonaventure University (SBU) from 1967-1969. I left there for a job in Canada as soon as possible after Martin Luther King's assassination. But while there, I became the president of the local AAUP, a union job nobody else on the faculty really wanted.

Because of my AAUP role, I was invited by the administration and the hosting English department faculty to come to an after party for a visiting poet, one Allen Ginsberg. Allen had already earned fame as a Beat poet and as one of Kerouac's group. But to SBU admin, he was more noted for being a homosexual, Jewish, and especially for his last public reading in which he had dropped his pants for emphasis. Even in the late freedom-oriented 1960s, this was a lot for SBU. When Allen actually did his reading there, audible gasps occurred frequently from many priests and nuns whenever his hand moved anywhere near his belt, but no unveiling happened that time.

At the after party, Ginsberg was surrounded by English faculty who, for at least an hour, deluged him with nonstop conversation. Never once in that hour did I see him get an opportunity to speak. Apparently they were more interested in impressing him than in getting to know him. Finally I walked through the crowd to him in his hostage chair, leaned over, and quietly asked him if he had been given anything to eat yet. He looked up, smiled, and whispered "No! Get me out of here!" So I announced that our guest would be going for a walk with me and we would be back soon. Allen stopped briefly in the kitchen where his partner was trying to forage and let him know we would be back soon.

TIME STATUES

Once sitting in a nearby diner, quiet reigning at last, I asked him about his visit to St Bona. Between bites, he said his interest in coming was to visit our library, an important archival source for a book he wanted to write. But that afternoon, on arrival at our library, the librarian priests refused to give him access, swearing at him profusely. According to Ginsberg, their hostile verbage was the worst he had ever heard. I told him I was glad to hear there was something superlative about his experience at our Catholic university and, possibly, these new words and phrases might be the basis for another book. He shrugged but smiled. Another great idea bypassed by reality.

As to the era, my union role allowed me to become friends with Father Jerome, the Vice President for Academic Affairs. He was a gentle, well-read elder statesman, wise and kind. His attempts to convert me were interesting but unfruitful, yet still we remained friends. As we were walking across campus, a young woman walked by with the words "FUCK" in lipstick red on her forehead. Jerome looked to me and nodded at how life had grown to be so full of this suffering for him, the accelerated decline of civil discourse as he gently experienced it. I waited for him outside as he entered an auditorium to do a brief introduction. Ten minutes later he was back but without his clerical coat. When I asked him about it, he just resignedly said it had been stolen while he was speaking.

On the other hand, women had just been admitted as students in the university. They had a 10 PM curfew and their women-only dormitory was padlocked every night until morning daylight. One of my students for her project surveyed the coeds on their sexual practices, discovering a bi-modal distribution in which about half stated they were celibate while the other half claimed so much sexual experience that not even the dorm's kittens or parakeets were safe. This senior class presentation drew so much attention that our classroom had to be moved to the auditorium to accommodate interest. The presenter began her talk with a brief pornographic film excerpt, followed by some comment on the exploitation of women. After all of this, I sought out Father Jerome. Only the week before, a Notre Dame Professor had been fired for showing such a film in class. Jerome reassured me, not for the first time, that he and his peers accepted psychologists as a necessary evil, a cross between physicians and perverts.

I also agreed to debate birth control with a very devout biology professor. Again a full auditorium but this time mostly priests, seminarians, and nuns. After the usual comments on both sides, I asked the males in the audience to please stand if they had never been sexually attracted to an available woman. Nobody stood up (gay priests stayed secret in those days). I then asked them to stand if they had actually had sex with every one of these women. Again nobody rose. I wondered out loud: how many unborn children had been aborted by this abstinence? To my surprise, some applause and a few cheers. (As a therapist, I soon learned that few priests stuck to their vow of abstinence other than abstaining from vows.)

A final memory. Saint Bonaventure University or SBU was mostly a white male rural Catholic university. The exception was recruitment for their championship basketball team. For this, recruiters scoured the black community in Buffalo, Syracuse, New York. Thereby recruiting a few very large athletic black male students who, due to the academic standards at the time, were also straight A students. These few black males were the first such students the white majority had ever known. As such, the white students generalized, an important basis for prejudice, and assumed these Olympian ebony athletes were typical of their race. The fear to compete with anybody of color (see Bert Karon's book) was prevalent. (I do remember student Bob Lanier, eventual pro NBA center, crammed into my car and commenting on how amused he was by this stereotype.)

My Department Chair was a very fine person and psychologist. He was also a priest. As such, he was ordered at the beginning of Fall classes to move to New York and staff the diocese there. Many of their priests were dropping out and the Bishop thought a good psychologist might stem the flow. Actually the psychologist in time became convinced of the wisdom of his patients and dropped out himself to marry a nun who dropped out with him. This meant I took his place to run the psychology course for seminarians. So it was I taught my only course for students about to become ordained priests, one on Pastoral Psychology.

Once again I noted the emphasis on obedience that the church militant had demanded of my Department Chair, that was now manifested in my seminary students. (Another memory about absolute mental obedience comes to mind.) When, in the first class meeting, I asked them for their own ideas on what would be useful to learn about psychological counseling, I was told that their Bishop had ordered them to learn and obey whatever I chose to do as the teacher. Hmm. I asked them to consider how they would respond if a little girl, one who had benefited from their counseling, gave them a flower in thanks. Many said they would not accept that or any other gift—they were doing counseling for Christ, not for themselves or for the girl. Others said they would take the flower and say thank you, identifying their primary client as the girl. I confirmed once again that they were all bound to do as I ordered while in this class. Affirmed. At the close of my class meeting, I ordered them not to come to the second class or any other of my classes unless they genuinely wanted to learn about counseling. About helping the people who came to them for help.

The next week only a little less than half the class arrived. The ones who would spurn the girl's flower were gone. Now we had a great Pastoral Psychology class. Also the last one I would be asked to teach. Years later the follow-up was gratifying. Now, let's look at another religious educational setting.

Marcy's Tale

Marcy lived in a rough urban setting. Here teenage girls often became pregnant as soon as it was physically possible.

Marcy's mother decided to send her daughter to a residential Catholic Convent girl's school for her final years of high school, ages 13-18.

Reluctantly but obediently, Marcy complied.

The academics were competent but the greatest emphasis was on rules and rewards.

RULE # 1: Thought obedience.

> The class exercises in thought obedience went like this. The teacher held up a colored piece of paper. If it was blue, the girls were told to look at it until it became the color their teacher said it was, until the blue became red because they were told so. Interesting molding of young minds.

RULE #2: Erotic pairing denial.

> The girls were told they must never be alone with another girl or great punishment would follow. This puzzled Marcy and her friends, not understanding the frustrated sexual

projections of the nuns. Good behavior did have its rewards at the end of each week.

The top two: REWARD # 1: One hour alone with another girl.

REWARD # 2: One hour standing by the west wall of the convent at a specific time and day. When this was done, the girl could hear the boys from the military academy marching by on the other side of the wall.

All the girls came home for holidays in November. By Christmas they returned a home a second time, many now pregnant from their first visit. Marcy's mother was quick to reverse her mistake. Marcy was re-enrolled in a public school where she excelled. She went on in life to be a top administrator at a major university. At the Convent girl's school, she had never allowed the nuns to make her mind see red when the paper was blue.

Subliminal Commercials

Auto-hypnosis is a natural state we move in and out of all the time (Morgan, 2005). For example, when we realize that we have been driving safely and successfully for many minutes but without much thought about it, that is a light trance. Visualizing an imagination scene clearly is another self-induction technique. And not paying attention to ongoing speech puts it directly into our uncritical memory. Commercials on radio or television count on this. Best to either pay attention to commercials or kill the sound lest you wind up buying things you neither need nor afford.

And what about those constant online ad demands, ever more invasive.

Well, maybe pay attention and even have fun with them?

Fun with product reviews

Here follow some I was asked to review and enjoyed doing so.

"Thanks Dr. Robert Morgan, Your latest customer review is live on XXXXX. We and millions of shoppers on XXXXX appreciate the time you took to share your experience with these items":

Aug 23, 2017

[Tea Tree Oil Foot Soak With Epsom Salt, Refreshes Feet and Toenails, Leaving Feet Feeling](#) Comfortable and effective. For feet. Not to be drunk as tea, particularly after foot use, despite advice from the neighbor who will drink anything.

Jul 29, 2017

[The Virgin Homeowner: Essential Guide to Owning, Maintaining, and Surviving Your Home](#) Full of very helpful ideas and well worth the price. Except for the price of being a virgin, an abandonment of essential pleasure far too steep for me or most readers.

Jul 10, 2017

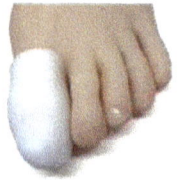

[ZenToes 6 Pack Gel Toe Cap and Protector.](#) Best protection so far. Comfortable. Use for toes only. Rumors that these were initially meant as condoms for our current (2017) president are completely unfounded.

TIME STATUES

Jun 27, 2017

Nature's Path Hot Organic Oatmeal Variety Pack, 8 Count Prime mover.

Great product. Better for your daily movement than North American Van Lines.

May 17, 2017

Clinical Forehead Thermometer FDA Approved Instant Read Sensor for Digital Fever Measurement Temporal Professional No Touch Readings Baby Adult & Children Best Infrared Scanner

Arrived on time and works well. Can read a temperature from an inch away so no direct contact needed. Caution to avoid injury: on a crowded beach do not use on strangers without their permission and no need to go below the neck.

Mar 17, 2017

Men's Heat Holders 0.61 tog Microfleece Thermal Base layer Leggings/Bottoms

Fit me well, great for warmth on cold days. Mixed reviews for relaxed clothes Friday at work.

Mar 17, 2017

[Jockey Full Rise Briefs - 4 Pack (9965) 44/Black](#)
Consensus. Fits well, looks good, great product. 6 out of 7 passersby came to same conclusion.

Jan 3, 2017

[Rainbow Pom Pom Ball Tactile Fidget Stress Ball Autism Special Needs](#)
Effective with a caution. Beautiful, comfortable, and effective but avoid use as an IUD.

Jan 3, 2017

[White Fang](#)
A beautiful read from a legendary author although somewhat of a surprise. From the title I thought it would be an expose of somebody in the current (2017) White House cabinet.

Dec 2, 2016

[Staples Shredder Lubricant Lubricating Sheets 24/pk](#)
Sheets that lubricate is a very creative idea. But each is far too small for a normal bed. Maybe just use for a shredder.

Dec 2, 2016

[Chili Pepper Ristra From TheCraftyCrocodile](#)
Not safe as an adult toy. Enough said.

Dec 2, 2016

[Chakra Stacked Layered Healing Heart Crystal Dowsing Pendulum](#)
Very very small but beautiful. May be inhaled if it approaches the nose. Yoga usage as holistic suppository is not encouraged.

Dec 2, 2016

[Generic Wooden Toys Magical Mini Kaleidoscope Bee Eye Effect Polygon Prism Classic](#)
Fun for children. Dissuade adult use as inexpensive colonoscopy.

Dec 2, 2016

[Sunnyside up; (An Island heritage book)](#)
Beautiful unique classic book. Challenging to follow the egg recipe though.

Nov 30, 2016

Hanes Men's Short Sleeve Beefy-T with Pocket, Black, X-Large

Shirts are fine and as advertised. Pocket may be too small for replacing carry-on or checked luggage at airport. Forensic note: in public, pants need to be worn with this shirt.

Nov 15, 2016

Bali Women's Active Lifestyle Extra Cover Wire Free, White/Blushing Pink, 42DD

Good product. Fit 9 of 10 passersby, not all female.

Nov 1, 2016

Tapp C. Classic Adult Size 22" Long Opera Length Satin Gloves - Black

Perfect classy anniversary gift for the proctologist or spouse.

Nov 1, 2016

Rachael Ray ChillOut Thermal Tote, Black

Spacious. Most body parts will easily fit.

TIME STATUES

Sep 16, 2016

[Kwok Girls Petticoat Rainbow Pettiskirt Bowknot Skirt Tutu Dress (L)](#)

Very beautiful. My granddaughter loved it as did the man who delivered it. It was too small for him to model and he left with only a few tears.

Sep 5, 2016

[Gold Bond Ultimate Comfort Body Powder, Aloe, 10 Ounce Bottles (Pack of 3)](#)

Effective use but permission required prior to using on others. Beach etiquette.

Sep 5, 2016

[Harris Roach Tablets (4oz)](#)

Safe to be used around humans. Assuming not to be consumed before or after meals. Or during. Very honest seller to put the main ingredient on the product name. Bland taste.

Sep 5, 2016

[Light Blue Fuzzy Slippers for Women L 8-9](#)

Arrived on time and as advertised. Attractive especially to neighbor's Chihuahua who was prevented from mating with them several times, not to mention his owner's similar attempts.

Maintenance pest control attempted to spray them. Friends took up a collection assuming slippers were a dramatic sign of poverty. Nice color.

Aug 29, 2016

[Decorations for Wedding, Silk Brocade Rustic Wine Bottle Cover in Set of 3, Decorative Wine Bottle](#)

Beautifully made. For that essential first impression of his marital contribution, it is useful for a groom to wear it there on the wedding night. With two backups for return performances.

Aug 29, 2016

[Jitterbug Flip Cell Phone Turtleback Black Leather Fitted Case with Heavy Duty Rotating Removable Metal Belt Clip - Made in USA](#)

Lilliputian holder too small for the Jitterbug Flip cellphone but ok for belt-clipped paper clips, tooth picks, cotton swabs. The Jitterbug would never fit in this. It is far too small and narrow for a cell phone. Looks cheap but it does have a metal belt clip as advertised. Maybe it could attach to your belt while carrying, oh, those paper clips, tooth picks, or cotton swabs. Too narrow for credit card. I wonder about those few positive reviews. Did they get a different product? Did the Turtleback holder shrink in transit? Buyer beware.

TIME STATUES

Aug 16, 2016

Do it Best 431125 Do it Rubber Sink Stopper, 5-Inch, White

Came fast, inexpensive, and did its work well. Great buy for the price. Although not for use as diaphragm method of birth control. Normally.

August 9, 2016

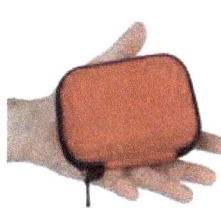

First Aid Kit – 66 Pieces – Small and Light Soft Shell Case - Packed with hospital grade medical supplies for emergency and survival situations. Ideal for Car, Camping, Travel, Sports, Home

This product came quickly and just in time. The sudden epidemic of cuts for husbands, fathers, children, DMV staff, store clerks, meter maids, supervisors, landlords, construction workers, and aggressive parking lot users has grown. I'm not sure but this has been attributed by some to the newly popular purchase and usage of the Tiger Lady gloves, ones that turn into claws when the woman wearing it makes a fist. Our first aid band aids are here now to help.

Thanks, *Your latest customer review is live on Amazon. We and millions of shoppers on Amazon appreciate the time you took to share your experience with this item.* **Subject: Thank you for reviewing Handcrafted Wine Bottle**

August 2, 2016

Beautiful and useful

Beautifully made, inexpensive, and has dual use as jockey short addendum for cold climates.

Subject: Thank you for reviewing Out-of-Body Experiences: on Amazon.

★★★★★ on August 2, 2016 Excellence

This is an excellent book and is not to be filed with laxative texts. Bookstore still wrong about that.

Subject: Thank you for reviewing Qhiti Mosquito Repellent Bracelets

★★★★★ on August 2, 2016

Direct action. Worked best when brought down abruptly on top of the mosquito.

Subject: Thank you for reviewing Excelvan Solar Ultrasonic Animal Repeller Dog Cat Pest Deterrent

★★★★★ **on August 2, 2016**
Effective. Crowded children's pool emptied quickly.

Subject: Thank you for reviewing Darkfin Webbed Power Gloves.

★★★★★ **on August 2, 2016**
Works well. Puppies appreciate this nontoxic nonverbal warning when placed in front of businesses that seem pet friendly but do canine neutering.

Subject: Thank you for reviewing Sperm Stress Toy – 6 Pack on Amazon

★★★★★ **on August 2, 2016**
Ice breaker Great ice breaker for competitive swimming events.

Subject: Thank you for reviewing FINANCIAL ABUSE OF THE ELDERLY on Amazon

★★★★★ **on August 2, 2016**
Not a fundraising guide.
Full of great ideas but meant for protection and not as a fundraising guide.

Subject: Thank you for reviewing Monte Bene Tomato Basil on Amazon

 **on August 2, 2016**

They appreciate the effort. Delicious and portable to bring to Italian restaurants. They appreciate the effort. Eventually.

Subject: Thank you for reviewing Owl Pellet on Amazon

 **on August 2, 2016**

Fun

Fun but do not hand out on Halloween or Easter. Some parents do not applaud the creativity of nature.

A Little Bit More

A few years ago, a Safeway grocery chain store in San Diego made the national news. Somebody left an extortion note claiming that jars of pickles and other products had been poisoned. When the marked jar specified in the note was checked, this turned out to be true. No money was paid and there was no way to know what if anything else on the shelves had been poisoned. Faced with the large cost of restocking everything, the manager decided to leave the stock on the shelves just as it was. He re-opened the store with only a disclaimer sign posted on the doors.

Amazingly, ignoring this danger completely, customers went right back that very day to purchase the stock. Safeway's motto at the time was **"ALL YOU COULD WANT IN A STORE............ AND**

A LITTLE BIT MORE."

Words to Heal: Selective Reframing and Happy Sleep

In San Francisco, one of my clinical clients was nearly through achieving her therapeutic goals. Little remained to do but address her persistent insomnia. Otherwise she was ready to begin her life and its challenges or, as Oprah Winfrey recently put it, "A new day, there on her horizon."

An avid reader, she rode her transference enthusiastically by reading some of my books. Therein she came across psychologist Leonard Elkind's hypnosis work on physiological aging reduction (Elkind, 1972, 1981; Morgan & Wilson, 2005).

Learning that he was still in private practice in San Diego, she wanted the same hypnotic intervention for herself. Following some discussion of how well this might fit into her best future, I agreed to make the referral.

Leonard graciously agreed to see her for a session that weekend. (Leonard Elkind taught his therapeutic clients to do their own auto-hypnosis. He was so effective at this that issues like stage fright or exam anxiety could usually be dealt with in a single session. This hypnotic mastery meant that he rarely made much money from so few sessions. Luckily his other skills allowed people with more serious issues, those needing more meetings, to also inhabit his practice. What this meant for my client was that her trip was very affordable.)

On her return to our regular sessions, she reported that the Elkind experience had been well worth the trip. She also admitted it helped that he was handsome and reassuring, although always professional.

In addition to the physiological work, he had taught her how to go into a light trance whenever she chose, to reduce discomfort or for any other reason. Her visualization for this was imagining a light blue fog filling her room, her safe place, until she would see only the fog but still could hear Dr. Elkind's voice saying whatever she wanted to hear.

She proudly said that this had the serendipitous effect of curing her insomnia. As she retold it: *"I was wide awake and lying in bed, so I invited in the blue fog, and once bathed in it, I heard Leonard Elkind's voice, strong and comforting, saying as he had in San Diego, 'You will sleep beautiful!' And then I did."*

This phrasing intrigued me. Leonard uses highly competent grammar. He would be unlikely to have said that phrase in that way. A follow up call confirmed this. He had said *"You will sleep beautifully."*

In exploring this reframing with her, she recalled that when her marriage had begun, years before, her new husband had teased her continually about how, to him, she seemed ugly when she slept. She laughed along with him but it deeply hurt her feelings, making her self-conscious when she slept with him.

Since they had been married for years, she still slept with him and so she still slept poorly, if at all. Until now.

Now, in the privacy of her own mind, she could lie in bed, bathed in the warm blue fog of her imagination, and hear the handsome hypnotist say (as revised by herself): *"You sleep beautiful."*

And she did.

TIME STATUES

Maybe we should visualize our own version of blue fog in a safe place and listen to the wisdom of our own mind. It beats commercials.

If we do, what then is our purpose?

Not long ago I was asked why I did what I did in my past life at work by two different people, an adult graduate student, and then by a gifted little girl next door. The answers were different but not incompatible.

To the Adult: *"Our primary client is neither faculty nor student but rather those members of our human family that receive the services of our graduates. Let's do the math: If a licensed practitioner sees only two new clients a week, in a year 100 different clients would be assisted. In a 25-year career, that would be 2500 people. Each client, on the average, will have major impact on at least 4 people in their life (children, spouse, parents, friends) meaning that we now have 10,000 people impacted by the career of one of our graduates. If a specific degree program has 25 graduates a year, it would take only 4 years of such a program to impact a million lives. The impact of* *course can be either helpful or unhelpful. In either case it has ripples across generations. Herein lies our greatest responsibility to graduate competent and caring human beings, able to meld their commitment to social justice and client care with a through and effective education. A successful teacher or administrator, over a 20-year career, can impact the training and professional lives of 500 of these program graduates (each one directly impacting 10,000 lives) and therefore, indirectly, we might improve the course of life for as many as five million people. This is in addition to those graduates who themselves become teachers, modeling their work on this instructor. Such an impact can genuinely change the course of human events for the better. It is well worth doing."*

To the Child: I said *"We help people to change their nightmares into their best dreams. Then we do our best to help them make these dreams they chose come true." "That's what I thought you did,"* she said and smiled.

Back to Paul

Paul made a great career out of advertising.

When you are amused or touched by a commercial, that one may well be his work.

He has learned from the inside about the subtle hypnotic influence of the selling tsunami and its attractions.

So he always mutes the sound track of such bait when he can. Especially when he is not concentrating on it.

His very happy family gladly helps him remove the leftover "remains" from their holiday feast, once the "kitchen autopsy" carving is complete.

TIME STATUES

His children like to use the word "allegedly" in their history classes and in discussing holidays. Their teachers rarely call upon them now.

Paul's children are especially happy about that.

Chapter 24. Silent Language

Ernst Beier was a celebrated expert on body language.

His popular book "*People Reading*" was a best seller. His book "The silent language of psychotherapy was a key volume for practitioners.

Ernst's day job was as a psychology professor in Salt Lake City, Utah.

In the summers he would travel to exotic locales like New Guinea, following the cultural variations of body language there. Not bad for man in his eighties.

When I met Ernst, he looked a lot like the mustached man about town in the *Esquire* magazine.

On the other hand, he spoke with a strong German accent. Add to that his military history in WWII, and my first impression was that he had fought on the Nazi side.

As we got to be friends, I asked him how he thought of that experience. He seemed startled. No, he was on the American side. The German accent? What accent?

In fact Ernst had been a Jewish refugee, immigrating as a young man to America and fighting as soon as he could against the Nazis. He had joined the US Army, Tenth Mountain Division, but was sent overseas with the 28th Infantry division. He was captured at the Battle of the Bulge by the Germans and had harrowing experiences in a POW camp. After liberation he received the silver battle star.

Now a Jewish professor in predominantly LDS Utah?

"*Exactly!*" he confirmed with a broad smile.

A few years later, he was my invited keynote speaker at a professional psychology school graduation in California.

Ernst and a restless audience waited for his turn through about an hour of preliminaries.

When I finally could introduce him, I reviewed his outstanding body language contributions briefly. Much of that was beginning to appear in television series and in books on poker tells.

I told the already restless audience that if they had read his books, they would have been able to follow his speech already. Since while he was waiting he had given it sitting there on the stage silently twice now. (Laughter.)

Now awake, they were focused. Actually, once using real words, he gave a fine talk. Lots of insights graduates could use.

Still with a great German accent though.

Ernst founded the international Division 52 of the American Psychological Association. I worked with him there for its earliest years.

Until suddenly he was no longer there.

Or anywhere. Nobody that I asked knew.

There was a rumor that Ernst, now in his late 90s, had Alzheimers.

Or, my favorite, that he had run off to New Guinea to marry a tribal woman.

One day I finally succeeded in tracking his phone number down and called.

Frances, his wife of 65 years, answered.

Once she knew who I was, she apologized: *"I'm sorry. Ernst is bedridden now. His mind is fine but he no longer can speak. You can talk to him on the telephone but he can't answer you. We are told he won't live out the week."*

I knew he would answer me just fine without speech if I had been able to see him. But I took what I could in the time we had, being thousands of miles away.

I talked one-way for a while, reminding him of past good times and wishing I could be there to enjoy his stories, even if by body language.

When I was done, his wife took the phone again.

She said: *"He's smiling now."*

III. CITIZENSHIP

Chapter 25. Bastille Day 2020

BASTILLE DAY 2020 FOR CAGED IMMIGRANT CHILDREN IN AMERICA

In France on July 14th their Independence Day holiday celebrates the release of innocent prisoners. It is still cause for celebration. There.

Chapter 26. Actualizing Democracy

My wife Becky and I are very close. This bond came to mind when she advised me to try acupuncture. I looked for acupuncture on my internal priorities list but, despite being a recognized valid and valuable technique, it was nowhere to be found. Maybe unfairly, I always thought that part of its success might have been motivated by a desire to not be stuck with needles any more. So. I thought: what if she tried it herself and then we looked for improvement measures in me? In this way, my concept of Vicarious Acupuncture was born. (Still waiting for the research to come since my wife so far has decisively declined this invitation to move science forward.)

I found Vicarious Acupuncture as a concept to be very congruent with a contemporary quantum entanglement perspective. This can be far too simply described as: what is done to one of two separate elements impacts the other, with or without any apparent connection and independent of distance.

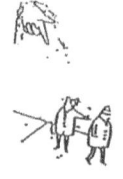

Second order or vicarious effects in psychology have long been well documented, even if these effects are unexplained, explained, or assumed. Some early examples: Shapiro (1970) demonstrated that the sensitivity training of nurses improved outcomes for their patients. Brandt

(1973) found that doing play therapy interventions with parents helped their parenting skills and raised their child's self-concept. This can also apply to the generation of democracy in a system. Chaos theory tells us that even the smallest intervention can have dramatic and systemic consequences, good or bad. Causality is not always clear and is often displaced. But first to definition.

Defining Democracy

"A rose by any other name won't know the difference" (Slattery, 2005)

Eugene Jacobson (1964) defined democracy as *"those most directly affected by a decision, make that decision."* Far from the simplistic concept of "majority rules," Jacobson brought his focus to a just, fair, and specific impact, one that might be considered developmental maturity or psychological health. And it is, in a very good way, contagious.

This can be a very powerful way to look at life's choices.

I taught at San Francisco State University for four years in the early 1970s. When this topic came up, I asked my students in a large class to define democracy. A lively group, some said *"Majority Rules!"* or *"Power to the People!"* These can be very good things, I agreed, but it's not the essence of the idea.

"The opposite of fascism!" somebody said and somebody else yelled *"Democracy is Anti-Fascism!"* (Today named *ANTIFA.*) So I digressed long enough to explore what fascism is: an enmeshment of the biggest corporate business with government such that they are functionally the same thing, consequently only a very few people decide for all the rest, the 1% ruling the 99%. But not enough to define democracy by what it *isn't*.

So time to put some examples on Jacobson's definition.

The early 1970s in San Francisco was a time of freedom, especially for the younger adult generation, in sexual or romantic explorations. The transition was farther along for some than for others. Still, here is the example I gave:

"If this class decided to have a backyard basketball game and divided into two teams of equal numbers. One first choice would be how to tell the two teams apart without uniforms. One of the guys wanted it to be 'Shirts versus skins' where one of the teams played naked from the waist up. Somebody else wanted to take a vote right away where majority rules. Now the males outnumbered the females by a 2 to 1 ratio. While a few males (very few) might not want to be distracted during the game by topless women and a few women (very few) might enjoy being topless as an equity gesture or to gather some interest, suppose that most women in that time would have voted no while most men, of any time, might have voted yes. Majority rule would mean the females, despite being directly affected from an emotional point of view, would lose. That would not be real democracy."

Class discussion followed. Fun for the class. One female student asked me what I would think if she decided to be topless then and there. I said I would know faster if the classroom temperature was too cold.

Hmm. Time to change the subject before we became an indoor Woodstock without music, or a Burning Man gathering without fire (hopefully). Time up. Saved by the bell.

I could well have given this other example of the Jacobson definition from a decade later:

TIME STATUES

"A president of a small graduate school in Palo Alto wanted to avoid lawsuits from students or their families over sexual hook-ups with faculty. He took the initiative to appoint a "Presidential Commission" to decide on an ethical policy for student-faculty dating. To cheat and make sure he got the outcome he wanted, a prohibition, he populated his commission entirely with older female graduate students. To his chagrin, their deliberations resulted in a DEMAND that students, as legal adults, date anybody they chose, especially including any faculty. The president charged me, as his Academic Vice President, with bringing the faculty together to come up with their own policy. This I did. The American Association of University Professors (AAUP) already had a policy on this: no dating within your discipline or major but freedom anywhere else. The essence of this was to avoid a conflict of interest where a supervisor or person of coercive authority over a student could not really have an equally free consent from the subordinate student. One of the faculty suggested that any of them having had sex with a student should just leave the room when faculty were discussing that student's progress. Another asked what would happen if everybody left? And so it went. We finally agreed that sex with a faculty member actively supervising a student, class or in any other way should be prohibited. Otherwise the decision of the female students on their Presidential Commission would be honored. Eventually, following the AAUP, any core or fulltime faculty of this single discipline graduate school would also be prohibited from dating a student. Since everybody was affected by this choice, with consultation from both groups, the decision stood. In time it was enforced and a few faculty lost their jobs. (Of course that very President had married one of his own students. No consequences for him)."

Maybe not the best example after all. Though I enjoyed the memory. Let's get back to applying the Jacobson definition of democracy.

Of course, democracy is not a panacea. While creating a very healthy psychological atmosphere, some human applications would not work well. A felon about to be sentenced for a violent crime will most directly be impacted by that decision, but that decision is better left to the judge or jury. Nor could a military function as a complete democracy when it is fundamentally designed to be hierarchical.

A toddler heading for a hazardous crossing:

Definitely needs a parent to intervene.

Still, democracy in most other cases is usually the most successful and peaceful way for decisions to be made. And should be encouraged. National movements toward this all across the globe should be actualized.

Being Inductive

Every community has its own collective personality. Rigid adherence to predetermined expectation may be misleading at best. Gathering data first, combing the literature, observing carefully and systematically can provide a more inductive approach to a better outcome.

Democracy is change that is by its nature inductive; in hierarchical systems it operates from the bottom up.

Now applying a good theory is very practical. But even these theories can be modified in unexpectedly helpful ways when those most directly affected provide feedback. How about an example from education?

Example from Education

I thought I made a mistake but I was wrong

Building on the decades of work by pioneers like A.S. Neill (Neill 1978; Neill & Lamb 1995, Reich 1981) and Jonathon Kozol (1967, 1985, 2006), Dr. Thomas Toy and I evaluated a 3-month program in which high school children tutored grade school children one-to-one a few hours each week during study hall. While the grade school children learned twice as much as their controls, the high school tutors learned three times as much as *their* controls.

We recommended an Educational Cooperative model where each child briefly tutored a younger one on a regular basis each week (Morgan & Toy, 1970). Such a model substitutes generational collaboration for antagonism, not only between children but between the teenage tutors and their teachers. The threat of their being embarrassed by not being able to explain what they were teaching to the younger children was reduced since the tutors now chose to learn the material to 100% mastery before they tried to teach it. We predicted that, in addition to enhanced test scores, bullying would decline and disciplinary problems for tutors would decrease. This occurred but was not really noticed by most of the high school teachers.

When I prevailed on Tom Toy, my graduate student at the time, to do the extra work of evaluating the tutors as well as the outcome measures for the younger students they tutored, it was because of my pre-existing theory. I believed that this antagonistic gap between adolescent students and their teachers would be far less combative once these adolescents experienced the role of teacher themselves. In this way they would begin to see their teachers as masters of the very educational skills they too needed to succeed in their mission. To test this hypothesis, I predicted the tutors would also improve, possibly even more than those they tutored. When this occurred, to the surprise of many, I considered my theory validated.

I met with the adult teachers and shared the study results, suggesting they use an Educational Cooperative Model (Morgan, 2012). In this model the child's learning was enhanced by teaching younger children one-to-one, at least a few hours each week.

My role identification theory led me to suggest the young tutors should even get a small paycheck, just like an adult teacher, and even be on a first name basis with their adult teachers.

This did not go over well. One teacher proclaimed that he had as a child sat in the very classroom he was teaching in now. Instead now that he was the teacher and not the student, he demanded to be called by his formal name. If not, he would feel he had made no progress, that he would lose control or dominance over the children in his class. I pointed out that he was much bigger than the children in his classroom now. No luck. The teachers wanted the gap to continue.

At this point I added a key component to the study, one I have urged adding to every one of my 121 supervised doctoral dissertations since. Post-study participant feedback. We decided to meet with the participants directly affected by the study, the adolescent tutors, to discuss why their improvement had surpassed the children they had taught.

Tom Toy and I met with them as a group, shared the study results, and asked them for comment. The feedback was not what I expected.

TIME STATUES

They had a better explanation than my role identification theory.

In the United States, the mass production group-in-a-classroom education model prevails almost completely over individualized instruction. There a scale chosen to measure success is a letter grade and percent score approach. In that, a perfect score would be 100%. A, B, C, D, F are the usual letters used with A the highest, and F the failing grade. In Singapore and many other British-style systems, letter grades give way to "Distinction" (70%) or "High Distinction" (80%), also based on a percentage where 100% is a perfect score. In the USA system, typically 90% success earns the A, 80% the B, 70% the C, 60% the D (barely passing), and 0-59% an F or failing grade. (Other countries can have far different interpretations of percentage; more about that later.)

Our cohort of tutors pointed out that even if they had earned grades of A through all their years of school, they had earned them with a 90% or so, leaving a mastery gap of up to 10% in every course. Those getting B or C grades had content gaps of up to 30%. Over the years, these gaps of missed learning accumulated. But then, in our study, they had no desire as a tutor to be embarrassed by any mistakes made in front of the younger children they taught. So they learned 100% of what they were about to teach before they taught it. In this way, they had discovered the mastery method of learning by teaching and it immediately enhanced their performance in their own classroom courses.

Their learning by teaching theory was far more valid than my own role identification one. It identified learning by teaching as a key education intervention. As good teachers know for themselves. Sharing this technique with students is a great next step.

Also clear was that, whenever possible, it is always important to share a study's results with participants for their feedback. This is not only respectful and just, but often essential to understanding the results. And it actualizes democracy.

The Keller mastery method (Morgan & Toy 1974; Sherman 1974) built on this model over the years, primarily in higher education. Today's educational milieu could benefit by a fresh look at the Educational Cooperative method in which teaching is a primary method for learning.

The Singapore Disruption

You recall that in Singapore and many British systems, success is measured by "Distinction" (70%) or "High Distinction" (80%), based on a percentage where 100% is a perfect score. When I was a Visiting Professor at an Australian university campus in Singapore, faculty were actually handed a written notice by the CEO that mandated not more than 5-10% of students in any class receive "distinction" or "high distinction" grades. Psychology doctoral programs in the USA instead typically mandate that students achieving anything less than a grade of 80% (B) can be dropped from the program. At my Singapore campus though, everything at 80% or above was *high* distinction.

Rather than doing a grading curve, I just told the students that their grade would be whatever they earned (0-100%). Further, I would do all in my power to assist them to learn all of the material needed to master the course (Mastery Learning). Since students in the Honours and Clinical Psychology programs were already highly selected for motivation/ability/knowledge, most did well. By USA graduate standards, there would have been some grade distribution:

As and Bs mostly. But by that university's standards, when all or nearly all the students achieved scores of mastery of at least 70% of the course material, I naturally awarded them their "distinction" grades. This, it turned out, was apparently a social embarrassment to the university administration. Even in my one undergraduate Honours class, of 23 students only one failed the course, while all the rest did very well. In a "distinguished" or "high distinguished" way. In many countries that would be expected, possibly celebrated, but then and there it led to much fury and consternation.

Once grades were in, the faculty member in charge of the Honours program sat in my office with tears of rage running down her cheeks. She said I had used up the 5% of high distinction grades allotted to her program in a single class. I realized then that, from her point of view, it was like I had arrived early to her picnic and eaten all the food.

Then came the administrative response to my Honours and clinical psychology students receiving non-curved grades. There was a review, all the way by technology from the Australian main campus. In this proceeding, the demand was for me to justify why my grades were not in line with other faculty. An official proclaimed that "it could only be grade inflation." Although comparison across different courses in different countries with different instructors with varying students in each class was not logical, my own students were objectively graded on a wide variety of written and performance standards in each class. They were actually some of the best motivated and educated students I have ever taught anywhere. They had earned their grades.

The pre-determined curve was an abusive application of theory. I had instead chosen a more inductive approach, one dependent on the performance of those most directly impacted.

In the exchange with the perturbed administrators, I wondered if my teaching experience (50 years then) might have made a difference. Instead, I then asked them: what level of mastery would they accept for their personal physician? Would he or she be considered proficient ("distinction") and safe if they had only learned 70% of what a physician should know? I suggested that we should have our clinical psychology graduates do their best to reach 100%, or as close as they can get, and not feel smug about the graduation of clinical students with only 70% of the essential knowledge or skills required for treating patients successfully.

Despite their administration, some of my Australian faculty counterparts expressed interest in this mastery learning, seeing that it had promise to enhance our ultimate professional mission of service to our patients. In its purest form, mastery learning steps away from a fixed time frame of academic quarters or terms: students do not move onto the next step until they reach complete (100%) demonstrated understanding of the step they are on. Some finish faster, some need more time. At their university, a modified version might just ditch the forced curve and attempt as close to mastery as possible in the time allowed, as I had done. One could also drop grades entirely and just use credit/no credit with a narrative (often done at some University of California campuses and many other university systems in the world).

When they were in elementary school, my daughters were once both put in a "Gifted Class" for high IQ children. Unfortunately they forgot to hire a gifted teacher to run the class. The non-gifted teacher immediately instituted a curved grading system yielding hierarchical grades by the end of the first term. A student with an IQ of 130 would fail the class if there were other students with an IQ of 140+. Some very bright and motivated students had their first failure experience in school despite excellent work, work just not as excellent as their competitors. A few lost interest in school. My own children did well, but another very bright child dropped out and never went back.

In rare occasions, I've never had difficulty, as faculty or administration, in providing a failing grade or facilitating departure of a student who, despite every reasonable opportunity, earned this outcome. Mostly though, I have had the pleasure of seeing substantial learning take place with the right set and setting. I do suspect the grading curve approach may well be one major component in reducing many a university's retention. If followed, it elevates the self-worth of the top 5-10% while diminishing that of the remaining majority. This outcome fits only when the destructive goal is perpetuating the hierarchical antithesis to actualizing democracy.

Education at its best requires a cooperative cohort to develop. Not a cutthroat competition reducing learning levels all around to create superior and inferior status hierarchies. But actualizing democratic alternatives is not universally popular. And so there and then my Visiting Professorship came to an end.

Other Examples from Adult Literacy and Rehabilitation

Such a principle was also practiced effectively in Martin Luther King's Adult Literacy programs in Chicago, the only federally funded programs given directly to a Civil Rights organization. Here the tutors providing one-to-one instruction, a key success component too long ignored in the mass production education model, had the prior experience of graduating the program, no longer illiterate. As part of their teaching role, they wrote their own community-friendly curriculum (Hoehn & Woolman, 1969). I was a psychologist brought in to evaluate its success. Success was defined as 6th grade level literacy and holding a subsequent job. I was delighted to see more than 98% success. A competing program run by the mayor had less than 10% success.

(Note: Woolman also used his technique to move integrated childhood education forward. He used his focus on individual tutoring along with meaningful locally-generated content (Lazar *et al*, 1982, Consortium of Longitudinal Studies, 1983). Not only was this **"*Operational Context Training*"** used to effect in Dr. King's adult literacy programs, but it was actually an impetus for desegregating public schools in the Southern USA. Woolman would allow use of his technique, the one achieving Grade 6 Reading Level in a few months, *only* for grades K-6 schools that accepted African American children. The fear to compete engendered in segregationist school boards by these 5-12-year-old African American children, who now read extremely well, was sufficient for them to open up their school system to children of all colors. Of course, recent educational dogma focusing entirely on mass education techniques has eclipsed this approach and consigned individual instruction to isolated special education. In fact, if re-awakened, it could be faster, cheaper, and transform the community in a generation.)

Our education is provided on the cheap and profoundly under-funded. Consequently, the individual is lost in favor of group education. But entire communities can have their survival skills upgraded by more effective education of their children, both as to content and learning to learn, critical thinking, and comprehension of the culture.

Illiteracy is a major and often overlooked causative feeder for our prison system. Educational transformation is cheaper.

Yet even prison can be transformational given these principles. Hans Toch's years of work on inmate governance and humanistic corrections (Toch 1980, 1995, 1997, 2017) presents a valuable educational cooperative model employing therapeutic community empowerment in a highly challenging setting. The most powerful post-prison community success of this model that I have found has definitely been the self-reliant entrepreneurial Delancey Street Foundation, where ex-convicts live together, run businesses and move to self-sufficiency, even building their own housing.

***

Vignette: The *DELANCEY STREET FOUNDATION*

Dr. Mimi Silbert is the founder and President of the *Delancey Street Foundation* headquartered in San Francisco, California. As a matter of fact, for over 25 years, *Delancey Street*, considered the nation's leading self-help residential education center for former substance abusers and ex-convicts, has transformed the lives of over 11,000 graduates into productive members of the community.

At slightly under five feet tall, Silbert slays her challenges head on. She does this by implementing the principle of helping others help themselves. *Delancey Street* was named after the section of New York where immigrants assembled at the turn of the century. Silbert, a criminologist and psychologist, modeled *Delancey Street* after her own extended family in an immigrant neighborhood of Boston. In 1971, Silbert, along with former felon John Maher, started the program for ex-cons with a $1,000 loan from a loan shark. They started small with only four drug addicts as residents. Today there are about 1,000 residents located throughout the country. There are now five facilities, including locations at their San Francisco headquarters, Los Angeles, New Mexico, New York, and North Carolina. Dr. Mimi Silbert explained:

"Our population ranges in age from 18 to 68; approximately 1/4 are women; 1/3 African American, 1/3 Hispanic, and 1/3 Anglo. The average resident has been a hard-core drug addict for ten years and has been in prison four times. Approximately seventy (70%) come from the courts, and about thirty percent (30%) have been homeless prior to entering Delancey Street.

Despite the violent and criminal backgrounds of our residents, there has never been one arrest in the 25 years we have operated, and gang members once sworn to kill one another are now living in integrated dorms and working together cooperatively and non-violently.

Although the average resident is functionally illiterate and unskilled when entering Delancey Street, all residents receive a high school equivalency and are trained in three different marketable job skills before graduating. The minimum stay at Delancey Street is two years; the average stay is four years. During that time, residents learn not only academic and vocational skills, but also the interpersonal, social survival skills, along with the attitudes, values, sense of responsibility, and self-reliance necessary to live in the mainstream of society drug-free, successfully, and legitimately.

Over 11,000 men and women have graduated into society as taxpaying citizens leading successful lives—including lawyers, truck drivers, sales people, various medical practitioners, realtors, mechanics, contractors, and even a member of the San Francisco Board of

TIME STATUES

Supervisors, the President of the San Francisco Housing Commission, a deputy coroner, and a deputy sheriff.

We have accomplished this at no cost to the taxpayer or the client. One of the most unique features of Delancey Street is that we have never accepted any government funds, nor do we have any staff. The entire organization is run by its residents in the process of changing their lives. The foundation supports itself primarily through a number of training schools which provide vocational skills to all the residents, and which also generate the Foundation's income through pooling the monies earned. Training schools include a Moving and Trucking School, a Restaurant and Catering Service, a Print and Copy Shop, Retail and Wholesale Sales, Paratransit Services, Advertising Specialties Sales, Christmas Tree Sales and Decorating, and an Automotive Service Center, among others.

In 1990, the residents built from the ground up their very own block, sometimes referred to as the Embarcadero Triangle, along the breathtaking San Francisco Bay waterfront. The monstrous task—a 325,000-square-foot, four-story building—was built at about half the cost of the current $30 million appraisal. Everyone worked together with pride. Over 300 formerly unemployed drug addicts, homeless people and ex-felons build their very own 177-unit Mediterranean-style masterpiece.

The Delancey Street Foundation testifies to what can be accomplished when the disadvantaged of society are afforded opportunity. Delancey Street has been featured on 60 Minutes, 20/20, Oprah Winfrey Prime Time Special, PARADE Magazine, People Magazine, and Time Magazine, to name only a few. The Delancey Street principle holds that ordinary people can transform extraordinary—even impossi-

ble—*dreams into reality by pooling their resources, supporting one another, and living lives of purpose and integrity."* (Bickford, 2002)

Violence Prevention and Interviews from Inductive Cohorts

I just received and read a fairly recent (2017) book from Hans Toch: *Violent Men: An Inquiry into the Psychology of Violence, 25th Anniversary Edition*. This is an intervention book. Nothing in print better illustrates how applied psychology can turn inductive data into democratic interventions.

Professor Toch wrote a jacket quote for me once. It was for my *Iatrogenics Handbook: A Critical Look at Research & Practice in Helping Professions* (Morgan 2005). This was a collaborative book that explored ways people can be hurt by health or educational professionals in the process of being helped, and how to prevent this. ("Iatrogenic" is a term sometimes boiled down to "the doctor's mistakes," now a top cause of mortality.) With a concise and witty scalpel, the final line of the Toch quote was for me the most memorable: *"If the shoe fits, it will hurt."*

This book of his may, at a distance, well be mistaken for a simple reprint of his original from 25 years ago, possibly with a new preface. Not at all. New sections and authors are added. I liked the risk assessment one, among others. This edition kept the original 1992 essence but, by adding fresh material, explodes into the current era with a mixture of new insights, useful contemporary applications, and compelling evidence on how prophetic the original book turned out to be. And 25 years of even more experience for the author didn't hurt. Brilliance becomes wisdom. Humor still brightens the reading, also illuminating the reader.

See. Hans could have said all those words in my last paragraph so much more concisely.

Hmm. I can try. Great read. Well worth the time in our finite life. Choices must be made and this book was a really good one. How's that? In considering his book, I am reminded of the two best interview questions I have experienced in my own more than half-century as a psychologist. At least the two that come to mind.

1. McMaster

At the onset of the 1970s, a group of McGill University psychiatrists moved from Montreal to run the McMaster University department of psychiatry and its clinic in so innovative a manner that it would be considered progressive even today. They had a successful rehabilitation program focused from the beginning on career/job development for their patients.

Since I was finishing a stretch as a Visiting Professor elsewhere in Canada, I was intrigued when they asked me to come give a talk. On arrival, they told me that they were considering an offer for me to join them. So now it was a job interview. One of them would sit in on my talk. The rest would be busy during that time contacting my references, but ones from a very special list. This list would be based on the question: *"Of the people you have worked for, which ones would give you the worst reference?"* Amused and fascinated, I fully complied. I had already been out in the field long enough to earn a few such antagonistic reviews. After my talk, which apparently they liked, they asked me to join them. As to the calls to the hostile referees, they concluded: *"What they hate about you is exactly what we are looking for."*

Reading the newest Toch contribution, his successful pursuit of this challenging subject while surmounting obstacles along the way, is exactly what we have been looking for.

2. Therapeutic Community

Also in the mists of the past, I was invited to audition as consultant to a San Diego therapeutic community program for patients diagnosed with schizophrenia. This too was a very innovative and successful program. Employing what we now know to call "Tochian" participatory methodology, the inhabitants had a strong say in the way they were treated. This included a pass or fail interview with me before I could become their consultant. After introductions all around, I was only asked one question: *"What is it that you do that gets you in the most trouble?"* I just opened my mouth to learn what would come out and it was *"My sense of humor."* They liked that. Agreed that was often their downfall too. I passed the test.

Professor Toch's work always has had this key ingredient. An essential unrelenting sense of humor. Also, you learn something new and useful in every chapter.

Actualizing Democracy in Clinical Psychology

Psychotherapy includes active listening, behavioral pattern recognition, ethical and legal context, compassionate empathy, inductive detective collaboration, diagnostic experience, follow-up consumer feedback, and interventions including intuitive humor and advocacy that actualizes democracy. The last has implications for international applied psychologists as it is explored here.

A Tale of Two Clinics

Some universities compete primarily and excessively with another one nearby. In my pre-doctoral training years at Michigan State

University, for example, I learned that its competing institution, the University of Michigan, would loan its bound dissertations to any other university *except* Michigan State. This was a rivalry that went beyond football. The rationale (rationalization) was that the driving distance was too close to justify loans, although closer institutions had no such problem.

In the state of Alaska, two major public universities had such rivalry. To attempt a bridge across this divide, the leaders of the system funded a joint program to train much needed community-clinical psychologists. The University of Alaska program brought faculty from the Anchorage and Fairbanks campuses together to train the first cohorts of what looked to be an exciting program. Faculty tele-conferences were held regularly in real time with split screen technology. (Today I would want virtual reality capacity.) Student cohorts were brought together as often as the forbidding geography and climate allowed. Indigenous healers, one a psychologist, were consultants and co-faculty. There was a strong research granted base and ongoing separate Clinical and Community practicum experiences.

I was brought in to the Fairbanks campus to teach and supervise the new training clinic. Time to actualize democracy in the training?

The clinic had six meeting rooms, a record room, a reception desk, and my office. White noise machines were outside each meeting room door to maintain auditory confidence. An indigenous ceremony graced the clinic on opening day. There were six interns, all excellent and mature graduate students, every one dedicated to the community.

One, an Alaska Native, candidly said she did not anticipate liking individual psychotherapy in the clinic but would do it as well as she could so she might return to her community with the PhD credential and better help them. (She did her best, which was superb, and in the end decided she loved clinical work because *"I was honored to hear their stories,"* and she did help them make their next stories better.)

I assigned each intern to a specific room, with a request that they decorate it in a way that would enhance their work, create a safe and comfortable environment for their community clients, and express their own personality. This they did, creatively and effectively. Each room had a strong but comfortable setting, one individualized to the choices of the intern. To better prepare for their eventual post-graduate career doing this sort of work, we had business cards made for each of them. Every week I did individual supervision of cases with each intern based in part on the video-taped sessions with a camera in every room. We also did a group supervision and another group meeting to share decisions on clinic function. Each client filled out a very brief evaluation after each session (satisfaction: yes or no, and a space for comment) and as a follow-up after conclusion of their intern experience. Based on this, the clients were very happy with the service and seemed to resolve their issues to lasting satisfaction. The Fairbanks clinical faculty were happy with the clinic and the Fairbanks campus students were pleased to tell the Anchorage campus students how pleased they were with their experience.

Which may have contributed to some problems. There were two program heads with equal authority, one for each campus. My program leader arranged a touring visit to my clinic for his Anchorage counterpart, and for me to make a subsequent visit to her clinic there.

The Anchorage campus program head was met with the traditional great welcome and, following a meal with faculty, she began the clinic tour. As we went through each aspect and met each smiling intern, her demeanor soured. She was polite but clearly unhappy. No concerns were expressed, even after my request for criticism. This I didn't understand until my later visit to her campus.

My wife and I arrived but nobody was there to meet us. We took a taxi to the campus but the head of the program was busy and said we should go to visit the clinic on our own. So we did.

In Anchorage it was a top-down hierarchical approach. The psychology doctoral students were on the bottom of this ladder. The clinic there belonged to another program and the doctoral students were sandwiched in as openings occurred. The supervision was done by a central monitor but individual supervision of cases was unsatisfying, said the students we spoke with. The rooms were identical and Spartan. No business cards. No client evaluation opportunity or follow-up. Despite this, they did use the same progressive technology that we did in Fairbanks, albeit in their own way.

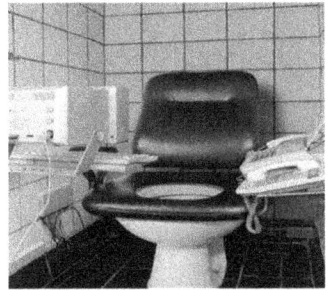

The doctoral students available said their program head was unhappy with the "coddling" I was giving to the Fairbanks students. Some had asked to transfer to our Fairbanks clinic practicum as they liked our model much better. But these requests were denied.

Looking for something positive, I asked how their community practicum was going. They liked this experience, but here too there was a fundamental distinction in perspective between campuses. The community practicum in Fairbanks defined community as indigenous native people. In Anchorage, the community practicum has mostly defined community as local organizations, businesses, and government entities. This all counted as advocacy and was undoubtedly useful experience. But not quite what our Fairbanks faculty, me included, thought of as Alaska's greatest community opportunity and need.

When it came time for me to leave, a cohort of doctoral students from both campuses petitioned the program to keep me on permanently. The petition was taken under advisement but, nearly a decade later, it is still apparently being studied. The intern students we stayed in touch with did graduate and went on to have successful careers as psychologists, most staying in Alaska. They continued our practice of treating their own clients and students with respect. Short term or long term, we can only provide educational oases in time, transient but beneficial while they last. And again, actualizing democracy in hierarchical systems is not always welcome. To say the least. Those who choose to actualize democracy always keep their bags packed.

Three years later I developed a similar clinical psychology practicum for interns in a Singapore clinic. It too was much appreciated by their community clients.

(Note: When I used to site visit community clinics, if they had no client evaluation feedback in place, I would do a telephone survey of past clients. Typical satisfaction percentage averaged about 60%. Then when I convinced the clinic to give clients a written feedback opportunity, subsequent year telephone survey satisfaction jumped to an average of about 90%. Just asking people if they are satisfied increased satisfaction. Businesses have become aware of this and successful ones routinely ask their customers for feedback. Having a say in what affects us directly, even post hoc, is actualized democracy.)

Election Systems That Actualize Democracy

Vote Ranking

The American Psychological Association initiated a vote transfer system for elections. With multiple candidates, the one receiving the fewest votes is dropped and those who voted for that candidate have their second choice vote counted. This continues until a single candidate is left and that person wins. This method allows voters to rank their choices, allowing more of their decisions to count. In contrast, systems requiring a single non-ranked vote may elect a poor candidate most voters don't want by splitting their votes among several excellent candidates. Priority ranking votes can be the future in any actualized democracy.

Note: One of the two first free-standing professional schools of psychology campuses began in San Francisco in 1971. Its 13 founding core faculty gathered to elect a representative by paper ballot. Although we had just met, it became clear that these psychologist pioneers were natural leaders. So much so that I suggested any traditional vote procedure might wind up undecided or unimpressive since my colleagues would likely just vote for themselves. After laughing agreement, I was challenged to recommend an alternative.

I said it might be better to vote for two candidates instead of one, a first and second choice. In this way anybody or everybody who wanted to vote for their self could do exactly that and we still would have enough second choices to get a majority. This we did. Sure enough, each of us had received at least one vote. Possibly because I had suggested this ad hoc voting system, most put my name down as a second choice, giving me the majority. This is how I became a

Dean in my first of four years at the California School of Professional Psychology. Democracy works in mysterious ways.

Belling the Cat

When I joined the faculty at a Pacific Rim university, they were profoundly and justifiably unhappy with their President. These faculty were generally quite gifted and articulate but rightly concerned about losing their jobs in any direct confrontation with this administrator. So it was that I was asked by the faculty union to do the formal evaluation. With my faculty team, we chose not to pinpoint the President alone. Instead we evaluated all the top administrators, including Vice Presidents and Deans. Again, the "Should this person be continued in their position" question was asked. With one exception, the administration received varying levels of majority confidence (although the comments were not universally friendly). The exception of course was the unpopular President, an outcome that had a vast majority (90%+ as I recall) wanting this President to resign. Which he refused to do.

Eventually the university's accreditation body intervened at our request. This led to the resignation of the President and the formation of a Faculty Senate. There I continued my charge with a faculty team that conducted an annual evaluation of the administration, Deans through President. Again it was not over-complicated. There were no hard to interpret nine-point scales. Every faculty member had the written opportunity to recommend or not recommend the continuation of their top supervisors. The yes/no recommendation was again coupled with an opportunity to comment. These results were tabulated and shared with faculty and all the administrative supervisors. Nearly all of them were recommended to continue although comments for improvement were more balanced this time between applause and criticism. Faculty morale rose even higher. The annual evaluation system became embedded in the Senate bylaws.

I did note that the Board of Directors did an annual evaluation of the President. The Board Chair liked my idea of using the evaluation from faculty as a key component of their assessment, further agreeing that annual continuation should be contingent on a majority vote of confidence from faculty.

(Note: When it came time to elect faculty to their Senate, they were voted for in their respective schools within the university. This led to some concern over partisanship. I suggested that we divide the total number of faculty by the number of Senators to be elected and use that number for a petition process. If, for example, the number resulting from the division was 25, then a Senator would be elected automatically with a petition signed by any 25 faculty, local or not. But no faculty member could sign more than one petition. I really liked this transparent process idea. Nobody else seemed to. Never mind.)

In earlier decades, going a rung lower on academic hierarchy, I joined the movement leaders in the service of having students in higher education evaluate their instructors at the close of each course, today a common event. This proved harder to do with teachers of children in public schools. I did enjoy suggesting to teachers of five-year-old children that they let their students give *them* a letter grade in each report card. Little applause from teachers for this.

As an administrator in many different capacities, I always had the people I supervise do an annual evaluation of me (stay or go, with comment) in addition to the one-to-one mutual supervision feedback most organizations now require. This is still not a universally used procedure.

At the very beginning of that time I was a Dean at the California School of Professional Psychology, San Francisco, I initiated a process where the students evaluated everybody who worked there, receptionist to CEO (stay or go, with comment) and the results were distributed to everybody on campus. I always promised I would step down as a supervisor if I did not have the confidence of the majority of my supervisees. I then had this done by students for their faculty instructor in each course (satisfied or not, with comment).

This was met with resistance from some senior faculty. *"If my students don't like my teaching, should I just shoot myself?"* said one. I said *"That or just improve the teaching—your choice."* Again all results were tabulated, typed and distributed with no screening. And here I found a limit. One student in one of my classes put in his evaluation: "*Morgan's teaching is fine but the class would go a lot better if Gene XXXX had a giant cork put in his mouth.*" Gene's actual full name was used. A former professional football player, Gene was quite vocal in class. He read the part of the evaluation about himself in our class for the first time. Well, he took it well for a few seconds, smiled, then turned red in the face and moved fast against the student he knew had written this. I barely prevented violence in the classroom.

After that, evaluators were warned that comments about other students would be removed, although anything about the teacher or administrative staff would remain. That worked much better. Pure democracies may at time require some focus.

In a recent year, I was invited to give a talk at a private Louisiana university. The state had recently changed the requirement for their endowed Chairs for Distinguished Professors. The recipients now, immediately, had to be demonstrably distinguished by publication and experience. The university had up to this time been using these positions to hire new PhD graduates, who then taught the courses no other faculty wanted to teach. Now they had some interest in my coming there to work as well as to speak, lest they lose the funding for the endowed Chair.

Before I could give my talk, I was scheduled for a two-day marathon, early morning to late evening, of meetings with all levels of university inhabitants. The students were interested and interesting as ever, the staff engaged, and the President, a man with impressive business and legal experience, cordial.

The faculty, though, were unhappy. The new President was liked well enough, but not his actions. These generally moved decision-making away from faculty. Decisions that directly impacted their work were now made at a variety of administrative levels. While this was congruent with the state's political leadership philosophy, it did strike the faculty as a substantial shift from their prior, more progressive role, one providing a sense of ownership in the organization, a somewhat actualized democracy.

By the end of the second day, I was exhausted. But it was time for my talk and the room was full. Faculty, staff, administration, students—every seat filled. I had planned to talk about educational group interventions in a state hospital, in the Peace Corps, in prisons. But as I stood to begin, I decided to talk about actualizing democracy, with abundant faculty examples.

The faculty and staff seemed fascinated, administrators appalled. By the time I was done, I had a feeling my welcome from administration had evaporated. The message waiting on my phone when I returned to my home state that night confirmed this.

(Note: For international perspective, my talk had included some linguistic examples of cultural double entendre. The biggest laugh came when I shared that the word "lawyer" in Canada's Nova Scotia and parts of the British Empire is pronounced "liar." I suspect not all were equally amused.)

Time Release Impact

In an earlier decade, I had interviewed at another Louisiana university, this time a well-known public one. The position was that of Department Chair in a large psychology department. Their major interest was in gaining accreditation for their doctoral program, something I have done many times over the years. I gave a talk and met with the faculty. Following an hour of questions and conversation, they shared that I was the last of three candidates being interviewed. Then their Dean would receive their rankings and recommendations of the candidates. I asked "Who would make the actual hiring decision?" Apparently nobody had asked that there before and the faculty response was surprised enthusiasm. I was told that this was an important question. I agreed. Discussion ensued.

I left my very friendly welcome from the faculty to meet with the Dean. He was primarily interested in a successful accreditation effort and suggested that my past success in this made my hiring something I should plan on. My wife and I were given plenty of time to look at housing and imagine a life there.

Once we were home, the days and weeks went by without a decision. I now and then called their hiring office but was told to be patient as the position was still unfilled and I was still a top candidate. Months went by and the seasons changed. Same response.

A year later I took another job, leaving the Louisiana mystery unsolved.

Then, much later, we by chance met some of the same Louisiana faculty at a dinner. Mystery solved. Turned out that the faculty had wanted to take no chances and just sent the Dean one name, mine, and not the three candidate names the Dean had expected. The Dean let them know that he thought I would be fine for the position but he found their approach to be insubordinate, to him a more important issue. The Dean demanded that the faculty recommend all three candidates to him as the hiring decision was his alone to make. The faculty said they were unanimous in their choice and the decision should be theirs. The Dean said he would approve no decision until the faculty recommended all three candidates. The faculty declined. Impasse. The position remained unfilled.

Eventually many of the faculty relocated to another university. Once there, hiring and other decisions directly affecting them returned.

(Note: I have been told I have "time-release humor" meaning it takes a while to get it, but the time-release impact of certain questions and discussions suggests we need some patience in assessing change. I have also been enjoying doing some 40+ year follow ups with former psychotherapy clients. Valuable lifespan feedback.)

Rights are Recognized

As shared in an earlier chapter: A priest from the university philosophy department, Father Angelus, arose and said in a voice that shook the rafters: *"Thank you Father President. But I do have a correction. Rights are not **granted**. They are **acknowledged**."* This has always stayed with me. So here it is again.

(Note: The philosophy faculty there at Saint Bonaventure University were quite brilliant. The theology faculty were seen as less shiny. The theology department Chair, a past president of the university, was sent to me so I could assist him to get his first publication. I suggested he just write down those original thoughts that occurred to him over his teaching year and then I would help him get some published. He mused for a moment and then said *"I have never had an original thought in my life, and I do not expect to have one."* I thanked him for his honesty. No publication ensued. Still, now I have at least put his words into print at last.)

Benign Noncompliance

In a Canadian public university in Nova Scotia, I was a young new faculty member. As such, I was rewarded with huge classes. One, my social psychology class, had more students than the assigned room could hold. That first day I asked the class, standing room only, for ideas on where we might find a larger (and better) room to reconvene. The best idea was to meet in the spacious gathering room of the student center. There we moved. The chairs were comfortable, non-fluorescent lighting and acoustics excellent, and all we had to do was sign up for the time and dates we needed it. Despite the large number of people, I particularly liked that we sat in such a circled way that there was direct communication between every person there.

A few days later I got an official note from the head of the Faculty

Senate. I was ordered to return to my assigned classroom and request Senate permission to move to the new space *before* actually going there. Now, some Faculty Senates are not really allowed to make the most important decisions affecting them. They instead are just permitted to regulate other faculty through Senate-generated bureaucratic barriers: they are geared to say no, not often yes. In any case, they have no authority to enforce their own significant choices as faculty members. This was my first experience with such a body.

Still in our excellent but unapproved new space, at our next meeting I shared the note with my class. Since we were studying social psychology, I told the class we would just not respond to the note, keep meeting where we were, and see what happens. I diagrammed the Senate and its decision-making process.

The class was enthusiastic. I suppose it was congruent with their young adult rebellion phase (it was the late 1960s) and my own age at 29 was not much past theirs. (In all fairness though, I would probably do the same now.) As the weeks went by, I received more notes, plus an intense conversation with my supervising department head and dean. Still we continued on in our nice new space, an update at the opening of each class meeting. The end of the semester still found us ensconced in that comfortable room. We had added water and chocolates for each student, a practice I have maintained since.

We had studied human behavior in context. We had studied systems theory and organizational process. We all learned. In this instance, those most directly affected by the decision of room choice were the students and their teacher. The Faculty Senate was a level removed. Actualized democracy did not favor the faculty senators that time.

Relating to Other Species

Humane and just treatment follows from developed empathy. I could cite here the important work of Milgram and Zimbardo on the disastrous consequences for individuals who think they have no responsibility for their actions or no perceived power to determine their fate. Or, one could look at the growth of individual decision-making as a developmental process: the older the child, the more self-impacting decisions. Hence, lack of self-impacting decisions for adults invites regression or impairment. But, being classically trained in the psychology from the middle of the last century, I will give an example from a rat study.

As an undergraduate student at Michigan State University, one of my part-time jobs was to run each of 40 water-deprived male and female white rats, night after night, in a study. Well, here is our abstract:

TIME STATUES

"Forty water-deprived albino rats ran a straight alley with differently textured and colored start box, runway, and goal box (GB) for 35 acquisition trials and were then extinguished to criterion. After random assignment to four conditions, Ss received three trials of 30 sec exposure to either regular GB with reward (Group LRA-1), novel GB with reward (Group LRA-2), regular GB without reward (Group C-1), or hold box without reward (Group C-2). Three test extinction trials in initial runway followed. All acquisition, extinction, treatment, and test trials were given one per day. Control group speeds did not differ significantly at any test trial. LRA-1 group medians exceeded controls at all test trials on both starting and running speeds, significantly so only on the former. LRA-2 group medians were slower than controls on test trial 1, but not on later test trials, and significantly so only for running speed." (Barch, A.M, Ratner, S.C., & Morgan, R.F., 1965)

Each rat was different in how long they took to leave the start box and get their drink. Many just froze for what seemed to be a very long time to me (I was 19). Stanley Ratner, my major professor, had always said that reading all one could find about an animal was always prerequisite to working with them. So I read about rats. Therein was my solution. Rats avoid being in curved structures. So I cut a curved metal semicircle in the back of the start box. This helped a lot. All rats moved out and forward with no more freezing. I could finish in time to study or enjoy the evening.

This study went on each night for two months. As you might imagine, or not, I got to know these put-upon animals as individuals. Females were more anxious and liked to try to nibble on my hands. Males were more calm but meant business when they tried to bite. Eventually they relaxed with me, learning that I was usually a Pavlovian prelude to their drink.

Now, months to us are years to rats so the study was a very long time for them. Spending their life in cages was bad enough but males were kept grouped in their own compound and females were grouped together in another. They could smell, see, and hear each other but the sexes never met. Nor were they given enough water, as prescribed by the study, or any excess food.

Finally, the study concluded. It was on a Friday. I asked a staffer what would happen to the rats. He said somebody would come and kill them on Monday morning. Either with chloroform or throwing them against a wall to break their neck. I wondered why they couldn't be kept alive to be used in another study. I was told they were no longer "naïve," which meant this study's graduate rodents, impacted by their experience in the first research, apparently forever changed, wouldn't do in a second different study. Well, here was by definition a captive group of beings, I concede a non-human one, with no say over their lives or the demise thereof. An existential challenge for sure.

Rats have an intelligence not substantially different from dogs or cats. They can be pets, although by adulthood that long scaled tail discourages ownership. Or so I found (another story). I had a fantasy about harnessing enough rodents to a wagon, like little horses, so I could be transported in this unique way across campus to my classes. But neither time (nor reason) would allow this.

So, I got a very large holding cage, filled it with lots of food, water, and toys. Then I emptied all 20 males and all 20 females into it. Turned off the lights. Left them undisturbed by humans for the weekend.

TIME STATUES

Sunday evening I came by and found them sleeping, many of them coupled in each other's arms. Others sprawled exhausted over little mountains of food or toys. What a party it must have been.

With me was another student who had a large farm nearby. He took the large rat-filled cage, put it in his car, and drove off to release them in the tall grass of fields on his acreage. He did warn me that his farm had dogs, cats, and falcons. But at least they had a chance there, much better than if we kept them in the cages where they had spent their life so far.

Monday came and went without their mass execution.

Rats are not people. Not the other way around either. Usually.

Nor could they tell me what their decisions would be about the things in their life affecting them most directly.

But, considering their weekend party and subsequent freedom, I think I made a good guess.

Opportunity's Traumatic Shadow

In September 2006, Secretary of State Condoleezza Rice was asked about the deteriorating and traumatic situation in Iraq, deadly to so many of their citizens and so many of the troops from so many other countries. She responded with a smile and pointed out that the Chinese symbol for crisis included the symbol for opportunity. She urged the world to look on the war in Iraq as both.

That evening on television's **"The Daily Show with John Stewart,"** a new correspondent named Aasi Mandvi performed a powerful parody. Seeming to stand in war torn Baghdad, he agreed with Secretary Rice that the bombs bursting around him were each an opportunity for a better life. He deadpanned that the deaths of hundreds of thousands of Iraqis could be seen as a valuable gift for productive community change.

After ducking an opportunity bullet and a nearby opportunity explosion, he asked an incredulous John Stewart:

"Well surely the Americans see their own destruction on September 11th **as just such an opportunity?"**

"No, I think not" said John.

"Amazing!" said Aasif Mandvi.

An interesting implication. Dr. Rice's metaphor reflected the unpleasant reality that for her and the administration she served, the traumatic American tragedy of 9/11 had truly been a crisis full of opportunity.

Other

Voting

Clearly today, democracy in elections must be geared to a fair and honest procedure. Is there a role for modern technology?

Will DNA matching eventually have a role in accurate and open voter registration? Will virtual reality (VR) bring together decision makers at great distances from each other for discussion and voting in a virtual meeting room? (Much international classroom education in this way is possible with VR. Already happening in business.)

On the dark side, there was the election for governor on a Pacific Island. It turned out that the only election vote tally computer, housed in their only university, suffered a suspicious power outage the evening after voting was complete.

Once the vote was counted the next day, the outcome was the opposite of exit polling. I believe it was Stalin who was quoted as saying that he completely supported democratic elections so long as he counted the votes.

An honest count is more important than ever today. In national or local elections, we should have paper ballots that allow for recounts, access to all those who qualify to vote, removal of the burgeoning restrictions that are meant to inhibit or suppress or reverse voting access, all these protections are essential.

Acknowledging individuals

For example, Joe, the head of maintenance at Hawaii State Hospital, supervised more than 300 people but each was recognized by him on their birthday. He did the same when he moved on to run the Leper Colony on Molokai.

Another example: I found this useful for Head Start teachers to carefully observe, evaluate, and recognize each child on their birthday (with un-birthdays for those born on a day Head Start was not in session.) All democracy begins with respected and acknowledged individuals.

Being accurate

I still treasure a photo of actress Rita Moreno on her 70th birthday. I had just congratulated her on that special day, adding that the most riveting and emotional performance I had ever seen on the Broadway stage in New York was her performance in West Side Story. The photo shows her shock at what turned out to be my ignorant statement.

It was her rival Chita Rivera that I had heard on stage in 1957. Rita had only been in the movie. So acknowledgement good, accuracy better. Sorry Rita.

In sum

Are we getting lost in the dark woods of un-actualized oppression that we see throughout today's international experiences? Or is there a path forward for our human family?

In my contacts with elders in their last stage of their life, ongoing review of their lifespan experience usually occurs. (Something apparent in my own writing as you have seen.)

TIME STATUES

Author Alex Haley once noted that *"the death of an elder is like the burning of a library."*

In this life review process, regrets are much more often about actions *not* taken than any that were. Opportunities missed. Knowing this in advance is important. Actualizing democracy is one of those actions best *not* to be missed. The path is just ahead if we take it.

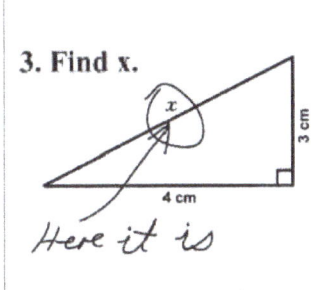

Chapter 27: A Columbus Perspective

Never having seen the stars, they dny the stars. Never having glimpsed the shining ways nor the mortals that tread them, they deny the existence of the shining ways as well as the existence of the high-bright mortals who adventure along the shining ways.

The narrow pupils of their eyes in the center of the universe, they image the universe in terms of themselves, of their meager personalities make pitiful yardsticks with which to measure the high-bright souls saying: 'Thus long are all souls, and no longer; it is impossible that there should exist greater-stationed souls than we are, and our gods know that we are great of stature." Never having seen the mountains, there are no mountains.
— Jack London 1916 (published 1986)

TIME STATUES

When I was in 3rd grade, we read that Columbus discovered America in 1492.

I raised my hand and asked "What about the people already here?"

"Those were Indians," said my teacher, "but Columbus was a white man from Europe."

I raised my hand again. "I saw a man about to eat a sandwich in the park last weekend. He laid it on the park bench next to him and then started reading the paper. But when he reached for the sandwich it was gone. A hungry stray dog was eating it on the grass. The man was very angry at the dog."

My teacher asked "What is your point Robert? What did you learn from that?"

I answered "Well, I thought that the dog had stolen his sandwich and he was right to be angry. But now I realize that, like Columbus, the dog had just *discovered* that man's sandwich so it must have been okay to eat it." She gave us recess early then.

(Response from Hans Toch: *"The moral is NEVER LEAVE YOUR SANDWICH ON A BENCH."*)

The Cultural Genocide Chart

Columbus killed and enslaved the indigenous people he encountered in his trips to the Caribbean: *In an era in which the international slave trade was starting to grow, Columbus and his men enslaved many native inhabitants of the West Indies and subjected them to extreme violence and brutality. On his famous first voyage in 1492,*

Columbus landed on an unknown Caribbean island after an arduous three-month journey. On his first day in the New World, he ordered six of the natives to be seized, writing in his journal that he believed they would be good servants. Throughout his years in the New World, Columbus enacted policies of forced labor in which natives were put to work for the sake of profits. Later, Columbus sent thousands of peaceful Taino "Indians" from the island of Hispaniola to Spain to be sold. Many died en route. Those left behind were forced to search for gold in mines and work on plantations. Within 60 years after Columbus landed, only a few hundred of what may have been 250,000 Taino were left on their island. As governor and viceroy of the Indies, Columbus imposed iron discipline on what is now the Caribbean country of the Dominican Republic, according to documents discovered by Spanish historians in 2005. In response to native unrest and revolt, Columbus ordered a brutal crackdown in which many natives were killed; in an attempt to deter further rebellion, Columbus ordered their dismembered bodies to be paraded through the streets. https://www.history.com/news/columbus-day-controversy

History repeats these atrocities throughout the eras. In modern days, attention is increasingly being paid to the intergenerational trauma of the survivors.

Edison Uno was a professor at San Francisco State University and the California School of Professional Psychology. He was himself a survivor of WWII concentration camps for California's citizens of Japanese descent. From this he lectured on the contrasting community survival strategies of subsequent generations of Chinese and Japanese Californians.

For the former, the strategy (facilitated historically by apartheid laws) was to cluster in "Chinatowns," maintaining language, culture, and safety.

For the latter, the strategy was dispersion, so much so that Uno observed **"If a Japanese American inhabits a home and the house next door is up for sale, another Japanese family will not buy the available home, will not live next door."** (Uno, 1970, 1974, Uno & Maisie, 1992).

Facing hostile and dangerous ethnocentric forces, cultures have faced these challenges as charted here on the next page.

LEVELS OF CULTURAL CHALLENGE

Annihilation   (Genocide, "Ethnic Cleansing," Holocaust)

Evacuation   (Deportation, "Removals")

Isolation   (Ghettos, Reservations)

Assimilation   (Cultural Removal)

Celebration   (Intact culture welcomed in larger community, gifts and differences appreciated)

These are listed in terms of greatest to least generational trauma, with only the last being a healthy outcome.

I developed these categories for a lecture, following conversations with Edison Uno and American Indian psychologist Arthur McDonald, when I was in my thirties.

McDonald spoke directly after my presentation, beginning with this response: *"The Cheyenne believe wisdom only comes with age. Wisdom is not likely before 60. When a man who has lived only 3 decades says something like this that sounds like wisdom, it is considered a coincidence."* (McDonald 1978, Pond & McDonald 1997).

Chapter 28. Unknown and Known: Drs. Green and King

Understanding our key past events requires providing more attention to these two courageous pioneers, one far too unknown and the other celebrated now as a National Holiday in their own country. Maybe today's world is the best time to remember what they contributed then.

Dr. Robert Lee Green

Who led the visit to the Union of South Africa that sparked the economic boycott that ultimately ended Apartheid and freed Nelson Mandela to begin Reconciliation?

Who co-wrote with Martin Luther King Jr. the speech to the American Psychological Association that reshaped modern Community Psychology?

Who was the only full time psychologist working with Dr. King, and so closely that he was one of the six bearers of Dr. King's coffin?

Who was the African American psychologist who planted the American flag on Jeff Davis's Confederate monument? Who was the African American psychologist from Detroit to stage a sit-in protest against a barber shop owned by people with black skin who would only cut the hair of people with white skin?

When an entire county in Virginia closed its schools for 4 years to avoid desegregation, who took on the research to follow these thousands of children, re-open the schools, identify critical periods for learning, and develop an empirical basis for seeing measured intelligence as environmentally dependent?

Is this the same psychologist who helped found and develop Head Start along with Follow Through in the US (and Newstart in Canada) as well as modern schools of urban studies or special education or desegregation institutes?

Yes, and his name is Dr. Robert Lee Green, now a retired President of the University of the District of Columbia, author and professional speaker. Today living in Nevada with his wife Lettie, children grown and away.

I met Dr. Green on the Human Relations Committee of the city of East Lansing, Michigan. He had recently graduated from Michigan State University with a doctoral degree in Special Education and had been hired as a young Assistant Professor. When he attempted to buy a home there for his young family, he was told that the realtors had a written prohibition against selling property in their city to anybody of Dr. Green's race. As usual, Bob did not accept this: whenever faced with the alternatives of bad and worse, he always generated a third choice.

He went with me directly to the university president. Now this president, John Hannah, had been appointed by President Eisenhower as National Chair of the United States Human Relations Commission. He did not want an embarrassment in his own back yard.

President John Hannah's academic background was essentially a

B.A. in Poultry Science enhanced by marriage to the prior university president's daughter. He also had many high level friends in the national Republican Party. In record time he had substantial funds rolling in from other countries, international students, parents, governing families, and corporations developing resources for the growing war in Vietnam.

Hearing of Green's housing dilemma, Hannah called the Chair of the MSU Speech department (who was also the Mayor of East Lansing). The university president ordered him to put a Human Relations Committee together to look into Dr. Green's situation. Not to resolve it exactly, but definitely to consider it carefully, or at least publicly. While this phone call was being held, I noted a huge painting on President Hannah's wall depicting slaves picking cotton.

In any case, the Commission was formed. Besides Bob there were 8 other members, 7 of which were friendly to the realtors. The last and ninth seat was held open for a student at Michigan State University: that was me. I earned this seat because I was the only volunteer from MSU's 30,000 students – not a selection particularly based on merit.

As the press-covered public monthly meetings progressed in City Council seats, the other Commission members agreed that Bob had been treated unfairly. Yet they argued for change by persuasion instead of a new law.

They stated that we needed to create positive community change by changing attitude rather than behavior. A classic argument resolved usually by existential context or *"it depends"*.

In this clear case of injustice, attitude change alone as a first approach of course did not work.

It took Green and me half a year to get them to (barely by a vote of 5 to 4) move to behavioral change, let attitude follow, and to ask the City to pass a law ending racial discrimination in East Lansing.

How we did this is another story but it borrowed heavily on the work of a Social Psychologist, Solomon Ash.

Dr. Green took me under his wing and allowed me to bootleg an unofficial second pre- and post-doctoral internship with him that involved special education, innovative federal poverty programs, and assisting Dr. King in the last four years of King's young life.

Green's work on the vulnerability of measured children's intelligence made him famous, leading to changes in educational patterns in the USA and in Bermuda among other places. His Prince Edward County, Virginia, project included the organization of Martin Luther King Jr. who took Dr. Green on as his key Director of Citizen Education. Responsibilities included Adult Literacy programs in Chicago, Desegregation Institutes across the country, and innovative educational methods in and out of government throughout the world (Green *et al* 1964-1969, 2015; Morgan 1969, 2012, 2018).

It was Robert Lee Green who went to the apartheid Union of South Africa with Arthur Ashe and other African-American celebrities to see for themselves what actually was being done there.

Mandela was in jail and the press was censored. Green, Ashe, and the others received intense criticism from both left and right political figures for what they charged seemed implicit support of a rogue apartheid regime. But just as Mandela had been doing from his cell, Green was studying the opponent, knowing that information-based decisions were more effective.

It was Green that noted that the apartheid regime would fail without the continued economic support of some very visible western corporations. Not that these corporations responded immediately or willingly, but a broad-based economic sanctions campaign was launched to withdraw university and union retirement funds from any corporation doing business with South Africa's regime.

Eventually this worked, along with a growing (and music-influenced) rebellion by the mistreated South African majority in-country. With economic sanctions, racial rebellion, and a fear of a bloodbath, only Mandela and his Reconciliation plans held hope to the white leadership for a non-violent transition. Mandela was released and history tells the rest of his successful story.

Dr. Green now consults internationally here and there, but he chides me for assuming he's *"still only 35 years old"*. He no longer looks like a young Denzel Washington. He looks like an older Denzel Washington (smile).

Psychologist Green remains largely unknown to the public. Well, not well known enough.

If only more people knew of the national and international legacy of his lifelong applied decades of contribution to assessment, community psychology, the organization of Black Psychologists in the American Psychological Association, special education, urban psychology, and the career launching of younger psychologists like myself.

Well, with great good fortune, I know him.

And now you know him too.

Dr. Martin Luther King Jr.

September, 1967. Martin Luther King Jr. was only 38 years old but already president of the Southern Christian Leadership Conference and winner of the Nobel Peace Prize when he stepped to the microphone, not something he really needed, at the American Psychological Association (APA) Annual Convention in Washington, D.C.

Robert Lee Green and I collaborated in the development of this speech, suggesting some paragraphs, a few of which he approved. I learned later that Ambassador Andrew Young had said that he contributed separate input as well. When addressing a specific professional group, Dr. King always wanted to review what this group was all about, their issues and goals, so he could build an informed speech around core ideas that were entirely his own.

Dr. King never needed a ghost writer. Or a teleprompter. He was always on top of delivering his own speech, his own principles, and his own powerful delivery. Bostonian and calm at first; louder, faster tempo, and more emphatic in the middle; with powerful impact for the close.

The few sentences we suggested seemed reasonable but kind of mundane. To listen to what he ultimately delivered was hearing a script brought to life from this great orator. The speech was moving, persuasive. Even to an auditorium full of psychologists.

A re-reading of his powerful address today captures the urgent tone of the 60s, as he cajoled the nation's social scientists to 'tell it like it is', to invite them to join a crucial and just cause.

In fact, to APA's membership, whom he addressed as *'concerned friends of good will,'* his plea for help in changing a society *'poisoned to its soul by racism,'* seems now much more poignant in light of the tragedy of his death that struck only seven months later.

My minor portion and Green's went to him through a meeting Robert Green had with King. I was honored to see if anything we suggested had met with King's approval, and fit his message for that day. What a lifetime gift to contribute any part of this.

The full text of his speech is found at the end of this chapter. When you read it, please use your auditory imagination to hear him speak it. And if you can, see him on that stage in this everlasting live statue in time.

The words he spoke that Sept. 1, as the convention's Invited Distinguished Address, were reprinted in the *Journal of Social Issues* (Vol. 24, No. 1, 1968). While the speech was in galley proofs, the shocking and numbing news of his assassination was released.

**

Another time statue

It was 1964 in Atlanta, Georgia. Thanks to Robert Lee Green, it was time for my first visit to the main office of Martin Luther King Jr. At age 23, still a graduate student, I anticipated meeting this older man in his late thirties.

Now I was just outside his Southern Christian Leadership Conference (SCLC) office entrance. From the street I could see, just beyond the front door, was a woman at her reception desk. She was white. This I learned later meant racists were far less likely to shoot into the office as, at that time, such women were held in some esteem by gun loopy white supremicists. Some. Maybe.

Also from the street, I could see another office just past her on the side, still very visible. That was where Dr. King worked, where I would be with him shortly. Once inside, the receptionist told me that the other SCLC leadership and staff had offices not in any direct line from the front door or street.

The layout was "L" shaped with the receptionist and Dr. King in the smaller leg of that "L", the only ones in line from any bullets fired from passing cars. The rest were housed in the more secure larger leg of the "L". Not that they stayed there for long.

I wondered what kind of human family member, clearly lacking conscience or sense, would shoot into an office building in downtown metropolitan Atlanta and still expect to have no consequences.

Maybe dimwit ones who might do a drive-by shooting from a bus?

Well, we are all cousins in a much closer DNA family than people thought. Can't say I like them all. Like the two in the elevator that other time in Atlanta.

The Elevator

Green and I were on our way to a special SCLC Conference in Atlanta. The elevator was our last stop on the way to the Dinkler Hotel Conference Ballroom.

When we got on, two white men were already there. Both wore suits, as did we. The elevator door closed and began a slow ascent. They checked out the large SCLC Conference name tags we wore on our jackets. Sneered.

TIME STATUES

Well, not going to *our* conference.

One, the big one, just glared. He shifted to stand up very straight which most men do just before they fight.

The smaller one smiled but managed to make it hostile. Turning to me, ignoring Robert Green, he said: *"We live here in Georgia. We BELONG here. Now, where are YOU from?"*

Answering directly: *"Hawaii."*

Him, sneer widened: *"Ha-why-yeee?"*

I said *"Well, if you can't pronounce it right, they won't let you come there. It's Hawaii."**

This annoyed him.

"Why would I want to go there anyhow?"

I looked to Bob Green who seemed on full alert. Bob wanted no racial incident here to reflect badly on the nonviolent participants of the SCLC Conference. He nodded at me, meaning "Okay for you to take care of this."

Now Robert Lee Green, fit and feisty, had plenty of his own courage. He grew up in Detroit, drove a cab in San Francisco (where his fraternity brother Willie Brown became eventual Mayor following years of spectacular success as Speaker of the California Legislature). He was an adept at standing up to authority. I saw him once intimidate the legendary university football coach Duffy Daugherty for Duffy's disrespectful treatment of Black football players.

That was in Michigan, the North. Here we were in 1960s Georgia, the

South, safe home for even more white privilege. Bob was very protective of his joint mission with Martin Luther King Jr. No distracting incidents.

A San Francisco gay client of mine once advised me that his favorite way of dealing with narcissistic hate group citizens was to identify them as a member of the group they hated.

Still time to play. Two of us and only two of them. I gave it a try.

"*Check with your wife. She'd give her left anything to have you take her to Hawaii.*"

"Well, you are sure wrong there, kid. I don't have a wife."

"*Not surprised. Sorry, ask your husband then.*" I nodded toward the other quiet local, the one still glaring.

The speaking local, no longer sneering, seemed confused. I knew he and his friend would figure it out eventually in a time-release way.

The elevator door opened at our floor.

No time to have fun telling them that they would be unlikely to pass the IQ test required to enter Honolulu. No need to have fun telling them that my job was to make sure that the pro-boxer I had with me didn't fight when no pay was involved. And it didn't occur to me to end our conversation with that friendly Southern mocking "*Well, BLESS your hearts.*" Their tiny little hearts.

We walked out the elevator door. It shut behind us. We moved on in peace, Bob Green laughing.

–

*Note: It is said that a tourist couple newly arrived in this 50th state, approached an oldtimer resident sitting in his chair enjoying the ocean view. They asked him *"Do we say 'Hawaii' or should we call it 'Havaii'?* The oldtimer smiled and said *"Havaii."* They thanked him. He responded *"You are velcome."*

**

In His Office

Dr. King was ready to see me.

I entered his office. Stepping from behind the desk, he shook my hand. His hand enveloped mine like a glove, reflecting the welcome in his voice.

I was a head taller at 6'4" than the older man but he seemed much larger, seeming to fill the room. Green had told me of King's athleticism. I could see for myself that he was solidly built and, in his thirties, at his prime. All the more remarkable that he was truly nonviolent.

Most others around him bought into nonviolence as a strategy to achieve equity and justice. Not King. He lived it. I thought of him in later years where the best martial artists shunned fighting anywhere outside exhibitions.

We sat in comfortable chairs and spoke together for an hour. In that time, outside the content of our conversation, I noticed that he effortlessly sat like a king, deserving his last name.

There began my four year study of his regal posture, nonverbal leadership confidence, speaking tone shifts, and fully focused attention on whomever he was spending time with. What was it about this man, our human family cousin, to endear him so completely to those of us whose path he crossed? Existentialists might say it was his clear righteous purpose in life, a primary mission he was willing to die for. And did.

Coming from Buffalo, I grew up with an excessive disdain for celebrity. Even earned celebrity. I had also as a child lived across from a very lively Black church, amazingly beautiful in its own powerful way (the music!), but run by a Black minister who was also the local slum lord exploiting families fresh up from the South. I at that time shared my father's distrust for clergy of all races. Yet here I was in the presence of our most celebrated clergyman. He was the real thing, genuine, driven. I trusted him instantly.

With no tact whatsoever, I asked him what he thought of Robert Williams, a Black veteran whose gun club with other Black veterans was achieving initial success at desegregating parts of the South. Williams had a perspective that was the antithesis of Dr. King's. Williams threatened retaliation for injustice, freedom by strength. Wasn't this more congruent with the American spirit than the Asian Indian nonviolent approach of Gandhi?

King was patient and gracious in his response, explaining nonviolence as though I had just recently discovered it and could use some tutoring. In fact I did. What a fine teacher.

(The success of Williams ended when Freedom Riders came through, bringing after them cowardly white racists who expected no pushback from nonviolent people. They fired into residential homes randomly. To their surprise, Black veteran gun club members fired back. The battles ended with Williams a federal fugitive fleeing the country, labeled a dangerous "paranoid schizophrenic" by a local Sheriff.)

We spoke about our families. He was truly energized by this.

I asked him about the SCLC stress tests. For example, if they were to get to the airport in an hour in order to catch a plane, they would leave half an hour late and do their best. At least once, a plane had stopped in mid-runway to let King and the reverends on.

He laughed and said it wasn't so much of a test as it was his spontaneous repetitive oversight. But, on reflection, he could see that it was good preparation for handling crises. Of which there was no shortage.

King's resume or CV was only a few pages long but ended with a paragraph, very important to him, about his wife and children. Right after the listing of the Nobel Peace Prize.

Toward the end he spoke about my working at SCLC, even part-time as I was, assisting Dr. Green. He said he never made an important organizational decision without first listening carefully to each of his staff. Each one was heard out. Once that was done he would consider fully everything that had been said.

In the end though, much as King deserved his name, the decision would be his alone. The deciding factor would not be a majority vote or the persuasion of friends. It would be *"the right thing to do."*

This was exemplified by the discussion around whether he should go beyond his desegregation efforts, for which he had the full support of President Johnson, to move forward on economic justice or equity.

Even more controversial was the choice to oppose the war in Vietnam, an intrusion into a Civil War involving the invasion of another country with consequences being the deaths of thousands of young Americans. Yet, that would lose President Johnson's support completely, also magnifying the right wing hatred for King already led by J. Edgar Hoover's FBI. Consequences could be deadly.

Almost all staff advised against these initiatives, especially the Vietnam one. Robert Lee Green was an exception, supporting this antiwar direction. (I wasn't at this meeting but through Bob I was informed and agreed.) Very few others did. King reflected quietly. Silence. Then he announced that he would do the right thing. They moved ahead on all these initiatives.

In Michigan, the desegregation marches had not been molested. The police kept order and did their jobs. Years later, the anti-war in Vietnam marches had a different reaction. Police clubs came out, protester arrests in great numbers, public support was highly divided. By 1968, Dr. King had been murdered. He died doing the right thing.

Once my 1964 conversational hour with Dr. King was over, I met with Green and went to work. Program evaluation, desegregation institutes, an Adult Literacy program in Chicago, suggestions for speeches, whatever could be contributed.

This while and after finishing my doctorate in Michigan, an internship at Hawaii State Hospital, globetrotting consultations or site visits for government programs with Robert Green, and a young family of five to support. It was a very full and very enriched four years.

Never again did I get a one-on-one with Dr. King before the four years and his life ran out. We both were very busy, particularly him. Bob Green was a great observer though, always keeping me informed, involved, aware.

Dr. King's verbal and nonverbal leadership never let up. His was the first "Rainbow Coalition," insisting on a place for all races in his staff and in the movement.

I studied his command of a room, confidence in his goals and in all of us. On stage in a panel or on TV, he sat alert and focused. Should a staffer have an urgent message for him, he would keep looking forward, tilt his head slightly so the staffer could whisper the message in his ear without his shifting focus from forward. Regal. Effective.

Positive Psychology challenges clinicians to define the opposite of all those diagnostic categories. What can be at the other end of the human potentials spectrum? What would a totally healthy person, mentally and physically, be like?

Probably somebody athletic, compassionate, loving, eloquent, with a great sense of humor, a generous spirit, decisive, inclusive, definitely a higher primary purpose for living as a reason for gladly beginning each day as a gift.

Who always jumps to my mind is Dr. Martin Luther King Jr. And yes, definitely, Dr. Robert Lee Green as well.

**

The Role of the Behavioral Scientist in the Civil Rights Movement By Martin Luther King Jr.

It is always a very rich and rewarding experience when I can take a brief break from the day-to-day demands of our struggle for freedom and human dignity and discuss the issues involved in that struggle with concerned friends of good will all over the nation. It is particularly a great privilege to discuss these issues with members of the academic community, who are constantly writing about and dealing with the problems that we face and who have the tremendous responsibility of molding the minds of young men and women all over the country.

The Civil Rights Movement needs the help of social scientists

In the preface to their book, Applied Sociology *(1965), S. M. Miller and Alvin Gouldner state: "It is the historic mission of the social sciences to enable mankind to take possession of society." It follows that for Negroes who substantially are excluded from society this science is needed even more desperately than for any other group in the population.*

For social scientists, the opportunity to serve in a life-giving purpose is a humanist challenge of rare distinction. Negroes too are eager for a rendezvous with truth and discovery. We are aware that social scientists, unlike some of their colleagues in the physical sciences, have been spared the grim feelings of guilt that attended the invention of nuclear weapons of destruction. Social scientists, in the main, are fortunate to be able to extirpate evil, not to invent it.

If the Negro needs social sciences for direction and for self-understanding, the white society is in even more urgent need. White America needs to understand that it is poisoned to its soul by racism and the understanding needs to be carefully documented and consequently more difficult to reject. The present crisis arises because although it is historically imperative that our society take the next step to equality, we find ourselves psychologically and socially imprisoned. All too many white Americans are horrified not with conditions of Negro life but with the product of these conditions-the Negro himself.

TIME STATUES

White America is seeking to keep the walls of segregation substantially intact while the evolution of society and the Negro's desperation is causing them to crumble. The white majority, unprepared and unwilling to accept radical structural change, is resisting and producing chaos while complaining that if there were no chaos orderly change would come.

Negroes want the social scientist to address the white community and "tell it like it is." White America has an appalling lack of knowledge concerning the reality of Negro life. One reason some advances were made in the South during the past decade was the discovery by northern whites of the brutal facts of southern segregated life. It was the Negro who educated the nation by dramatizing the evils through nonviolent protest. The social scientist played little or no role in disclosing truth. The Negro action movement with raw courage did it virtually alone. When the majority of the country could not live with the extremes of brutality they witnessed, political remedies were enacted and customs were altered.

These partial advances were, however, limited principally to the South and progress did not automatically spread throughout the nation. There was also little depth to the changes. White America stopped murder, but that is not the same thing as ordaining brotherhood; nor is the ending of lynch rule the same thing as inaugurating justice.

After some years of Negro-white unity and partial success, white America shifted gears and went into reverse. Negroes, alive with hope and enthusiasm, ran into sharply stiffened white resistance at all levels and bitter tensions broke out in sporadic episodes of violence. New lines of hostility were drawn and the era of good feeling disappeared.

The decade of 1955 to 1965, with its constructive elements, misled us.

Everyone, activists and social scientists, underestimated the amount of violence and rage Negroes were suppressing and the amount of bigotry the white majority was disguising.

Science should have been employed more fully to warn us that the Negro, after 350 years of handicaps, mired in an intricate network of contemporary barriers, could not be ushered into equality by tentative and superficial changes.

Mass nonviolent protests, a social invention of Negroes, were effective in Montgomery, Birmingham and Selma in forcing national legislation which served to change Negro life sufficiently to curb explosions. But when changes were confined to the South alone, the North, in the absence of change, began to seethe.

The freedom movement did not adapt its tactics to the different and unique northern urban conditions. It failed to see that nonviolent marches in the South were forms of rebellion. When Negroes took over the streets and shops, southern society shook to its roots. Negroes could contain their rage when they found the means to force relatively radical changes in their environment.

In the North, on the other hand, street demonstrations were not even a mild expression of militancy. The turmoil of cities absorbs demonstrations as merely transitory drama which is ordinary in city life. Without a more effective tactic for upsetting the status quo, the power structure could maintain its intransigence and hostility. Into the vacuum of inaction, violence and riots flowed and a new period opened.

Urban riots

Urban riots must now be recognized as durable social phenomena. They may be deplored, but they are there and should be understood.

TIME STATUES

Urban riots are a special form of violence. They are not insurrections. The rioters are not seeking to seize territory or to attain control of institutions. They are mainly intended to shock the white community. They are a distorted form of social protest. The looting which is their principal feature serves many functions. It enables the most enraged and deprived Negro to take hold of consumer goods with the ease the white man does by using his purse. Often the Negro does not even want what he takes; he wants the experience of taking. But most of all, alienated from society and knowing that this society cherishes property above people, he is shocking it by abusing property rights. There are thus elements of emotional catharsis in the violent act. This may explain why most cities in which riots have occurred have not had a repetition, even though the causative conditions remain. It is also noteworthy that the amount of physical harm done to white people other than police is infinitesimal and in Detroit whites and Negroes looted in unity.

A profound judgment of today's riots was expressed by Victor Hugo a century ago. He said, "If a soul is left in the darkness, sins will be committed. The guilty one is not he who commits the sin, but he who causes the darkness."

The policymakers of the white society have caused the darkness; they create discrimination; they structured slums; and they perpetuate unemployment, ignorance and poverty. It is incontestable and deplorable that Negroes have committed crimes; but they are derivative crimes. They are born of the greater crimes of the white society. When we ask Negroes to abide by the law, let us also demand that the white man abide by law in the ghettos. Day-in and day-out he violates welfare laws to deprive the poor of their meager allotments; he flagrantly violates building codes and regulations; his police make a mockery of law; and he violates laws on equal employment and education and the provisions for civic services. The slums are the handiwork of a vicious system of the white society; Negroes live in them but do not make them any more than a prisoner makes a prison. Let us say boldly that if the violations of law by the white man in the slums over the years were calculated and compared with the law-breaking of a few days of riots, the hardened criminal would be the white man. These are often difficult things to say but I have come to see more and more that it is necessary to utter the truth in order to deal with the great problems that we face in our society.

Vietnam War

There is another cause of riots that is too important to mention casually—the war in Vietnam. Here again, we are dealing with a controversial issue. But I am convinced that the war in Vietnam has played havoc with our domestic destinies. The bombs that fall in Vietnam explode at home. It does not take much to see what great damage this war has done to the image of our nation. It has left our country politically and morally isolated in the world, where our only friends happen to be puppet nations like Taiwan, Thailand and South Korea. The major allies in the world that have been with us in war and peace are not with us in this war. As a result we find ourselves socially and politically isolated.

The war in Vietnam has torn up the Geneva Accord. It has seriously impaired the United Nations. It has exacerbated the hatreds between continents, and worse still, between races. It has frustrated our development at home by telling our underprivileged citizens that we place insatiable military demands above their most critical needs. It has greatly contributed to the forces of reaction in America, and strength-

ened the military-industrial complex, against which even President Eisenhower solemnly warned us. It has practically destroyed Vietnam, and left thousands of American and Vietnamese youth maimed and mutilated. And it has exposed the whole world to the risk of nuclear warfare.

As I looked at what this war was doing to our nation, and to the domestic situation and to the Civil Rights movement, I found it necessary to speak vigorously out against it. My speaking out against the war has not gone without criticisms. There are those who tell me that I should stick with civil rights, and stay in my place. I can only respond that I have fought too hard and long to end segregated public accommodations to segregate my own moral concerns. It is my deep conviction that justice is indivisible, that injustice anywhere is a threat to justice everywhere. For those who tell me I am hurting the Civil Rights movement, and ask, 'Don't you think that in order to be respected, and in order to regain support, you must stop talking against the war?' I can only say that I am not a consensus leader. I do not seek to determine what is right and wrong by taking a Gallop Poll to determine majority opinion. And it is again my deep conviction that ultimately a genuine leader is not a searcher of consensus, but a molder of consensus. On some positions cowardice asks the question, "Is it safe?!" Expediency asks the question, "Is it politic?" Vanity asks the question, "Is it popular?" But conscience must ask the question, "Is it right?!" And there comes a time when one must take a stand that is neither safe, nor politic, nor popular. But one must take it because it is right. And that is where I find myself today.

Moreover, I am convinced, even if war continues, that a genuine massive act of concern will do more to quell riots than the most massive deployment of troops.

Unemployment

The unemployment of Negro youth ranges up to 40 percent in some slums. The riots are almost entirely youth events—the age range of participants is from 13 to 25. What hypocrisy it is to talk of saving the new generation—to make it the generation of hope-while consigning it to unemployment and provoking it to violent alternatives.

When our nation was bankrupt in the thirties we created an agency to provide jobs to all at their existing level of skill. In our overwhelming affluence today what excuse is there for not setting up a national agency for full employment immediately?

The other program which would give reality to hope and opportunity would be the demolition of the slums to be replaced by decent housing built by residents of the ghettos.

These programs are not only eminently sound and vitally needed, but they have the support of an overwhelming majority of the nation—white and Negro. The Harris Poll on August 21, 1967, disclosed that an astounding 69 percent of the country support a works program to provide employment to all and an equally astonishing 65 percent approve a program to tear down the slums.

There is a program and there is heavy majority support for it. Yet, the administration and Congress tinker with trivial proposals to limit costs in an extravagant gamble with disaster.

The President has lamented that he cannot persuade Congress. He can, if the will is there, go to the people, mobilize the people's support and thereby substantially increase his power to persuade Congress. Our most urgent task is to find the tactics that will move the government no matter how determined it is to resist.

Civil Disobedience

I believe we will have to find the militant middle between riots on the one hand and weak and timid supplication for justice on the other hand. That middle ground, I believe, is civil disobedience. It can be aggressive but nonviolent; it can dislocate but not destroy. The specific planning will take some study and analysis to avoid mistakes of the past when it was employed on too small a scale and sustained too briefly.

Civil disobedience can restore Negro-white unity. There have been some very important sane white voices even during the most desperate moments of the riots. One reason is that the urban crisis intersects the Negro crisis in the city. Many white decision-makers may care little about saving Negroes, but they must care about saving their cities. The vast majority of production is created in cities; most white Americans live in them. The suburbs to which they flee cannot exist detached from cities. Hence powerful white elements have goals that merge with ours.

Role for the Social Scientist

Now there are many roles for social scientists in meeting these problems. Kenneth Clark has said that Negroes are moved by a suicide instinct in riots and Negroes know there is a tragic truth in this observation. Social scientists should also disclose the suicide instinct that governs the administration and Congress in their total failure to respond constructively.

What other areas are there for social scientists to assist the civil rights movement? There are many, but I would like to suggest three because they have an urgent quality.

Social science may be able to search out some answers to the problem of Negro leadership. E. Franklin Frazier, in his profound work, Black Bourgeoisie, laid painfully bare the tendency of the upwardly mobile Negro to separate from his community, divorce himself from responsibility to it, while failing to gain acceptance in the white community. There have been significant improvements from the days Frazier researched, but anyone knowledgeable about Negro life knows its middle class is not yet bearing its weight. Every riot has carried the strong overtone of hostility of lower-class Negroes toward the affluent Negro and vice versa. No contemporary study of scientific depth has totally studied this problem. Social science should be able to suggest mechanisms to create a wholesome black unity and a sense of peoplehood while the process of integration proceeds.

As one example of this gap in research, there are no studies, to my knowledge, to explain adequately the absence of Negro trade union leadership. Eight-five percent of Negroes are working people. Some two million are in trade unions but in 50 years we have produced only one national leader—A. Philip Randolph.

Discrimination explains a great deal, but not everything. The picture is so dark even a few rays of light may signal a useful direction.

Political Action

The second area for scientific examination is political action. In the past two decades, Negroes have expended more effort in quest of the franchise than they have in all other campaigns combined. Demonstrations, sit-ins and marches, though more spectacular, are dwarfed by the enormous number of man-hours expended to register millions, particularly in the South. Negro organizations from extreme militant to conservative persuasion, Negro leaders who would not even talk to each other, all have been agreed on the key importance of voting. Stokely Carmichael said black power means the vote and Roy Wilkins, while saying Black power means Black death, also energetically sought the power of the ballot.

A recent major work by social scientists Matthew and Prothro concludes that "The concrete benefits to be derived from the franchise—under conditions that prevail in the South—have often been exaggerated," that voting is not the key that will unlock the door to racial equality because "the concrete measurable payoffs from Negro voting in the South will not be revolutionary" (1966).

James A. Wilson supports this view, arguing, "'Because of the structure of American politics as well as the nature of the Negro community, Negro politics will accomplish only limited objectives" (1965).

If their conclusion can be supported, then the major effort Negroes have invested in the past 20 years has been in the wrong direction and the major pillar of their hope is a pillar of sand. My own instinct is that these views are essentially erroneous, but they must be seriously examined.

The need for a penetrating massive scientific study of this subject cannot be overstated. Lipset in 1957 asserted that a limitation in focus in political sociology has resulted in a failure of much contemporary research to consider a number of significant theoretical questions. The time is short for social science to illuminate this critically important area. If the main thrust of Negro effort has been, and remains, substantially irrelevant, we may be facing an agonizing crisis of tactical theory.

The third area for study concerns psychological and ideologi-

cal changes in Negroes. It is fashionable now to be pessimistic. Undeniably, the freedom movement has encountered setbacks. Yet I still believe there are significant aspects of progress.

Negroes today are experiencing an inner transformation that is liberating them from ideological dependence on the white majority. What has penetrated substantially all strata of Negro life is the revolutionary idea that the philosophy and morals of the dominant white society are not holy or sacred but in all too many respects are degenerate and profane.

Negroes have been oppressed for centuries not merely by bonds of economic and political servitude. The worst aspect of their oppression was their inability to question and defy the fundamental precepts of the larger society. Negroes have been loath in the past to hurl any fundamental challenges because they were coerced and conditioned into thinking within the context of the dominant white ideology. This is changing and new radical trends are appearing in Negro thought. I use radical in its broad sense to refer to reaching into roots.

Ten years of struggle have sensitized and opened the Negro's eyes to reaching. For the first time in their history, Negroes have become aware of the deeper causes for the crudity and cruelty that governed white society's responses to their needs. They discovered that their plight was not a consequence of superficial prejudice but was systemic.

The slashing blows of backlash and frontlash have hurt the Negro, but they have also awakened him and revealed the nature of the oppressor. To lose illusions is to gain truth. Negroes have grown wiser and more mature and they are hearing more clearly those who are raising fundamental questions about our society whether the critics be Negro or white. When this process of awareness and independence crystallizes, every rebuke, every evasion, become hammer blows on the wedge that splits the Negro from the larger society.

Social science is needed to explain where this development is going to take us. Are we moving away, not from integration, but from the society which made it a problem in the first place? How deep and at what rate of speed is this process occurring? These are some vital questions to be answered if we are to have a clear sense of our direction.

We know we haven't found the answers to all forms of social change. We know, however, that we did find some answers. We have achieved and we are confident. We also know we are confronted now with far greater complexities and we have not yet discovered all the theory we need. And may I say together, we must solve the problems right here in America. As I have said time and time again, Negroes still have faith in America. Black people still have faith in a dream that we will all live together as brothers in this country of plenty one day.

But I was distressed when I read in the New York Times of Aug. 31, 1967; that a sociologist from Michigan State University, the outgoing president of the American Sociological Society, stated in San Francisco that Negroes should be given a chance to find an all-Negro community in South America: "that the valleys of the Andes Mountains would be an ideal place for American Negroes to build a second Israel." He further declared that "The United States Government should negotiate for a remote but fertile land in Equador, Peru or Bolivia for this relocation."

I feel that it is rather absurd and appalling that a leading social scientist today would suggest to black people, that after all these years of suffering an exploitation as well as investment in the American dream that we should turn around and run at this point in history. I say that we will not run! Professor Loomis even compared the relocation task of the Negro to the relocation task of the Jews in Israel. The Jews were made exiles. They did not choose to abandon Europe, they were driven out. Furthermore, Israel has a deep tradition, and Biblical roots for Jews. The Wailing Wall is a good example of these roots. They also had significant financial aid from the United States for the relocation and rebuilding effort. What tradition does the Andes, especially the valley of the Andes Mountains, have for Negroes? And I assert at this time that once again we must reaffirm our belief in building a democratic society, in which blacks and whites can live together as brothers, where we will all come to see that integration is not a problem, but an opportunity to participate in the beauty of diversity. The problem is deep. It is gigantic in extent, and chaotic in detail. And I do not believe that it will be solved until there is a kind of cosmic discontent enlarging in the bosoms of people of good will all over this nation.

There are certain technical words in every academic discipline which soon become stereotypes and even clichés. Every academic discipline has its technical nomenclature. You who are in the field of psychology have given us a great word. It is the word maladjusted. This word is probably used more than any other word in psychology. It is a good word; certainly it is good that in dealing with what the word implies you are declaring that destructive maladjustment should be destroyed. You are saying that all must seek the well-adjusted life in order to avoid neurotic and schizophrenic personalities. But on the other hand, I am sure that we will recognize that there are some things in our society, some things in our world, to which we should never be adjusted. There are some things concerning which we must always be maladjusted if we are to be people of good will. We must never adjust ourselves to racial discrimination and racial segrega-

tion. We must never adjust ourselves to religious bigotry. We must never adjust ourselves to economic conditions that take necessities from the many to give luxuries to the few. We must never adjust ourselves to the madness of militarism, and the self-defeating effects of physical violence.

In a day when Sputniks, Explorers and Geminies are dashing through outer space, when guided ballistic missiles are carving highways of death through the stratosphere, no nation can finally win a war. It is no longer a choice between violence and nonviolence, it is either nonviolence or nonexistence. As President Kennedy declared, "Mankind must put an end to war, or war will put an end to mankind." And so the alternative to disarmament, the alternative to a suspension in the development and use of nuclear weapons, the alternative to strengthening the United Nations and eventually disarming the whole world, may well be a civilization plunged into the abyss of annihilation. Our earthly habitat will be transformed into an inferno that even Dante could not envision.

Creative Maladjustment

Thus, it may well be that our world is in dire need of a new organization, The International Association for the Advancement of Creative Maladjustment. Men and women should be as maladjusted as the prophet Amos, who in the midst of the injustices of his day, could cry out in words that echo across the centuries, "Let justice roll down like waters and righteousness like a mighty stream"; or as maladjusted as Abraham Lincoln, who in the midst of his vacillations finally came to see that this nation could not survive half slave and half free; or as maladjusted as Thomas Jefferson, who in the midst of an age amazingly adjusted to slavery, could scratch across the pages of history, words lifted to cosmic proportions, "We hold these truths to be self-evident, that all men are created equal. That they are endowed by their creator with certain inalienable rights. And that among these are life, liberty, and the pursuit of happiness." And through such creative maladjustment, we may be able to emerge from the bleak and desolate midnight of man's inhumanity to man, into the bright and glittering daybreak of freedom and justice. I have not lost hope. I must confess that these have been very difficult days for me personally. And these have been difficult days for every civil rights leader, for every lover of justice and peace."

— King, M.L. (1968) Role of the Behavioral Scientist in the Civil Rights Movement. *J. Social Issues* 24 (1).

Chapter 29. Are We Team or Equipment? Automation Windfall

Owners can be onerous. It's all in the name.

In the pro-football movie *North Dallas 40*, Burt Reynolds realized that the owners see themselves as the *real* team while the players are only seen by them as the equipment.

This is a business model readily found in how workers and even customers fare in modern corporations.

In the second Democratic Primary Debate of 2019, Andrew Yang introduced this challenge: the rise of automation, while generating windfall profits for owners, is accelerating massive job losses for their workers. Nor do these profits for shareholders often provide meaningful price reduction for consumers.

While the official job unemployment figures seem to be approaching an historic low, these jobs do include part-time and subsistence wages. Lots of jobs for not much money. More jobs but less pay. Far too often this means people must carry two or three such minimum wage jobs to keep their family from the homeless ranks. And now increased automation might make even these meager job opportunities disappear, leaving only those fewer human workers management deems as still needed.

Historically, early Americans worked seven days a week with a half day off on Sunday for church. Unions eventually achieved the 40-hour week to curtail this. Morale and productivity jumped. Yet now, those with several low wage jobs to maintain are back to working close to the seven day week. Especially with so many working from home. So how can the problem of automation be a solution?

As it enhances efficiency, automation can generate a financial windfall. How about sharing some of this? Instead of shedding workers as obsolete equipment, what if stakeholders or staff were considered essential parts of the corporate team? Therein is the business advantage. Identifying the company as their own target of success, employees can boost productivity and wellbeing for all.

And if a 40-hour work week is no longer needed? That is the very opportunity of automation. Automation allows for the work week to be reduced, with no salary or benefit reduction, to just the hours needed to be productive, say a 20-hour week.

If there are those, despite the reduced work week's hours, needing retraining for a new role, this will be freely provided so every employee who wants to stay can choose productively to do so. The company still retains a substantial windfall portion along with that second windfall profit from the enhanced and energetic productivity of their non-automated high morale human workers.

The reduced work week allows for better family time, educational progress, creative paths, better physical and mental health, adequate rest, life purpose progress, and even that "pursuit of happiness" that the American founders promised. There would also be an opportunity to direct some of this profit windfall to raise salaries to gender equity levels sufficient to support families, buy homes, give consumers a cost break, and consequently generate a thriving economy.

This only works if the non-automated company decision makers have a working human brain equipped with an actual conscience. Some do.

Reduce the workweek hours and pay fair salaries? Thanks Automation.

Supplemental Time Statue

In the early 1970s I was invited to the office of the Chief Financial Officer (CFO) for the world's largest bank, the Bank of America.

I was there for him to sign a lease for a home for our first freestanding professional school of psychology, of which he was on the Board.

On arrival, I found his office had no desk but rather a spacious couch and furniture. He explained that his job required him to be there for business only an hour or so per week. Of course, he added, in that hour, he made decisions involving billions of dollars.

In later interactions with billionaires Norton Simon and Laurence Rockefeller, I found the same brief flexible work week. Clearly, work week hours are defined far differently for those of wealth and privilege. (The Bank of America CFO decided not to sign our lease as I had neglected to bring my wife to our meeting, despite his eager invitation, to his office of comfort. Another story there.)

Bonus: How to Prevent a Government Shutdown over Budget

Pass legislation as follows: The government budget already in effect will continue indefinitely except as amended by congress, including additions or subtractions, on at least an annual review basis. If no amended changes are passed and signed into law, the government budget will continue as it has been, without a termination date. This rules out any government shutdown, thereby maintaining government services.

Chapter 30. Forrest Gump on Today's Box of Chocolates

L*ife today is still like a box of chocolates, half empty, crumpled, found in the park by a bench and smelling of something strange. Maybe somebody licked each of the pieces that were left and put it back in. Bite into one. You just never know what you're gonna get. Maybe become homeless, get flu, or acid reflux, or even humongous halitosis? But the chocolates each might turn out to taste REAL good. You never know until you try.*

Now for you and me though. WE have a box of chocolates with only a few left. Wait! Our chocolates are peppermint bark, every one. Know what we get when we bite into one of these each day?

Happy.

Bonus:

Chapter 31. OPENING NIGHT 2020

Most of the memories in this book are true, at least as true as memory allows. Which at times is not completely valid. A few though, like the one below, are fiction. In that this did not actually happen to the author. Yet, like most fiction, it can reflect a true core. Or even turn out to be actually just as described. It sure fits the world as it was when this was written.

The Bar had photos of DJ Trump everywhere. Yet these were upstaged by colorful streamers and OPENING NIGHT signs.

The Governor of the State of Georgia had declared, despite the deadly pandemic that surrounded the city, this night to be a time when bars, tattoo parlors, massage businesses, and more essentials could be open. Life here was second to commerce.

The bar owner strode into his business only minutes before the 8 PM grand unlocking of the door. He held a box in his hand carefully as though it held breakable diamonds.

He signaled Sam, his security man, to stand by the door.

Opening the precious box carefully, he confided: *"Donald HIMSELF sent me these. The very ones they use at his umm, White Supremacy House."*

Laughing at his little joke, he gave the Donald credit for not getting angry at all the jokes like this he had made at the President's expense on TV.

What a good sport! he thought. Besides the owner was one of the Donald's major contributors. So, smiling, he extracted a large thermometer from the Donald's gift.

To his security man, he instructed *"Be sure you test EVERYONE who wants to enter, staff, dancers, or customers. Only the ones with NORMAL temps can come in. I'm no damn fool! And Sam: follow the instructions in the box EXACTLY! Bonus if you do. Fired if you don't."*

With that the owner went home for a nap. A big night was expected.

At midnight he returned, rested and anticipant.

The bar was empty of customers.

Furniture was broken, bottles smashed.

A battered and bloody security man was the only one left.

"Sam! What's going ON here?"

Sam carefully pointed to the box at his feet. Crumpled and torn with blood stains.

He waved the instruction sheet and a stained thermometer between his bruised fingers.

He got out one word through broken teeth: *"Rectal."*

Chapter 32. Climate Change has Fingerprints

It's all a matter of proportion. I try to solve more problems than I create.

Climate Change in a Multinomial World

These days my own mornings do not begin untouched. They come with fingerprints.

On our planet's north and south hemispheres outside what we think of as the tropical zone, half the year is growing warmer in an accelerating manner.

The other half of the year is marked with extreme changes: sometimes even colder with heavier snowfall. Climate change has put more moisture in the air, leading to a redistribution of water on a global scale. Millennial floods in some places, severe drought in others. Insect species should thrive under these new conditions while other species, note the current devastation in our oceans, may find the new conditions more than they can survive.

The tropical zone is increasingly impacted year-round. Without the great seasonal changes elsewhere, the heat raises ocean levels to the point where many communities are threatened. Floods and droughts are found here as well. Our tropical boundaries are expanding with each passing year. The increasing heat and humidity adds ever more countries to what may be considered a torrid or tropical zone, eventually one that may cover the planet with very few exceptions.

This makes our successful human adaptations to a more tropical world more essential to learn and share. We must do our part to track the psychology being done in these expanding territories of heat and light.

Some of it may address behavioral strategies focused on coping or taking advantage of climate change challenges. Most will likely be the continuing progress of findings from psychologists in tropical regions that may be applied to enhancing human progress everywhere.

We usually think of our world as binomial. A forced choice between yes or no. Our computer code, so far, is binomial. Our statistics are largely based on this model of the world. We anticipate normal distributions. How often will the tossed coin land on one side or the other? Only two clear choices. In life, our coin sometimes lands on its edge. Neither heads nor tails.

Therein lies our advantage. Our human family has survived this long by not accepting a choice between two bad alternatives. Instead, we can seek a better third. Psychologists often assist our clients to do this. We know how to generate fresh alternatives for coping with challenges. This is the basis for realistic hope.

Hope. Rollo May corrected me once when I said I was mostly an optimist (Morgan, 2012). Optimists outlive pessimists: they each fulfill their expectations (Morgan and Wilson, 2005). Again, Rollo said that optimism and pessimism are classic mistakes. He thought that the best we can do is be hopeful. But I am sure that he did not mean a passive hope.

We can choose an active one, full of actions that can lead to hope fulfilled. From an existential point of view, we are fortunate to the extent that climate change is being caused by us, by our corporations, by our countries, or by us as individuals. If we are the cause of it, we have the best hope of creating changes to our advantage. Problems not caused by us are more difficult. If we are the problem, we can also choose to be the solution.

Luckily we do not really live in a binomial world. We live in a world full of new possibilities. It is in fact a new day, fresh and untouched, except for the fingerprints that can turn out to be our own. On a sunnier note:

A Sunny Day in New Mexico

Indigenous people lived here for many centuries before Europeans came along. Then New Mexico was owned by the Imperial Spanish viceroyalty of New Spain. It then became part of the newly formed nation of Mexico before eventually a US territory and now a US state.

New Mexico's sunny blazing hot summers qualify it as a Torrid Zone vicinity. Tropical minus the water. It often happens that people who live there are assumed to be residents of the country of Mexico. This holds true even more the farther away on the earth New Mexico residents travel.

Such a hot sunny day here in Albuquerque was April 13th 2015.

I walked the mile down Central to the bank, interrupted only briefly by various sad-faced panhandlers, although on this day they seemed to be college students searching for just some "spare change." Not having a supply of *Watch Tower*, Jehovah's Witness "Good News" pamphlets to contribute (the pamphlets work like garlic to vampires), I just wished them good luck and moved on. The people I saw on this passage today were generally self-absorbed and unsmiling. Not the usual friendly bunch I am used to here.

At the bank I cashed a check. Next to me at another cashier's station, an older man in faded jeans and a torn work shirt brought out a well-worn check book. *"I'm closing out my account,"* he declared. *"I know there's only 84 cents in it. But I have big plans for that money!"* I didn't hear the cashier's words but the customer responded with: *"You're kidding! I have to write myself a check so I can get my money? Hmm. Never wrote a check for 84 cents before. Sure you all will cash it? Okay."* And then: *"Can I have a little help with this? Haven't written a check to myself for a long time. And now this special moment is for 84 cents."* And then: *"Aren't you going to ask me how I want the money?"*

I was enjoying this new memory as I walked back home down Central. Coming toward me was a young crew cut man on a skateboard. Lots of college kids use skateboards to travel here. My favorite on this route was a man pulled on his skateboard by a German Shepherd.

The other one racing toward me on my sidewalk this time though was balancing on one hand a tray half full of Dreyers vanilla ice cream pints. As he came to a stop next to me, I declined to buy one. No: he said they were free and handed me one. They did not look tampered with. I put my still cold pint of vanilla in my shoulder bag and continued on.

As I walked the blocks I passed the same panhandlers and college kids I had seen before, each eating their own free pint of ice cream. But now street after street they were all smiling, content, fulfilled. Central Avenue had become a sunnier place. I like New Mexico.

The Shovel

At the University of Southern Colorado in the mid-1970s one of my psychology department faculty was in his last year of teaching. In those days retirement was mandatory at age 65.

An experienced and much-loved teacher, he was beginning to doubt his mental capacity. He told me he was beginning to forget things like where he had left his keys, what chapter his class was on.

As his department Chair, I convinced him to keep track for the next week on how many times he forgot something. Then I asked the other faculty to do the same.

At the end of the week, he did better than most of the faculty, many of them 30+ years younger.

He had been the victim of negative ageist expectations. Cheered up, he agreed to teach as long as he was allowed.

We, all of us faculty in the department, even started a nonprofit business so we could reimburse him through that to teach our psychology classes part-time after his 65th birthday forced his retirement.

But when the time came, he thanked us and said he was going to retire after all. Reassured that he still had his mental faculties, he looked forward to enjoying his next more flexible life.

Especially freedom from Colorado winters. We asked him where he was going to settle.

He said: *"I'm going to strap a snow shovel to the top of my car. Then I'm just going to drive south until somebody looks at it and says 'What's that?' There's where I'll retire."*

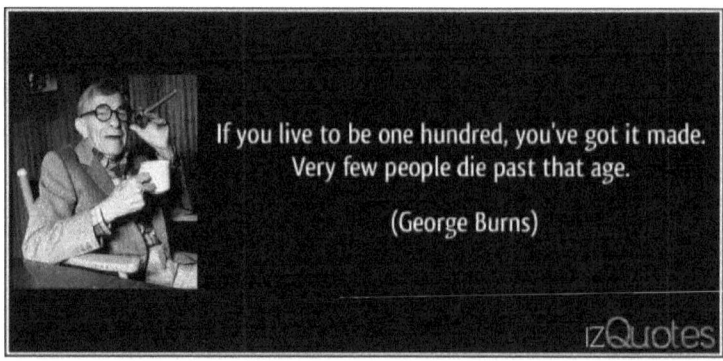

Chapter 33. Equity and Ice Fishing

"*WE WANT WHAT THE RATS GET!*" said one sign.

It is said that if three blindfolded (politically correct version) men were put in a room with an elephant, then each would describe a different creature based on where they groped the animal. We say "would" because an elephant groped in such a manner would likely object and survivors of this experiment are unlikely.

Self-aware elephants are unlikely laboratory animals for most psychological experiments. White laboratory rats are more traditional, although dogs and cats have been used in many parts of the world since Pavlov. Signing chimpanzees have also been used as experimental animals, but their own self-awareness and communications have led to a growing understanding that to treat them in a non-humane way should and must be discontinued (Fouts, 2003).

There was also a very famous gorilla named Koko who had been taught by Dr. Francine Patterson to communicate with sign language (Patterson 1987, 1999) and even, with Dr. Patterson as intermediary, holding an internet interview years ago. When the Scientific Organizing Committee of our 1998 ICAP world congress in San Francisco asked me for some original ideas, my favorite was to invite Koko as a keynote speaker: there was no apparent interest in this at the time.

In the 21st century, university students are often the key species of experimental interest. Yet the rat colonies survive and are normally protected by a series of environmentally friendly laws and ethical codes dedicated to the humane treatment of these animals.

One day, when I was a psychology department chairperson in a Colorado university, the department secretary complained to me of headaches and eye strain. Her desk was well lit by large fluorescent lights.

A review of earlier research (Morgan, 2004, 2011) suggested that fluorescent lights could cause headaches or even narcolepsy for some people by synchrony with the flicker. Another problem was the restricted light spectrum in most such lights which, over hours and days, could lead to eye strain. It would seem that fluorescent lighting, using less energy at less cost, might well be useful for areas requiring bright inexpensive lighting at short time intervals—places like library stacks. However, for people using this light all day long, it would seem that natural or incandescent lighting would be the far better choice. Health should not be a lost variable when considering contemporary economic choices.

Today cheaper fluorescents are often being mandated while the manufacture of equally cheap incandescent lighting can be overlooked, much less the enhanced use of natural lighting in buildings. Environmental psychology can contribute here.

As a first step, I told the department secretary I would get the fluorescent tubes in her lighting changed to full spectrum lighting, an array approximating the range of natural light. I called the appropriate university manager and asked for this.

He declined: "Those tubes each cost a dollar more than the ones we are using now." He was concerned everybody working in the university would want the better lights, thus multiplying his costs. After some thought I called him back.

"Are full spectrum lights being used anywhere in the university now?" I asked (expecting they might be in the President's office). But he surprised me.

"Yes, in the rat colony. These lab animals get sick with regular fluorescents." Having acknowledged this, the purchase request was still declined.

The department secretary was a very assertive individual. Learning of the priority of rats she, with my delighted support, organized the university staff in a protest march: "EQUITY WITH RATS!" was one sign and "WE WANT WHAT THE RATS GET!" was another.

The protest, with suitable publicity, succeeded and they got the full spectrum lights.

In recent years, as a visiting professor at the University of Alaska in Fairbanks, I discovered that the understanding of the environment was quite sophisticated on these issues, possibly because of half the year having little light and the other half having nonstop light. I recall the midnight parade in June and the 4 hours of daylight in January.

The Clinical-Community Psychology PhD program I worked in there was thoroughly advised by Alaska Natives, to its great advantage.

At one such week-long retreat, I shared the preceding episode of lights and rats. This was quietly accepted with smiles. Later, in the circle, each of us was asked to tell a very important memory that we did not understand. By then it was dark and only the campfire lit our thoughts.

My memory was about being in an apparently terminal condition where I retreated into the hypnotic "safe place" visualization in my mind to get away from the pain (Morgan, 2000).

To my surprise at the time, it was something new: I was in an ice fishing hut with a small fire and a hole in the ice through which I could see some large beautiful fish underneath. Strange, since I was living at the time in the American territory/colony of Guam, a place that never knows ice fishing. But my safe place had been as cold as an arctic night.

Whenever I needed to, I kept going back to this visualized hut where I gained energy and a sense of peace. What I did not get was better.

TIME STATUES

In what seemed like my final visit of many, I realized that I didn't want to catch these fish. I already had some sandwiches to eat and I didn't want to damage their beauty or take their life. I pulled the fish hook out of the hole. Then I dropped pieces of my sandwiches down the hole and fed the fish. The next day I began my recovery and eventually regained my health.

Now back in Alaska, the native advisors interpreted my visualization in this way:

"What you did with light for the secretary is what you psychology people are here on earth to do. In this memory you are told to come to Alaska and help, not hurt, the beautiful fish—which are most likely meant to be us and people like us."

May we all try our best to do so.

Chapter 34. Interview with Grover Hardscrabble

Radio Interviewer (RI): We are pleased this morning to be interviewing Mr. Grover Hardscrabble of Fragrant Bolus, Maine. He is a hardworking fertilizer farmer chosen from a national data base provided by the Right Wing Voter PAC. So he represents the typical right wing voter ("You can't go wrong when you're Right"). Good morning Mr. Hardscrabble.

Grover Hardscrabble (GH): *Mawrnin to you I spose. Ta me, I bin up fer half a day aready jest doin' my chores. Fer the critters dependin' on me.*

RI: *Well that's just so impressive. What exactly do you do for these farm animals?*

GH: *Umm. Well, first I feed the chickens.*

TIME STATUES

RI: *Please go on.*

GH: *I feed em to the pigs. Not all of em. Just some. A few that don't cluck good mawrnin to me when I get there.*

RI: *Oh. Please go on. You've fed the pigs.*

GH: *Yup. But then I have to feed the dogs. I feed them the pigs.*

RI: *Wow! All the pigs?*

GH: *Nope. Course not. Just the ones not oinking a happy good mawrnin to me.*

RI: *Phew! What happens to the dogs?*

GH: *Well, that's how I make muh money. I get big Grover's Farm bags and pack up the dog droppings' fer sale. Organic bagged farm fertilizer for West Coast and Arizona farms. Known for the feathers and bacon bits to show it's the real thing. A super spreader. East Coast, Midwest, and the South through Texas though have humongous stockpiles of their own.*

RI: *Maybe a change in subject? I never heard of your town, Fragrant Bolus, Maine. Where is it near?*

GH: *Not near anything. Ya follow highway til it become a dirt road. Then when ya pass where the post office used to be, before it was burned down, ya make a left off the dirt road. From there ya just have ta follow your nose.*

RI: *Fragrant Bolus? That's an unusual name for a town.*

GH: *Well, could be. Once it was the town called Cornucopia, Maine. People had hard time spelling it. Mail truck couldn't find it. No zip* code fer one thing. No post office any more when election time got close. Deep State dint get us. People round here figured my fertilizer farm deserved some notice. So name of town became Fragrant Bolus. In Maine. Well, gotta go now. Time past to feed muh kids.

RI: *Feed them to? Oh never mind. Thanks to Mr. Grover Hardscrabble for our morning interview.*

IV. FAMILY: NON-HUMAN RELATIVES

TIME STATUES

Chapter 35. Animal Clients

In Singapore, not long ago, I was a visiting professor at an Australian University located there. The guard at the entrance and I had both once been staff sergeants, each in our own country. Soon we were good friends. One day, as I was leaving, he pointed to a bird at the top of a large tree. "Did you know that here in Singapore we have the best talking birds in the world?" I did not. So far the bird songs I had noticed had only two notes and no lyrics. Apparently this simple male competitive mating music still was enough to attract female birds of the species. He waved at the bird on the tree to get its attention and said "Hello! I have an American friend here." The bird replied: "Hello! Food?" Much to the point. "Sing first," said the guard. The bird obliged with the standard two note song. I responded by whistling a little of the song "Staircase to Heaven." When I finished, the bird silently contemplated me for a few seconds. Finally it said "Go Away!"

What if an Animal Hospital was run by animals? Probably not. There is though such a thing as an applied psychological practice for non-human clients.

Comparative psychology is about the study of non-human species. It is useful for preliminary testing of hypotheses possibly applicable to human behavior. It allows an evolutionary perspective to gather behavioral data cross-species. It of course has long yielded basic research in acquiring knowledge of a species for its own sake (Ratner and Denny, 1964, 1970).

Often referred to as Animal Behavior, it is more than that. Add perceptual equipment and experience, neurological plus other physiological capacity, and even inferential consciousness or emotional aspects. These can also contribute to modern psychology.

Once one understands the perceptual world of another species, including its time perception (Morgan, 2005), this can lead to an experiential empathy. Among other things this is a great exercise for budding clinicians. If you can truly understand enough about a non-human species to imagine what their world must be like, how hard can it be to empathically understand another member of our own human family?

And yes, there is a clinical psychology practice that fits here.

Dr. Stanley C. Ratner taught the first psychology class I ever took and I continued with him as a key mentor through graduate school. A brilliant psychology professor with substantial scientific training (a former student of Thomas Kuhn), he was really more of an ethologist in that he loved learning about other species in their natural settings. He cared very much about the animals themselves. He was also a pioneer in comparative psychology (Ratner, S.C. & Denny, M.R., 1964, 1970).

Thanks to Stan Ratner, I became a thorn in the side of my first (also excellent) Anthropology professor. In our first Anthropology class, he listed on the board all those characteristics he believed that made the human species uniquely different from any other. One at a time, using examples from Ratner's class, I contested the notion that only our species was capable of language, self-awareness, higher intelligence, emotions, and particularly tool using.

In the end my friendly but frustrated instructor said he would write me a reference if I would undertake a graduate anthropology degree at Harvard, where *"they like to argue about everything all the time."*

About Monkeys

In Singapore it is illegal to feed the monkeys, of which there are multitudes. The government gets complaints from residents whose home has been burglarized or otherwise impacted by hungry monkeys. Once fed, they consider it an obligation and return reliably. There are other simian hazards.

The only other American teaching at my university was Keith. One day he was riding his bike and coming over the hill saw the car ahead of him hit a monkey that was crossing the road. The car sped up and was gone from sight, seemingly just as the unfortunate monkey hit the ground. A larger monkey ran to the body of his now deceased companion (mate?). He looked up in rage just as Keith reached the scene. The large monkey growled and ran at Keith. Keith later said he had never pushed the bike so hard and yet the large monkey almost caught up to this innocent victim of circumstance. Maybe a few minutes later though, the pursuer stopped for breath and Keith made his wheeled escape. Never to visit that piece of road again.

So not encouraging monkeys by food or otherwise to get too close to people made some sense. On the other hand, we did see an alternative to compliance. A young Indian family was picnicking on a blanket around the corner from our apartment. Next to their grassy location stood a tree, and at the very top of the tree was a family of monkeys. Hungrily eyeing the picnic food. The father gestured to his children to ignore the monkeys. The mother made similar gestures. They all focused on quietly eating their food. We watched the tableau for a few minutes, marveling at the restraint of the children and the hungry monkeys up in the tree. Turned out they all knew what to wait for. Once most of the food was gone, the family quietly got up and went for a walk, never looking up at the monkeys, leaving the remainder of the picnic unguarded. Once out of sight, the monkeys quickly descended and tore into the food left for them on the blanket. Once done they re-climbed the tree. In a few more minutes the family returned, quietly gathered up the empty baskets and blanket, never looking at the monkeys, and left. No law had been broken and the monkeys had been fed. Looked like this scenario had been done many times before.

The High Road

Monkeys kept raiding our Academic Dean's Singapore mansion. Joachim and his wife had invested a lot of their funds in a huge mansion located overlooking the edge of the jungle. The monkeys were as impressed as anybody else at its opulence, making it their top priority for midnight snacks.

Cutting their losses in this continuing struggle, he and his wife invited all of the faculty over to at least share the view of their home and surrounds.

It was a welcome break. The owners were gracious hosts. The food treats, despite monkey struggles, were diverse and tasty. The day was sunny and friendly. Then Joachim's wife led us on a guest tour of the neighboring jungle.

This was done first by our ascending to a high wooden pathway, maybe 20 feet off the jungle surface. As we walked along behind her, we could see the lush jungle clearly. We saw birds, we saw monkeys. These saw us too, radiating suspicion.

I had asked our hostess why we needed to be up high rather than just walking through a jungle surface pathway. She suggested I look down from the side of the platform walkway. I walked to the side of the platform as suggested. Looking down from the height, at first I saw very little. Just some dark movement of creatures about the size of cats. As one emerged from shadow, the sunlight caught its shape more clearly. Looked a little like an ebony lobster.

No, not a lobster. Just black and shiny with ... I turned to our hostess and said *"Is that an ANT?"*

She confirmed with a smile: *"Now you know why we stay here on the high road."*

I didn't think ants could get that big without lungs. Have they grown lungs here in this jungle? And the Queen ant would be much larger. Dog size?

We stuck to the high road for the rest of the tour. Without objection. On the way back we passed the monkeys again. Their look seemed to say *"There are things out there a lot worse than us."* And *"Next time we visit, have our treats ready."*

A Clinical Psychology for Nonhuman Species

Stan was the first stop for anybody needing assistance for any species in their care. This made him an early (non-licensed) clinical psychologist for challenging animal behaviors. For example, Michigan State University heavily funded its animal livestock programs. A hugely expensive prize-winning bull had been purchased to beget generations more like himself. A semen milking machine was acquired for this purpose and applied on a daily basis. The expectation was that sales of his seed would far exceed his initially impressive cost.

After some initial compliance, the bull began refusing to cooperate.

They called Dr. Ratner. (Note: many specialists in animal behavior had names like Fox, Tiger, and Ratner—none saw any connection beween this and their career of choice.)

Stan was very methodical in his approach to such matters. First he read whatever was available in the current scientific literature on the species in question. Then he spent careful observation time, usually 5 minutes per hour for a substantial number of hours, over a period of days, or in this case two weeks. There he observed the bull object powerfully, effectively, to any contribution of his to the semen milking machine.

Then came a diagnosis and a therapeutic prescription. The bull, much like any other bull consistent with its normal life cycle, required some access to real live cows. Ratner prescribed this weekly schedule: Cows on Monday, Wednesday, and Friday. The machine on Tuesday, Thursday,

Saturday. A day of rest on Sunday. All this worked as expected to the satisfaction of the agriculture department and, of course, for the bull (and, hopefully, for the cows). We need not imagine that we were creating erotic memories for the bull to get him through cow-less days. But we could.

Stan was also asked to help a colleague who had brought a newborn male puppy home for his children. It was fine at first. But now the puppy was a young adult. He kept attempting to mate with the vacuum cleaner. Further, if they hid the machine, the dog would howl in mourning until it was returned.

Again, setting aside his own suspicions, Stan took a full history of this puppy's life to date, reviewed the literature on puppies and on early imprinting, briefly observed its attempted mounting of the vacuum cleaner (moreso when it was turned on). He soon had a diagnosis and prescription.

The newborn puppy's eyes had first opened when the children were at school and the vacuum was busy at its cleaning purpose. Imprinting on the first large loud moving object had taken place. As a youth he therefore followed the machine around as a sad replacement for his missing mother. Coming of age, he now saw this vacuum as an erotic object (canine love at first sight you might say). Also, this pet had experienced no contact with others of his species. Raised as an outsider, he knew not what he was or what such a learning-based animal should be doing. Undoubtedly being heavily discouraged from mounting the legs of the humans he lived with, he had turned to the machine for his sexual needs. (Our species has been known to do this—we have stores thriving on these sales.)

The Ratner prescription was to bring other animals of his kind over for regular play dates. This puppy hated being squirted with a water pistol, so this was used to discourage (extinguish) approach behavior to the vacuum cleaner. In time the furry client was content to play and court (very briefly) female canine visitors.

The therapeutic behavioral prescription was effective. Problem solved. Yet, when vacuuming took place, he watched intently from a distance. Fantasy from a Canine American? Hard to infer a puppy's thoughts at a time like this. Probably not thinking about leaving on a puppy-centered airline like Puppitalia. Or a complaint to be filed with the Puppy Union (PU). Longing for forbidden love then? We'll never know.

Applied Comparative Communication

The field continues to be fascinating. Chimpanzees have been taught to communicate meaningfully with humans by sign language (Fouts & Mills, 2003).

For several decades there was a popular signing Gorilla named Koko who had much to say to us through psychologist Penny Patterson (Patterson, P. & Schroeder, B., 2010). Dr. Patterson even held a Q&A with Koko and her human admirers over the internet with the psychologist translating.

When I was asked to generate ideas with the organizing committee for the 1998 IAAP World Congress to be held in San Francisco, I suggested Koko as a keynote speaker but it was not to be. My theme idea of *"The Bridge to the 21st Century"* was adopted but apparently no talking gorillas were welcome to cross this bridge with us.

In a classic applied comparative psychology study, psychologist Carl Gustavson effectively discouraged wolves from eating domestic sheep by adding aversive tastes to the sheep wool.

Eventually the more secure sheep even chased the wolves. (Gustavson, C.R. & Gustavson, J.C., 1985, 2006; Morgan 2012).

Spinning Chickens

My most internationally popular publication was on a solution as to why NASA livestock were dying on a simulated space station.

My hypothesis was that they were being stressed by continual stops for assessment. We demonstrated this inexpensively on a spinning brooder for baby chicks versus another still one for a random control group. The spinners were never stopped throughout the study and without that trauma they all survived. They even thrived. They had the usual stages of development to go through but, after a slow adaptation to their bizarre environment, they used it to their advantage. They grew larger than the controls and, when two of the control chicks were added to their spinning world, these newcomers were not attacked—very unlike normal chicken behavior (Morgan 1964, 2012). The spinners even had larger legs, aka drumsticks.

TIME STATUES

I am not sure if the popularity of this 1964 article was due to our building a substitute for a multi-million dollar NASA centrifuge for less than a hundred dollars, showing that intermittent trauma can be lethal, or for the commercial value of the larger legs and breasts of the spinners.

In any case, nothing I have written after this has generated so many reprint requests or responses from all over the world. All downhill since then.

As for Comparative Psychology, it has diminished in popularity over the years.

Yet this new century could productively see a revival.

Imagine the psychologist's waiting room.

Chapter 36. L'escargot Sauvage

"I owe much; I have nothing; the rest I leave to the poor."
(Francois Rabelais, 1533)

Mike Acree was a San Francisco chef before he saw the light and became a psychologist. Still, he brought all his skills with him. Each day he would fast until dinner, looking forward all day to that special meal he would prepare to meet all his needs. That, and walking the full length of Golden Gate Park to work and back each day, kept him trim, healthy.

Eduardo Duran and I, Mike's faculty colleagues, were one day invited to enjoy his special home-created dinner. We rightly anticipated an outstanding meal. But. There on my plate as a first appetizer was *l'escargot*—snails in white sauce. I politely declined.

Now it is hard to merely say no to many psychologists. They want to know the why.

Further, Mike was at that moment a Chef, standing by the prelude to his art, clearly a sensitive socio-cultural moment, although Mike was of an exceptionally friendly disposition. Still...

In early childhood, I had some unfortunate experiences with animals.

For example, here are my notes about a temporal visit from age five.

Doris Ducker and the Duck

Made it at last! Grade number one! First place! After grade 1 is 2, then 3, and so on... all downhill from there.

My first grade teacher, as I recall, was Miss Doris Ducker. I remember her more clearly because she became friends with my mother, a former teacher now on leave due to child care (me).

Doris was an older woman (over 30) who lived alone on a small farm just outside the city. The summer after that first grade, my mother took me to visit Doris. By now I was six, used to playing on city streets, but interested in the new universe just outside city limits.

Doris had a pond with ducks. As we left she gave me an actual duck egg, and said I could keep it as a pet once it hatched. Early responsibility. I held the egg carefully in its little basket all the way home. What we would do with a duck in our tiny apartment was not something I gave much thought to at the time. Still, the next morning, a Saturday when my parents were sleeping, I wondered how I might best protect my little egg from harm. Then I remembered what my mother did to keep eggs safe.

So I carefully put the duck egg in the back of the refrigerator. Now, relieved that it was safe, I went out to play. On a late morning the next day, my mother noticed a bad smell in the refrigerator. A funeral followed in the back yard. I was the only one there to say goodbye. I think my parents were relieved. Doubt that the baby duck's mother would have felt the same if she knew. Only recently, as I remembered this, did I finally notice that Doris had a last name suggesting kinship with my victim's family.

Later when I was grown and I had two little daughters of my own, I would take them to a small lake and we would feed the ducks. When we were done, I would take them to the Chinese restaurant next to the lake and I would order the pressed duck to eat there. I didn't ask where they got their ducks from. Circle of life.

*

Some years earlier I had been at an international psychology conference in Amsterdam with my 14-year-old daughter, Angel KwanYin. An acclaimed Netherlands psychologist asked me to his home for dinner, through an interpreter (a former Belgian Ambassador), to discuss the founding of what became the Benelux

University, particularly as to how American psychology might play a role. He spoke no English and I spoke no Dutch.

That evening my daughter and I sat in his living room next to a very busy interpreter. Our host proudly brought out a large tray of cigars, cigarettes, and other smoking possibilities.

I respectfully declined as I didn't smoke and my daughter had no choice in the matter. This was lengthily interpreted. Most likely with apologies and explanations.

Then followed another tray, even larger, full of alcohol options as a before-dinner drink. But I don't drink alcohol nor again did my daughter have a choice in the matter. So again I declined and again the diplomatic interpreter took a fairly large amount of conversation to explain my unexpected recalcitrance.

Finally, our host wheeled out a wide table full of pastries and other sugary temptations. I was on a longevity diet at the time that precluded sucrose (my daughter referred to it as "our long vacation from sugar") but both my daughter and the Ambassador shook their heads negatively—a third and final refusal could be truly insulting. I took the diplomatic route and we ate dessert first. (This is a great gift from the Dutch; a possible weight loss technique if we agree with our mothers that it will spoil our appetite.)

Now, in Mike Acree's home, I tried to avoid another diplomatic blunder.

So I searched my memory for some honest traumatic episodes with snails. I remembered growing up near a creek that had snails and brought some home to inhabit our front porch. Since I was only 3 years old I forgot they were there and noticed their trampled remains far too late. Hmmm.

And the time I bought three huge snails and put them in a bowl of water. I thought they might be lonely so I went out to the creek to find them a companion. This particular creek emptied off Lake Erie, so polluted with arsenic and other poisons from the steel mills that all the fish in the Great Lake had died. Yet there in the creek was a tadpole which I fished out and put in the water bowl with the snails along with some fish food. The tadpole may have mutated from the pollution-although it was small you could see tiny teeth, unusual for a tadpole. I hoped the giant snails would not eat the little creature but, after all, it was faster. Two days later I noticed that the three snails all had empty shells—the tadpole had eaten every one. (I still wish I had kept it to see what the frog would have looked like.)

So I shared these sad stories as traumatic explanation for my denial of an *escargot* treat. To no avail—Eduardo and Mike were amused but not satisfied. Reaching deeper into candor, I just shrugged and said I guess I'm just squeamish about eating snails. Eduardo is a brilliant therapist (Duran, 2006) and Mike a natural one—they both asked what I was going to do about this gustatory barrier.

I remembered that Jack Kerouac had given William Burroughs the name for his novel "The Naked Lunch" as that moment when we realize what it truly is that we are eating. I also recalled being in a San Francisco Health Food store and asking if they had any fish or chicken—only to be told by an indignant clerk: *"WE DON'T SELL FLESH!"*

So I came up with an empathy exercise so we could all understand my rejection of snails for dinner. I suggested we all try dining on "*L'escargot Sauvage*" which, in my invented recipe, would be live snails on a leaf of lettuce. The subject was dropped and we went on to an otherwise outstanding meal.

Moving small creatures or large from life to death, even as food, reminds us of the limited lifespan we all have. Most of us would rather not be reminded of this. But denial or repression can be existentially deadly.

In graduate school, Milton Rokeach lectured that the best way to learn what people feared the most was *"Just ASK them and they will tell you about their fear of ladders, snakes or spiders."* In the next class, Bertram Karon followed this with *"People will never tell you their greatest fears if you just ask them; put a gun to their head and they will climb the ladder holding the spider to feed it to the snake."*

Bert was revealing that our worst fears are often hidden from ourselves, particularly the existential truth of universal but personal mortality. Seeing life as it is, with an expiration date, allows us to shine a light on our future and better live it.

This is also an international approach to suicide prevention—yes: *None* is the loneliest number (Morgan, 2008). I have even seen the therapeutic confrontation of death to improve the cognitive functions of withdrawn elderly inpatients (Morgan, 2012a), although dealing with anticipatory grief to get to that point takes substantial clinical technique (Neimeyer, 2012).

Social psychologist Carl Word found that adult high-risk needle sharers also significantly often shared an early childhood experience of seeing somebody close to them murdered, suggesting early or late intervention on understanding mortality can be essential to survival, and a full life (Morgan, 2012b)

So: Avoid regrets at the end of life and eat dessert first.

Feel free to say no to *L'escargot Sauvage*.

Chapter 37. Guam & Singapore, Brown Tree Snakes & Bee Moths

I. Cultural adaptation to a brown tree snake invasion

Guam, where America's day begins, is a beautiful tropical western Pacific island with a rich multi-cultural history. Residents often give driving directions along the lines of "go past the corner where the school used to be." Although it is a United States territory, it is nearly in Asia, as far from Hawaii to the west as California is to the east. In this land of super typhoons, military buildups, and irresistible courtesy and friendship, chaos theory applies at least as much as anywhere else. And yes, Guam has earthquakes. Something to consider when surrounded by the world's deepest ocean.

We were living in a leased 4th floor condo when the earthquake hit. Our building had about 20 floors of residents. Earthquakes meant we all had to take the stairs and get outside. Happy we weren't, navigating staircases from a higher floor. The building shook but didn't fall. Soon we were able to return home. There a hotel-wide message let all residents know to look for cracks in the wall. If we had any of these, we were to notify management immediately. We did find some in our condo wall and alerted management right away as instructed. It was impressive how fast management responded. Within minutes from our alert, a maintenance team had painted over the cracks in our wall.

Anybody familiar with science fiction knows that going back in time is risky for the future. The accidental death of a small animal or the crumpling of a tiny piece of vegetation could, over sufficient cumulative time, change everything. Today the public is well aware of this possibility as the *"Butterfly Effect."* The flapping of a butterfly's wings could, with enough time and distance, lead to a typhoon or … nothing of consequence.

The butterfly lives a short, decorative life, mainly to reproduce, and along the way does some useful pollination. If flapping its wings ultimately brings about a major storm, it really doesn't care. Its collective impact is not aggressively purposive. Any grand consequences of its actions would be part of a pattern so complex humans have yet to understand it. The intentionality of a butterfly on world events is neutral (Butz 1997; Butz and Schwinn 2004).

On the other hand, the Bee Moth has a more focused destructive effect on others. Like the Butterfly, the Bee Moth lives to reproduce. It neither eats nor drinks in its short life span of three to four weeks. A single female with only about a 4 cm wingspan lays up to 1000 eggs. In a few days these hatch into voracious caterpillars. The diminutive mother lays them in a bee hive, usually one weakly defended (possibly due to some external stressor). When the larvae hatch, they begin burrowing through the hive walls in search of food. Eventually they will destroy the entire hive. The Bee Moth, a small creature, has a powerful ultimate impact on the hard-working bees. In this it has specific purpose, useful for its own survival, but at the parasitic cost of another community.

While the *Butterfly Effect* is initially neutral and without specific eventual outcome, the *Bee Moth Effect* is one with specific purpose, initially through small effort, that over long chains of events can become a behemoth in damaging others. Danger can be an impetus for transcending trauma. But applied to the human species and magnified by the ripple effect of billions of individuals, the *Bee Moth*

Effect is the shadow side of this opportunity. Undercutting human progress, it is a manipulation for the gain of a few in a way that is exponentially destructive for others (Morgan 2008).

(Note: As early as 2007, it was noted that more than half the American domestic bee population had suddenly disappeared and that this seriously threatened the food supply for humans across the globe. This crisis was variously blamed on pesticide or cell phone towers or a warming climate, but at least metaphorically it certainly fit the accelerating zeitgeist of traumatic corporate Bee Moth greed across the planet.)

When the communities of a species confront crisis, their survival may depend on how long the crisis endures. Unresolved crises are exhausting over long periods of time. This chronic trauma can be deadly. The emergency system of living organisms can battle so long that its hyper-metabolic response becomes locked into high gear. This is why birds, for example, surviving an unusually long harsh winter, tend to die in the spring when the weather is warm once again.

Leaving the bees and the birds, communities of people have a similar response. They can be so locked into conflict that it becomes a way of life and, eventually, reach death by exhaustion. Benjamin Tong (2005) discovered high early mortality among Chinese American males, linking this interestingly to a life-long destructive "positive racist stereotype" which, when combated effectively, saved lives. In our present Procrustean culture, we have traveled many years into an era of terrorism, both from genuine external enemies and from the Bee Moth political manipulations of fear from within.

At this writing, the crisis has not been transcended. Although we have become used to stress, we seem to have almost lost, as a national community, the essential belief in ourselves to return to a more secure and generative life. After years of externally induced stress, lethargy sets in. With each new alarm, real or manipulated, we are again "shaken but not stirred." An existentialist community therapist might say: What will we do about it?

Guam was having an epidemic of Brown Tree Snakes. In the early 1990s these aggressive animals were to be found everywhere on this United States territory. They were seen on public streets, private lawns, and in what seemed like every tree. There were no birds anymore to be seen on the island, the snakes having eaten them all.

A psychologist friend had seen one jump from the plumbing of her toilet where she immediately dispatched it with a ready machete. Children were warned away from them as they attacked anything that moved in their direction. Tourism, particularly plentiful from Japan in prior years, was declining rapidly as word of the swarm spread.

But by the time I came to work at the University of Guam in 1999, the epidemic was over. In my years there I saw only one Brown Tree Snake and that was in a cage. It was thought that, running out of birds, they had begun to eat their own young and so had reduced their numbers drastically. Others thought they had just stopped reproducing so prolifically. The frequent power outages were regularly still blamed on the snakes, but with a smile, as most Guamanians knew the faulty equipment and maintenance was the true culprit. My students asked me, since I was new to Guam, if I was afraid of Brown Tree Snakes. No, I told them, I just stay away from brown trees.

Where had these snakes come from and why had they swarmed? Why had their numbers retreated to near invisibility? My answers were heavily based on a Guam history book called *Destiny's Landfall* (Rogers 1995) that was cheekily referred to locally as "Destiny's Landfill." In that helpful volume we have these disparate facts:

1. Aggressive Brown Tree Snakes first appeared in Guam in the 1940s after stowing away on planes from Indonesia.

2. These stealthy hitch-hikers settled quietly into a small colony near the airport and were curiosities.

3. Decades later the radioactive refuse from nuclear submarines was stored near the home of the snakes.

4. In time the surviving traumatized snakes multiplied and swarmed the island.

5. Once relocated throughout Guam, particularly in the jungle habitats friendly to snakes and away from people, they eventually stopped over-breeding and faded into quiet lives.

This may sound like a grade B movie: radiation creates monsters! Instead, the behavior of these animals is quite typical for many living (surviving) populations, including humans.

The traumatized snakes were likely all but destroyed by the radiation dump. The survivors did what animals do under decimating conditions. They moved away and reproduced exponentially. In animal populations this would usually lead to larger families and shorter life spans. The aggressiveness may have come from pain or fear: attack as a defense.

Their swarm of the island was partially reversed by a unique intervention: a project by the US Department of Agriculture Wildlife Service used mice stuffed with acetaminophen -- the active ingredient in many headache medicines -- to poison the snakes in an effort to cut down the population of the invasive species. About 280 mice were dropped from a helicopter with their legs glued to cardboard "flaggers," which are designed to hook on the jungle canopy and suspend the mice in treetops, where only the snakes can reach them. The 80 mg of acetaminophen in each mouse is enough to kill any brown tree snake and took out a large swath of survivors (*Pacific Daily News*, September 20, 2010). The remaining survivors of the brown tree snake population are hard to find, and may well avoid mice in trees. Once safe again, they may well have done what human populations do: smaller families and longer individual life spans.

Human populations that face deadly trauma produce extra progeny (remember the Baby Boom of post-WWII?) and extraordinarily larger families reduce longevity (Morgan & Wilson 2005). In quieter eras, less "interesting times," families are smaller and interest in life extension proliferates. Applied Gerontologists know this.

In thinking about our own future as a species, facing the recurrent challenges of 21st century eras, we see a time of struggle between liberal and conservative philosophies, science and scientism, ecology and greed. The Trump era was definitely an "interesting time" where traumatic crisis is equated with opportunity (but for whom?) and even this opportunity has its shadow. The Butterfly of chaos theory fame was in danger of extinction by the devouring Bee Moth of contemporary chaos emergence (Morgan 2008).

II. Suicide from the top and its prevention: None is the loneliest number

On February 1, 1990, hours before Ricky Bordallo was scheduled to report to a minimum-security federal prison, the popular former Governor of Guam committed suicide. He had wrapped himself in a Guam flag, chaining himself to the statue of Guam's first native chief to adopt Christianity, a statue located on the island's primary thoroughfare, and shot himself in the head with a .38-calibre pistol, all during rush hour traffic. In addition to wrapping himself in the Guam flag, Bordallo had set up four placards, one of which said: *"I regret that I only have one life to give to my island."*

Despite the Catholic disapproval of suicide, the much-loved Governor was given a church burial with honor. A decade later, during my work with mental health counselors at the University of Guam, the graduate students said the island community's number one prevention problem had become teen suicide. Even a depressed homicidal citizen, before gunning down people at his former workplace (and then himself), loudly proclaimed *"I do this for the people of Guam."*

My counselor education graduate students did some good prevention work by a media campaign recognizing that suicide is not glamorous and is, in fact, a "loser's choice." They promoted quick counseling intervention, including ventilation of bottled-up rage and compassion from friends. Not only did their interventions prevent some suicides, but the process of organized intervention transformed the students, helping all to generate more and better choices. *"Confronted with two dismal alternatives, choose a third"* was a slogan and they became adept at generating many more.

Yet, in January 2009 a survey called "A Profile of Suicide on Guam" noted that there was an average of 23 suicide deaths per year on the island between 2000 and 2007, or about one every two weeks. The survey also stated that nearly 60 percent of all suicide deaths on Guam in that time involved people younger than 30 years old. (*Pacific Daily News,* September 20, 2010).

Clearly, despite ongoing effective interventions, the trauma remains, probably intergenerational by now, and there still is work to be done,

Teenagers are so far from a time of old age and death that they can develop an illusion of immortality: what is distant seems non-existent. From that perspective, should they be in a circumstance, continuing or acute, that is overwhelmingly traumatic, they may feel trapped in an eternity of suffering. A good therapist will help them see fresh options for action and the temporal reality that situations often change over time. Absent that intervention, that key insight, suicide may appear to be the only exit from pain.

Of course such sad feelings can be magnified iatrogenically by a psychiatrist's mistakes.

In nearly every school shooting incident in the United States in the past 20 years, the children involved were already taking one or more psychiatric drugs, had the dose increased, or had just stopped taking them abruptly (Ross, 2006). As we have seen, recently published evidence suggests that the death rate on the more expensive newer drugs, the "atypical" anti-psychotics (Risperdol, Zyprexa, Seroquel, etc.) is twice that of patients taking the older much cheaper typical anti-psychotics (Haldol, Thorazine, etc); even though multiple studies have verified this (Whitaker, 2005), these drugs are still on the market and are the drugs of choice for current federally funded suicide screening programs (Ross, 2006).

David Healy, the psychiatrist whose research was responsible for the British banning antidepressants for children and the United States placing Black Box warnings on them, found that the suicide rate for "treated" schizophrenics has increased *20-fold* since the introduction of psychotropic drugs; he also found major increases in diabetes (Healy, 2006).

Is the crisis the diagnosis or its treatment, cause or effect? Clearly, this is a factor to consider in understanding the multiple causality of contemporary suicide. Drugs are definitely a key component of the Propane Decade: their use is exponential, heavily marketed directly to the consumer. Legal or illegal, the epidemic use of toxic drugs can be a Bee Moth for suicide-challenged communities.

Psychiatrist Leonard Miller took a more nonlinear existential approach to a community's suicide prevention. At San Francisco's Center for Special Problems, he held a Contact Group the same night each week. Contact groups are walk-in opportunities for people in crisis: no paper is ever filled out, no records kept.

Leonard was ahead of his time in many ways. He prescribed drugs only as a last resort. He was the most articulate and acidic critic of any prevailing iatrogenic practice of the medical community, of which the targets were many.

Dr. Miller lived on a houseboat in Sausalito with an eclectic community of thinkers including Alan Watts. The staff at the Center could choose any client group to work with and the Contact Groups were organized accordingly. If a sly intern wrote in that his group was only for "Left-Handed Hermaphrodites," then the group might still fill with left-handed hermaphrodites, drawing on San Francisco's legendary diversity.

Another psychiatrist, who we will call Harvey (much as his mother did), suddenly announced that his cooking could cure any diagnostic category and offered a Contact Group afternoon picnic to test his theory: Harvey challenged Leonard to find him clients for this healing picnic without Harvey knowing in advance what their problems were. Harvey was a great believer in excessive medication and eternal slide shows of his vacations. Leonard was a poor choice to mediate this opportunity for poor Harvey. Dr. Miller chose all self-identified bulimics for the picnic. We looked forward to Harvey's slides but none were forthcoming.

In his own group, advertised for those considering suicide, Leonard Miller excelled. We sat in and watched him take walk-in clients from *"I have no reason to live"* to the search for their own specific best reason to live. In very Ericksonian fashion, he would say: *"Congratulations. Not having a reason to live is a great insight. Finding the best reason to live is why we are alive. Your search can begin now."*

The group helped each member, session after session, find their own individual purpose for living. The choices varied but were all admirable and suicide was quickly discarded as a good path. Leonard promised them that they would all die and most sooner than they meant to: the purpose of life was to use the window of opportunity we have to find our own purpose. Leonard was an Elder, semi-retired, and had clearly found his own purpose.

At a more recent event in 2010 for Suicide Prevention Week at Australia's James Cook University in Singapore, a very moving presentation was made by a suicide survivor. She was the mother of a much-loved teenage girl who had killed herself unexpectedly at the age of 15, and mom now wrapped herself in the best memories of this child while sharing her most effective methods of trauma reduction.

This was followed by two more such presentations from trauma survivors of the families of attempted and completed suicides. In the very large crowd, many were tearful and struggling with their own survivor trauma. The mood was intense and to many it was overwhelming.

I began my own serious remarks with music from Peggy Lee's depressing *"Is that all there is?"* record which didn't help much. So I detoured the mood with the following story, recently circulating from unknown origins on the internet:

* * *

The Reframe

"There I was sitting at the bar staring at my drink when a large, trouble-making biker steps up next to me, grabs my drink and gulps it down in one swig.

"Well, whatcha gonna do about it?" he says, menacingly, as I burst into tears.

"Come on, man," the biker says, "I didn't think you'd CRY. I can`t stand to see a man crying."

"This is the worst day of my life," I say. "I'm a complete

failure. I was late to a meeting and my boss fired me. When I went to the parking lot, I found my car had been stolen and I don›t have any insurance. I left my wallet in the cab I took home. I found my old lady in bed with the gardener and then my dog bit me. So I came to this bar to work up the courage to put an end to it all, I buy a drink, I drop a capsule in and sit here watching the poison dissolve; then you, you jack-ass, show up and drink the whole thing! ... But enough about me, how›s your day going?"-Anonymous

The entire massive audience roared with laughter and the laughter continued on, uninterrupted by me, for what seemed like a minute or two.

I knew this was not a particularly funny joke, kind of sadistic really. But this release opportunity is one of the elements of successful healing from suicide trauma, as well as other fairly traumatic events.

Fighting back in a good way and on target humor can be powerful access signs to healing, both in therapy and in lecture halls. The feedback after the event was that this was a very helpful comment, although many were somewhat puzzled why that might be.

Sometimes, trauma and depression so suppress the joy in life that the right combination of turning the tables and laughter can be liberating. It can help prevent suicide or the impact of secondary trauma from a family suicide. Or so it seemed that evening.

On the other hand, sometimes even some health professionals "assist" suicide. To live or die is a fundamental existential choice. So who gets to decide, if not you? For me, the best choice is life, brief as this unmatched opportunity is once again:

TIME STATUES

"If that's all there is, let's keep on dancing."
(Peggy Lee, 1969)

Chapter 38. Lepidoptera Wars & the Month of the Moth

That day in May was sunny and hot with a UV so high it would burn any uncovered skin. Roscoe stood in the shadows where it was cool and hard to see him. His whisper was hard to hear too. He spoke through the side of his mouth, gangster style.

"Psst!" he said to me. Said it again and yet a third time until I came over to hear him better.

"So you have this Moth problem here. Suddenly they're everywhere. You open your mail box and moths fly out, right?"

I agreed with a nod. He continued.

"I can fix your little problem real fast and not for too much cash. Up front. Deal?"

I confirmed the price was affordable. Paid him. He was suddenly gone from the shadows.

Roscoe had noticed the hummingbirds in our yard were fast, faster than the moths, and pretty aggressive around their feeder.

For their good will he filled the feeder to the top with a sweeter mix. Then he dressed each one in a little pirate outfit, tiny pirate hat, and added to their beak a small but very sharp cutlass. To finish the costumes he pasted an eye patch on their right eye. They definitely looked piratical.

For motivation, he had caught some moths, not hard since they were everywhere, and put them on the hummingbird feeder. The flying pirates raced into battle.

"Psst!" said Roscoe once again, still in the shadows.

I looked around and the moths were still mating everywhere.

The hummingbird pirates were just flying in circles until they flopped to the grass in exhaustion.

"I'd give ya yer money back if I could but it already went for expenses. No profit for me. Sorry about the birds. I think it might have been the eye patch I glued on them. These hummers are just as fast and deadly as I knew they would be, right motivated too. Can't really undo the eye patches though. Good luck!"

And Roscoe was gone. Moths remained

* * *

The house in Pueblo West was just what I was looking for.

It was June of 1975 in southern Colorado, mile high desert with very few neighbors. Only two houses on our street and the other almost out of sight. Yet the university and the city of Pueblo were only a 20-minute drive away on the highway.

The realtor was enjoying the sale. So she took me on a tour of Pueblo near the university. She first parked her car in front of an art gallery.

As we entered the front door, we could see down a long corridor to the back end of the building. Rooms off this corridor had varying collections.

I saw on the wall at the far end of the corridor what seemed to be a portrait of a large face. From this distance it clearly was built out from the canvas to give it extra dimension. Intrigued, I walked closer.

The realtor smiled and kept up. Halfway there I realized this was no ordinary face, something not human about it. Closer I began to see what it was. The face of a moth, human size.

The realtor explained. "Moths here own the month of May. They swarm to mate. Part of their life cycle. Their sex is going on everywhere. So moths unending. We try to kill them. Some leave a bucket of water under a kitchen light all night. In the morning the bucket will be full of drowned moths. Yet still even more are partying elsewhere. Anything poisonous enough to kill the moths kills us too. The birds and snakes are gorged with them, spiders happy too. Not us. Feast or famine, flash flood or drought. But we endure. It *is* only for a month. The moth month of May. That's life in the High Desert. Your new home."

She continued. "By June, lucky you, they will have mostly died out by now. Sure, if I open my car's glove compartment, dead moths fall out. Same for my sock drawer at home. And the toaster. But now we are free of this swarm for the rest of the summer."

"Just the summer?" I asked.

"Well, the moths won't be back until next May. We do have to avoid rattlesnakes when they shed their skins and then they can't see well. Or mountain lions with cubs. But in October it's the mating time of Tarantulas. They will be everywhere here for their month too."

Chapter 39. RITTERS CRITTERS

This never happened. It was a dream.
This DID happen. It was a dream.

Maybe Boomers still remember John Ritter. He was in their living room every week as the lucky young man, John Tripper, in the ABC sitcom *Three's Company*. For that he received a Primetime Emmy Award and a Golden Globe Award in 1984. John had successfully moved into serious acting such as playing author L. Frank Baum in the film *"Dreamer of Oz."* He died suddenly at the age of 54 from the rare disease of a torn heart aorta. On learning of his friend's death, Henry Winkler said ""It's like there is a big tear in the world's heart. He was extraordinary in every aspect of his life, especially as a father. His children were there at every moment of his life."

John's father was the singing cowboy Tex Ritter. In the Country Music Hall of Fame, called *"America's most beloved Cowboy,"* he sang the theme in the film "High Noon." Despite his movies and records, Tex is the voice of the biggest bear in Disney's Country Bear Jamboree: *"There was blood on the saddle, blood all around, and a big puddle of blood on the ground."* https://www.youtube.com/watch?v=qG5EqP1nyr0&ab_channel=JohnEagen

In 1974 Tex died of heart failure in Nashville. His son John was only 26.

In the dream John was 25. He came to my office in the early 1970s when I was a San Francisco psychologist, only seven years older than he was. His father was increasingly ill and John wanted to do some project with him while they still could. Might cheer his dad up he thought. He problem was that he didn't want his father to be too active as he was already doing far too much for his health. I suggested he raise that question before he slept that night and wake up with the answer (David Cheek taught this method to a generation of psychologists. Called "dream incubation" it goes back to the ancient Greek healing temples of Aesclepius.) John came back the next day bemused. He had dreamed about a family Petting Zoo. He knew his dad loved animals but still. We developed the idea of a Disney-like place called *"Ritter's Critters."* To add drama, John had some unique thoughts. So *Ritter's Critters* became a real thing. Known far and wide especially for the trio of Gray Parrots that sang *"Blood in the Saddle"* as Tex had. In time a fourth parrot was added to do the music accompaniment so the parrots could entertain *a cappela*. The parrots soon moved to BeeGee songs that better fit their falsetto range. I was reluctant to wake up from this one.

In Singapore, not long ago, I was a visiting professor at an Australian University located there. The guard at the entrance and I had both once been staff sergeants, each in our own country. Soon we were good friends. One day, as I was leaving, he pointed to a bird at the top of a large tree. "Did you know that here in Singapore we have the best talking birds in the world?" I did not. So far the bird songs I had noticed had only two notes and no lyrics. Apparently this simple male competitive mating music still was enough to attract female birds of the species. He waved at the bird on the tree to get its attention and

said "Hello! I have an American friend here." The bird replied: "Hello! Food?" Much to the point. "Sing first" said the guard. The bird obliged with the standard two note song. I responded by whistling a little of the song "Stairway to Heaven." When I finished, the bird silently contemplated me for a few seconds. Finally it said "Go Away!"

Chapter 40. Puppy Unleashed

As to a Siberian Husky named Chort, he followed my Golden Rule of Proportionality, solving more problems than he created.

She was last on the San Francisco street car and it was rush hour. All the seats were taken. Her arms were full with shopping bags. Thoughtful, she stood in front of a young man looking appropriately pitiful but he ignored her. She finally said "I'm pregnant. Please let me have your seat." Other seated passengers began looking his way. He scowled but got up and traded places. Now the streetcar was moving and he, clutching the pole where she *had stood, had a good view of her above the bags at her feet. "You don't look pregnant" he complained. Then "How far along are you?" "What?!" she replied. Annoyed, he said to her and the increasingly interested other passengers, "What I want to know is, if you really are pregnant, just how long you claim you have been pregnant." She smiled up at him sweetly and said "About an hour now."*

Time is an important dimension in applied psychology. To psychoanalytic psychologist Dr. Al Talkoff, it was a key issue for psychotherapy. In fact he was teaching a course for clinical doctoral students at psychology's first free standing psychology school entitled "<u>Where do you put your clock</u>?" I never did ask Al where he thought the clinician's clock should go, but I eventually decided it had to be where both therapist and client could see it. The year was 1971.

The 13 of us hired as the first core faculty at the California School of Professional Psychology's San Francisco campus, including Al, had no core curriculum yet. Our students were often older than we were and had only come in from an active MA-level practice to secure a PhD. Consequently, faculty and students collaborated to develop courses amplifying what they already knew and also what they needed to learn.

This led to substantial creativity and experimentation. I was particularly pleased about inviting David Cheek MD to teach hypnosis to beginning students (and for us faculty too). Often held as a last year elective in today's doctoral programs, if there at all, David showed it to be of great value as a basic skills course. Students used it for speed reading, enhanced comprehension, reduced test anxiety, and a helpful tool for client success. They also learned, importantly, how not to use it since altered states can make patients under stress very suggestable.

In fact, David demonstrated that hospital operations can be deadly with negative medical staff comments or helpful with positive ones. Patients under these conditions typically develop involuntary hypnotic states. So, all in all, the placement of hypnosis training and other human potential offerings at the beginning of the program were of great value. Timing again.

The Early Years: Puppy Unleashed

Dr. Al Talkoff (a great last name for a psychoanalyst?) employed his sense of timing to have me solve a domestic problem of his. He invited me and my young children to come over and meet his canine family. Al bred Siberian Huskies as a major hobby.

I was leery of bringing my children to this since we already had two cats. I had a feeling the children would not want to leave without a puppy. Al guaranteed me that he would not sell me a puppy so we went.

There it was that we first met Chort.

He was a beautiful male Siberian Husky puppy with two-toned blue and brown eyes. Yet he was not one that Al could show, sell, or breed. This puppy had one testicle undescended which, apparently in the dog show world, ruined his value.

Further, according to Dr. Talkoff, the puppy was "overcompensating" for this missing testicle by behaving in a very oversexed manner. Once he was separated from the female puppies he had begun mounting the males.

San Francisco, then and now, is very comfortable with bisexuality. But for this psychoanalytic psychotherapist such behavior was less than welcome.

And there was more. This puppy, like so many Siberian Huskies, was an escape artist.

And a very successful one. He had learned to spring locks and gnaw through cages until Al despaired of ever containing the libidinous puppy.

So he named him "Chort" which, Al confided, was the Russian word for Devil. We took the devil home with us but free of charge as Talkoff had promised.

Chort seemed to understand immediately that he was now part of a family pack, despite our many non-canine shapes and smells.

To our pleasant surprise he got along with—well, *tolerated*—the young cats already part of our family group.

TIME STATUES

More important than that, he understood immediately that he was to protect our human puppies, playing with them somewhat but always keeping a watch on their wellbeing.

This was very important in an era when young children were free on weekends to play in a not always safe city.

This was especially so for the youngest ones including an infant girl, and then later when she was a toddler.

I established my alpha role with Chort early on. Not only was I the one to feed him during his earliest days with us, including treats for good behavior, but I was also the one to negotiate his freedom.

Chort was superb at reading body language and, in my failure to learn formal sign language, I had developed some fluency in just plain gestural communication, later enhanced by body language expert Dr. Ernst Beier.

On our first walk together, I removed Chort's leash and signaled that he was to stay next to me. When he began to stray, I held out and waved the leash: he came back.

Except for one rare circumstance years later (discussed following), from then on he always walked free of leash. He thrived and grew. Puppy unleashed, he was free to explore San Francisco.

The Urban Chort

Now a young Canine-American, he roamed the city for adventure, as most dogs domestic and feral (including the tie-dyed ones) did in those days, but he always returned in time for dinner.

Apparently through some Skinnerian event, he had learned to ring doorbells. I could imagine the surprise in some homes when they opened their door to a wolf-like animal that calmly entered and helped himself to goodies.

Once he came home with a cooking pan filled with chicken, handle firmly in his teeth. One of the children wanted him to bring back toys while an older one thought jewelry might be nice. Then I got calls on an election day that he was following voters to join them in their booth to see what they were doing in there. He was retrieved.

Down the street from us was a cement front porch slab on which two large dogs, let's call them Ma and Pa Barker, plus a posse of several smaller pet canines, growled and menaced the children as they walked to and from school. So Chort and I took a walk that led us by them.

True to form, as we approached at a distance, a cacophony of barks met us. Then all stopped suddenly as Chort came into closer view. Huskies have jaws like jackals, very powerful. The Siberian varieties have speed and intelligence plus a certain confidence bordering on royalty. By now we were close and all the porch growlers had grown silent, frozen in place.

This may be too anthropomorphic for some, but Chort definitely laughed silently.

He ascended the cement platform and strolled among the dogs, still as statues. Then Chort lifted a leg and marked the Barkers as his territory. Finally, my canine samurai returned to our walk, the job well done.

Silence followed us from behind.

TIME STATUES

The Middle Years: Salute to the High Desert Regions of the World

At the end of four years we moved to the high desert of Pueblo West, Colorado.

I was a psychology department head at a university 20 miles from our new very remote home.

The nearest visible neighbor was a home in the far distance. The rest was open land, including rattlesnakes, most dangerous when shedding their skin (and visibility) but also attracted to any open water. We had a swimming pool in the back yard, the only outside water for many miles.

Our neighborhood was also inhabited by coyotes, scorpions, night-shades, and also the tarantulas that roamed in October to mate.

Every May there was a mass infestation of moths, so dense their bodies were eventually still found months later, even inside desk drawers and glove compartments.

But between Chort and the growing family of the original two city cats (now more than a dozen and counting) they kept the outside area around the home free of varmints. A delicate ecology but it worked.

Now free to roam as outside residents, the cats expanded their population with every new generation: youngest stayed in place while the oldest ventured farther.

Chort was allowed in-house privileges when the weather warranted it, but normally preferred the free outdoors. He gathered together bushes in a shady place far from the house for his own excretory contributions (we considered this his way to copyright his puppy short stories and adventures for other dogs within olfactory range.)

The fenced acre around the house was his territory to guard, although he left it at will to explore, walk the girls to their school bus, meet them when the bus returned, and never went so far he could not respond to my calling his name.

Chort was now an adult of both years and experience. Also with immense self-confidence, this based on years of mastering any and every challenge. Except for that first night in our new high desert home.

The sky was open and beautiful. Sunsets were spectacular, often rivaling the beauty found in the Pacific.

Following a sunset, the moon could dominate the sky. On a moonless night there would be dramatic sparkles of stars and other celestial art.

Unless, of course, a night without a moon was overcast.

It was on one such dark moonless night, that first night in our new home, that the sky was too overcast to see any stars. So naturally, visibility on the ground was nil.

Once the children were asleep, their mother suggested we take a walk around the desert block, possibly an hour round trip. She held the flashlight and Chort led us on the path.

He was fearless as ever. Until...

He whined, put his tail between his legs, and backed away to move closer to us. This was the first and the only time I had ever seen him frightened.

I turned to ask my companion what she thought had spooked him. Only to see that she and my flashlight were already halfway back to the house.

I decided Chort must have a very good reason, so I turned and walked back toward the receding rays of my flashlight, the Husky, fearless again, leading me toward home.

Afraid or not, he had stayed with me. But he was also delighted to lead us in an apparently much safer direction.

He had been right.

The next day I found the tracks of an adult mountain lion and her cubs directly in the path we had been on.

He did soon get a new opportunity to excel. On a daylight walk about a mile from our home, we saw two huge farm mastiffs in the distance, also roaming free. Once they scented and saw us they charged.

The two distant dots fast came close enough to see clearly that they were at least twice Chort's size and quite ready to bite. I got ready to defend myself with a walking stick, but no need. I hadn't even seen Chort leave my side, but there in the distance he was racing toward them. Then there was a cloud of dust.

As I was running to help him, Chort emerged from the cloud head held high, almost prancing.

The two mastiffs were running away from us, one limping.

As we moved through the four seasons, Chort became ever more at home, seemingly ready even to co-exist peacefully with any willing high desert predator.

I imagined him in Winter with a friendly bear.

Chort Finds Romance

Then there was his love life. At first it was a beautiful thing to see. He had very diverse taste in his companions. Huskies are never antagonistic to diversity—in fact they literally don't even see color.

One particularly beautiful female Collie was brought home often by Chort, usually to lounge by the swimming pool. Once she was running after him and slipped, falling into the deep end of the pool. Chort had never shown any interest in this domestic body of water. Now though, he jumped in after her and floated her to the shallow end where he and I could retrieve her.

Note: My daughter, psychologist Dr. Angel Morgan, added another memory I had forgotten. She recalled this from when she was five years old: *"I remember a handful of the kittens once walked right into the pool. Without question Chort jumped into the pool after them, and swam them to safety on the deck one by one by their scruffs. We were like, 'Our hero! Good job, Chort!' and I imagined him thinking, 'Yeah. No problem. Don't make a fuss.' And then strutting off like, 'I know I'm a badass.'"*

Huskies, like wolves, tend to develop lifelong pair bonds with a mate. But Chort remained unattached, except for brief liaisons with many different partners. Which led to his next major problem.

Our only neighbor down the road had a female Saint Bernard. She was a source of his income as a breeder of purebred Saint Bernard puppies, valuable sales in that region. Whenever she was in heat, he would rent a Saint Bernard male and generate more revenue.

One day he called to let me know his female was in heat and I needed to keep my oversexed Siberian Husky away. He promised that, even though he loved dogs, he would sadly need to shoot Chort should he try to take advantage and mount his furry meal ticket at that delicate time.

I believed him capable. I told him to keep her inside the house then.

Just to make sure, I did my best to let Chort know he had to stay away from that house.

Chort understood "no" and understood my gesture to the house. He also was clear in his body language that he was not in agreement, even quietly taking a few steps in that wrong direction. I tried to get across the idea of being shot but that was either too abstract or too unconvincing. After all, the scent of a female like the Saint Bernard in heat was the real Call of the Wild for free-roaming Chort.

So, gesturing my "no" again and my sadness, I reluctantly put him on a leash and tied it to a fence post at the front of the house. He was stoic about it as he took on the stance of a Ulysses lashed to the mast so as to resist the song of the Sirens. Then I left for work 20 miles away.

On return I saw a very tired Chort leaning against the fence post, his fur all tangled. Around him was a mixture of blood and multiple Coyote paw prints. Some pack had taken advantage of his lack of mobility.

Chort had only a few scratches but it was clear that I could not leave him so vulnerable again. The lack of dead coyotes suggested they might come back.

Explaining by gesture again that he was in trouble if he went to the neighbor's home, I set him free. He settled that evening for a quiet meal, some petting by family, and a good night's sleep.

The next day I set out once again for work. Chort walked the girls to their school bus as he always did. On coming home, my neighbor was waiting for me.

He had kept his Saint Bernard inside his house just as I had wanted him to. But then, in the afternoon, his doorbell rang. Once he opened the door, Chort flashed by and mounted the female before our neighbor could stop him.

Rather than shoot our dog he had a monetary alternative. So I agreed to compensate him for the lost litter opportunity and even take one of the puppies.

Chort was left to live another day, free and wanton.

Saint Bernard dogs are strong and bred to be fully focused on one task at a time (guaranteeing they won't drink the rum themselves while on rescue trips). Sadly the female puppy had her father's combat skills and her mother's mission focus. Might have worked out if it had been the other way around. As sweet as she was, she still decided it was her goal to liquidate the kittens. After the second one, I had to find another home for this puppy before her serial killing could continue.

A New Wolf

In our second year of high desert living, Chort became even more valuable.

We were halfway between the state prison and the state mental hospital's maximum security wing. Periodic escapes and subsequent road barricades were far too frequent. His vigilance was an impressive safety factor.

Visitors from Canada had to stay in their car for hours until I came home from work to welcome them. They said a wolf had kept them in there. I introduced them to Chort, not really a wolf, yet, and then they got along fine.

Feeding Chort had now been delegated to my teenager, the eldest of the three daughters remaining at home. She, at that age, had other more imperative interests to address and apparently Chort began missing meals. One evening I saw Chort dragging home an opened

10-pound bag of dog food. I asked my teenager when she had fed him last. "What day is this?" she responded. Oh.

I began again doing the feeding. But it was no longer enough.

During his weeks of sporadic home meals, Chort had learned to live off the land, and not just for bags of dog food. Soon there were stories of some wild wolf taking down sheep and goats in the region's farms at night.

One weekend afternoon I decided to take Chort with me to visit friends on a nearby farm we had visited once when we first moved there. In an earlier visit, the livestock had ignored Chort and he reciprocated. This time when they saw him, the livestock panicked. Chort was calm but that smile of his was there again.

Circumstantial evidence but…

Chort's Latter Days

About then, a series of life changing events happened.

For one, I had been instrumental in getting the state mental hospital to stop giving weekend passes to maximum security former rapists and serial killers which, as you might gather, was not popular with them. My ability to protect the children, even with the formidable help of Chort, was increasingly less apparent.

I also had just become a single father with daughters to care for.

I took a year off to consider the choices.

I decided to look at a university job in Perth, Australia.

But taking Chort with us to Australia would have been an overwhelming hardship for him. Legally, he would have had to be confined to a kennel prison for months in the process. Years to a dog already now in midlife.

Instead, one of my students agreed to take care of Chort in our absence.

The university job looked well worthwhile but their academic year was the calendar year. So I would have had to wait nine months to begin and collect a first paycheck, hard as the sole support of a small family.

We stayed and considered.

It was there, sitting with three daughters, that we all first saw the *Fiddler on the Roof* movie. About three daughters leaving home.

Eventually though, an opportunity arose to come back to the United States and run the professional mental health continuing education in Nevada. This would be in a system that was accidentally progressive and way ahead of its time: psychiatrists would not work for the lower state wages so psychologists and social workers were running things.

This too though would be a wait, but not for as long.

We had enjoyed Australia. In the end, we chose Nevada.

When we returned to our former high desert setting, much time had passed.

Experiential dog years for Chort.

My student had passed Chort on to live with his mother in the city of Pueblo, a kind woman the Husky had in time bonded with.

She was an elderly woman with no other caring companion. Chort was no longer young himself. Given the far too short lifespan of Chort's species and the similar remaining life expectancy of his new human, they seemed temporally matched.

They certainly both seemed content to grow older together.

So we accepted this new arrangement and wished that these last days be their best.

For them both.

Final Note

As we know now, If Einstein and Vonnegut were right, time is a place. If so, then every moment of our life continues to be always there, vibrant in those coordinates of time and space. It follows that each day of our existence creates these eternal statues in time.

Some of these sculptures are best forgotten and others well worth remembering. This creation is our temporal art. Chort was clearly a very fine artist.

Should life ever give us another chance to add a Siberian Husky to our family, I would welcome this. But only if this intelligent, resourceful, and loving being can each and every day still roam free.

A puppy forever unleashed.

V. FAMILY: HUMAN

*"Here is a new day, fresh and untouched.
What will we do with it?"*
— Native American Church

Room to move
Becky Owl and Craig Menteer perform a modern dance at a Friday afternoon

TIME STATUES

Chapter 41. Tomato Soap, a Fantasy

He was new to speaking English, poor, and hungry. Nor could he tell the difference between words like soap and soup.

Nor could he tell the difference between words like soap and soup.

Which is why he asked the waiter in his hotel restaurant for Tomato Soap.

He could only afford a bowl of soup but he could not ask for it by accurate name.

The waiter smiled and said *"Well now, you need to go to that high end bath and beauty store across the street to see if they have any of that there. Cute idea though."*

Shrugging, he stepped across the street and entered the expensive bath and beauty store.

To puzzle the clerk who considered very carefully if she had ever heard of tomato soap. She asked her supervisor who also thought the idea was cute. So she gestured carefully that her store sold only things for men to be had in the bath or shower, things you use to get clean.

He understood but made soup eating gestures. The two women pointed him toward the inexpensive soup and salad restaurant across the street next to his hotel. They also wrote out "**Tomato Soup**" on a piece of paper for him to show at the soup and salad place.

And therein he went, showing his paper. Received a big container of Tomato Soup in exchange for all that was left of his pocket money. Took it home.

Remembering the two kind women in the bath and beauty store, he put the soup container on the bathroom counter. Should he bathe with it or drink it?

He was still hungry but in need of a bath, so he decided not to drink soap and instead have a great bath with tomato flavor.

Pouring the liquid into the hot water-filled tub, he had enough left to put in a hotel glass on the bathroom sink. He understood what liquid soap was. In fact he was quite smart but here in this new country his poor language skills led people to assume he was not. A common mistake.

There was still some tomato soup left. Having just seen a television ad for blue pellet toilet flush, he emptied all the remaining soup into the top of the toilet flushing chamber, flushed, and laughed when it all came out red and tomato scented. Then to the tomato bath.

Meanwhile back at the bath and beauty store, their distributor had been watching the man try to buy tomato soap. Stunned by the originality of the idea, she also was attracted to the man.

Her preference had always been for fixer-uppers, whether in homes or men, and clearly this man needed her renovation skills. She had flashed him a big appreciation smile as he left the store and he had returned a surprised but grateful one.

To the distributor this also seemed like a great business opportunity. She had taken on a much challenged business that promised by contract 2% of the gross sales for any new successful product idea she discovered.

The company had already gone all out on competing with the blue toilet flush fad.

It had introduced *Sunshine Lemon* tablets with lemon color and scent.

It had introduced *Bronze Macadamia Nut* tablets with a salty nutty scent.

Of course, when flushed, the one came out in the toilet bowl as yellow and the other as brown. Possible sales on Halloween, April Fools Day, or as another prank product. Not a beauty bath product, not a winner.

But Tomatoes! An inexpensive local product, cheaper than the lemons and berries that were running out of fad time. Not a fruit but a healthy vegetable.

And who could complain about the *Tomato Rouge* flush, a red the same as popular shades of lipstick or nail polish. (Eventually though, at various times of the month, university sorority sisters and upscale single women would have harsh words.)

TIME STATUES

A tomato is even called the "Love Apple," which reminded her she liked the Tomato Man, as she thought of him. She had to act.

Quickly she crossed the street and followed the Tomato Man to his hotel.

A small bribe for the desk clerk and she knew his room number and name.

Then quickly to her office nearby to get a contract and some cash.

The Tomato Man had just sunk into the bathtub of tomato flavored warm water when somebody pounded on his hotel room door.

He rose, wrapped a towel around his waist, and strode dripping to the door.

The distributor woman appraised him again with that smile, appreciating his scent from the bath, and followed the tomato aroma to the hotel room's bathroom.

There she took in the red tomato filled toilet bowl, the liquid tomato soap by the sink, and the red tomato scented warm bath water. Genius!

On impulse she stripped down and sat in the tub.

Always intrigued by the strange customs of this new country, he gladly joined her.

After the bath they had a very tomato consummation.

Later she had him sign a contract for half her 2% of gross sales for the new tomato soap and accessory products. She gave him a thousand-dollar cash advance.

Not long after that they moved into their very own fixer-upper condo and were married.

Bride and groom wore tomato red with fragrance at the ceremony.

–

Cherokee wedding vase. Wedding incomplete until
both bride and groom have drunk water
from the vase. Making this happen calls for
cooperation and consideration. She drank
from her side first. Set stage for a lasting marriage.

Chapter 42. Who Killed Andy Curry?

I was at the ceremony to honor Andy Curry's passing. Flanked by Eduardo Duran and Bonnie Guillory Duran, we had with us some of Curry's writing to share when the time was right.

Andy had no enemies. He was the most friendly, creative, and quietly charismatic man I ever knew. More than that, he was a world class expert on group dynamics. And he was one of the founding core faculty of the first free-standing school of psychology in California.

It was Andy that interviewed me, along with Dick Metz, to join that first faculty group in San Francisco. Dick was a clinical psychologist and Andy a social worker. Dick was white and Andy African American. This appealing diversity in race and discipline was not misleading. These were the early 1970s in San Francisco and a highly creative time. What also came across: both of my interviewers were welcoming people, despite great credentials and experience in the field. Everything was new and adventurous. Joining them was a pleasure.

In that early year of the school, Andy raised everybody's morale. He led the inventiveness and made the hard work fun. His leadership added spice to everything extra-curricular for the students. A dance group became the *"Tantric Feets Ensemble."* The campus newspaper became *"Freedom from Disabling Pathology."* In the absence of the yet-to-come core curriculum, courses were innovative, often years ahead of their time. Curry taught and covered fascinating non-psychology courses as well as the clinical ones. The very classes you always wished to take. The faculty in general was superb but Andy Curry was the heart of the enterprise. From Dr. Ben Tong, his student then: *"That walking sunshine of a man."*

As to time statues, I have a vivid memory of the glowing afternoon Andy brought me to Felicia's apartment. There we listened to the first album of Cheech and Chong, followed by Felicia's look-alike, Minnie Riperton. (Today, in the 21st century, Riperton's daughter is Maya Rudolph.)

This was an era when we could sit in on Santana rehearsing in Aquatic Park or Dan Hicks in Sausalito. But that specific time with Andy and Felicia stands out.

Felicia herself had a story, one about the successful changing of her last name. She had been besieged by calls from threatening creditors. In response, she had detoured their unwelcome and constant barrages by changing her last name to "*Newme.*" As the new me of her fresh identity, none of the credit callers got it, and she celebrated their silence with us that afternoon.

Andy in turn, recognizing his equally Melanin-blessed friend Felicia's probably temporary success, shared with us one of his own racial experiences: A young white family lived next to his own apartment. The mother of a three-year old boy persuaded Andy to stop by. Turned out that her son would run to their living room bay window any time Andy walked by. He seemed to love Andy and was excited at the very idea of meeting him. Andy graciously agreed and now sat in their living room, one decorated with Easter material, it being that very Sunday. Not waiting to be introduced, the child ran up to Andy, arms out as though for a hug. Andy leaned forward to reciprocate. And the little boy bit into his face. Turned out that the boy was convinced that Andy was a huge chocolate bunny. Typical of Andy to share that story on himself, replete with humor and pain.

By the time I left, four years later, the school had expanded from its original two campuses in San Francisco and Los Angeles to a four-campus system with new sites in San Diego and Fresno. It was later, in the early 1980s. I was the Dean at the Fresno campus of the same free-standing professional school.

The provost from the San Francisco campus called me about Andy. He said they were letting him go. A new president didn't think a non-psychologist should be on the faculty and the provost had agreed.

I argued: Even though Curry was once your teacher, a founder of the school, and valued by everybody? Yes, he agreed, the faculty and students were outraged and protesting. To no avail. It might help Andy (and provost) to get some distance. Could I bring Curry to the Fresno campus to teach a class?

So I could and did. I hired Andy to teach a night class in Fresno, hours of commute from his San Francisco Bay area home. Now his only job.

Meanwhile: Andy had a student, a white woman barely in her twenties, who on graduation married him. Although Curry was decades older, he responded to his wife with exceptionally intense love, one reminiscent of desperate adolescence. She was far more relaxed but seemed happy as well. This was Andy's *Hail Mary* pass, and, at first, it tempered the trauma of his lost career job.

But this was a time in San Francisco when women were under pressure to "sleep with a sister," whether or not their sexual orientation leaned that way. Andy's wife was no exception. Not long after their marriage, she ran off with the woman she had sistered with. Andy took it very hard. He began drinking.

Even though he had been through these double traumas in his life, he was an instant hit with this new group of students. Andy in his youth had studied with Fritz Perls and other equally famous psychotherapy pioneers. His remembered stories were outstanding, not diminished by the alcohol radiating from his breath. All part of the mystique.

I had talked with Andy about a move to Fresno, sharing a practice, and beginning a new phase of life. No- He saw himself though as always living in the San Francisco Bay community where he thought he belonged.

When the course was over, he thanked me for the experience, said goodbye to the students, and drove home to see the ocean again. He was living now in Alameda where his much-loved school had moved. Months went by.

On one devastating day I was called and invited to a ceremony hosted by the San Francisco campus provost to celebrate Andy Curry's life and passing. He had been found in his apartment, shot to death, the gun in his hand. Police called it suicide.

There must be more to it than that.

Andy, depressed and drunk, might have left it to the gods, losing at a kind of Russian roulette. Still, it was a terrible choice, one in lesser beings than Andy that would be an absence of imagination.

We all die someday. Isn't the basic point of life to find something worth living for? Had alcohol in that moment frozen his spirit, his clinical skill? What could have so misled this brilliant man? *Who* killed Andy Curry? Now the question was *Why*?

As Eduardo, Bonnie, and I arrived at the provost's ceremony, we saw our former founding faculty, friends, and students. And all seemed to be sharing my own sense of responsibility.

True it was Andy's choice, Andy's action. But what might any of us (me) have done to prevent this from happening?

As we listened to long tributes for our departed friend, a pattern began to emerge.

Andy was an expert on community. The community he was part of was San Francisco. He was revered by the street people he knew. He made them feel like they belonged, using all the group dynamics he had mastered, plus his uniquely charismatic spirit of fun.

This had energized him throughout the early years of the school when I worked with him.

After I left, the San Francisco campus had moved to Berkeley.

Here Andy had to adjust to a new street community. This he did. It took a while, but between the street people and the inhabitants of the school, he was again established as the heart of all who knew him.

Then, the campus was moved again. This time to Alameda, a military family community. Not much street community there.

So instead Curry redoubled his involvement in the professional school, now his main remaining source of purpose.

In addition, he had his marriage. Until he did not.

Freud said that his therapeutic work was done when his patient was happy in both work and love. For Andy it was the opposite outcome. He had lost both.

On his last day at the school, Andy had said to the provost: *"Take good care of my school!"*

So now we knew the Who and the Why. His school and wife had abandoned him.

Had he chosen to leave his fate to the gods of chance? If so, we all lost that gamble.

Eduardo, Bonnie, and I left the provost's ceremony once we understood what had happened.

The provost did not deserve any more of Andy's words.

Chapter 43. When Time Goes Faster

> *"We stand in life at midnight; we are always on the threshold of a new dawn."*
> — (Martin Luther King Jr.)

In San Francisco, a young woman ran for the cable car, arms loaded down with groceries. She succeeded in boarding and, arms loaded with groceries, made for the last free seat. Suddenly, a teenage boy shot past her and, with a triumphant smile, sat in her space. She stood in front of him as the cable car started up, maintaining her balance as best she could. He clearly had no intention of surrendering his seat. But she had learned the hypnotic art of time distortion, slowing the experience of time to give herself more room to think in a crisis (Morgan, 2004). After several minutes of reflection, using up only seconds in real time, she said *"Would you please give up your seat to an exhausted pregnant woman?"* This was said in a loud voice and the other passengers turned toward the teenager who, reluctantly, stood up and let the young woman have his seat. Looking at her intently as she settled into his former spot, he said *"You sure don't look pregnant. How long have you been pregnant?"* She smiled benignly: *"Two hours."*

Since Paul Fraisse of France penned his classic Psychology of Time in 1963 and the International Society for the Study of Time began in Europe in 1972 (or the London based Association for the Social

Studies of Time or ASSET in London), global psychology has held episodic interest in this key variable.

I have had particular interest in the clinical stressor of the "birthday nine." When one approaches or enters their 29th, 39th, 49th, 59th, 69th or any birthday taking us into an age ending in 9, this can be a major life stress. While the measurement of time is an arbitrary concept, its experienced passage is not. We have many self-inflicted (or society/parents-inflicted) expectations of what we were supposed to have accomplished before beginning another decade of life.

An experienced clinician can be aware of this process and guide clients through it, knowing that reaching ages ending in zero signify a resigned acceptance of another decade to inhabit and accomplish a fresh set of expectations. The key is to assist the client to merge into a new decade of life with productive hope.

If this were also true of our human family on a global scale, then we should have expected 2019, a year ending in a nine, to have been an exceptionally stressful time. One magnified by the vast but disappointed expectations for a new century and a new millennium. Much less that the early 21st century decades included epidemic racism along with a triple threat: Covid, Climate, and Corruption.

Made every month seem to last years but each day seemed *way* too slow.

I do remember this from the last century: Margaret Mead walked to the podium. She carried an impressive walking stick to help and was followed by a younger man. I could see that she looked her advanced age but her words were strong, youthful as her companion.

Addressing a crowded audience of psychologists she began, as I recall, by nodding at her young male friend:

TIME STATUES

"Yes, we get old... but sex does not. Unless, like you psychologists, you just talk about it. Nothing is more boring than TALKING about sex." (Crowd laughter.) *"Now I notice that many in this audience look my age or older. You likely have noticed that time seems to go ever faster. Some of you may be concerned about it, life spans being finite as they are. Here is one reason why—a mathematical explanation of fractions. If a child one day old had a wet diaper for half that first day, it has been wet half its life. The dampness must seem to have gone on forever. Then again, once that child has lived an additional 90 years or more, if his adult diaper were wet for half a day, this experience is such a tiny fraction of his total life experience that fortunately this unpleasant memory will soon fade into the rocketing of time's passage. Of course, while he wore the wet diaper, time may not seem to have moved fast enough."* (Crowd laughter, applause.)

Ever since that day, I have noticed whenever a passing car's bumper sticker read

"PSYCHOLOGISTS *TALK* ABOUT IT"

What about the experience of feeling that time is dragging way too slow on a day-to-day basis yet a look back shows time has continued to rocket, seemingly when each week past feels more like months. This can occur when world/environment events are rapidly changing each day but one's own days are predictable, same, uneventful compared to the outside world.

It's like being on one of those bullet trains shooting along to its destination in record time. You would be impressed by how much mileage it accumulates so quickly. Yet sitting in the train seats reading or eating or conversing, time passes slowly, too slowly. Just as we can feel both hot and cold at the same time (separate sense receptors), we can experience time moving too slow and yet too fast.

Charlie was a teenager. He had been framed by the local police who left a marijuana brick in the trunk of his car. At the urging of the university's Dean of Students, Charlie was sentenced to three years in the federal penitentiary.

Once there, because of his age and intelligence, no prior felonies, he was placed in an "Honours" holding. No locked cell door, daily access to the prison library, scheduled events. Charlie was a fine artist and sent us beautifully illustrated letters that first year. Eventually a more experienced prisoner, a lifer running the library, had a talk with Charlie.

"*Charlie. Do you like being here?*"

"*I like the library. Overall it's okay. But two more years is a very long time. Moves very slowly. Wish I could get out faster.*"

"*You can. How about two more weeks and not two more years?*"

"*How?*"

"*Get out of my library, get out of the Honours program. Move to a locked cell, do the same routine every day. It will seem to be two weeks—time will fly by when every day is the same.*"

It worked. Still two years more passed in external time but to Charlie it flew by, seeming like two weeks as every day seemed like the next.

Charlie returned home on schedule, cheerful and focused. He married Sarah, the Dean's daughter, got her mother high on weed realizing she should and would divorce the Dean. Charlie and Sarah moved to Vancouver where he became a much loved artist.

TIME STATUES

Keeping each day unique and rewarding can slow time down for the elderly, make their experiential lifespan longer. On the other hand, keeping it the same each day rockets to that final destination. The alternative goal: each day unique, productive, wonderful in its own way.

More on how the experience of time can be chosen, read:

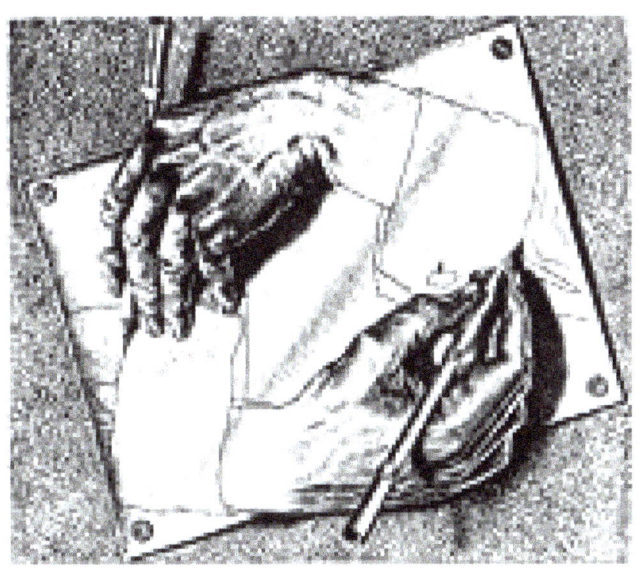

TRAINING THE TIME SENSE: HYPNOTIC AND CONDITIONING APPROACHES

Dr. Robert F. Morgan

Chapter 44. Another Golden Pond

This might have actually happened. Somewhere.

My mother liked to say "When you say the word 'pneumonia,' the p is silent as in swimming." In the house she grew up in, one of 13 brothers and sisters, the nine boys and their father all shared the same upstairs bathroom while the five girls and their mother shared the downstairs bathroom. The boys lined up their shoes, one pair to a step, on the stairs leading to the upstairs bathroom for a quick exit later to school. One pair each was all they could afford. One of the younger boys, five-year-old Danny, was last in line for the upstairs bathroom one morning. He was too old to wet himself and too young to wait. His solution was to relieve his bladder inside each pair of shoes on each step of the stairs. Consider the care and rationing of liquid involved in this five-year-old's protest. The consequences were unusual but typical for this family. Little Danny swore he would never do that again, his paddled bottom agreed with him, but the marking of the shoes feat became a celebrated family legend, following Danny right to the end of his adventurous adult life.

My mother's family had good reason to seek humor about this aspect of our biological function.

TIME STATUES

Another Pacific sunset. Best ever here on this tropical island resort, just off the coast of Asia. Quick now, we race to that outdoor hot tub in time to see the golden finale. Ahh! And there we sit in hot water up to our neck, waiting for the moment. Deep silence.

Broken when she asked me to fill this time with conversation. Something maybe about life and death. I would have preferred quiet. Still, indulging her choice fit this shared wait as much as anything else. Love matters.

Hmm. I considered how I taught life and death to my Life Span class. Not the normal birth to old age. No, mine went from early preparation for beginning a baby to pre-natal to old age to the ultimate exit. For that last part we each wrote our own obituary and even the tombstone epitaph. Mine, recalling my teenage post office job, was: *"Outgoing Male."*

We even, as I told her, described our own best funeral. She wanted to know.

Well, I wanted a gathering of best friends including family that cared about us. The opening music would be a performance of *"Oh what a beautiful mourning"* (my spelling) from the musical *"Oklahoma."* The childhood theme music of *Peter and the Wolf* would be played. Tumblers and jugglers. Wonderful food treats for the mourners. The eulogy following might best be described as amazing, witty, fun, and moving.

Of course all this was to be filmed while I was still alive, not there, but able to see it at home eventually. Why waste all those fine words and actions if the deceased subject can't hear them?

She added: Why not also use that gathering to do a tribute of happy mischief? Fits our approach to life. What might that be? Something this beautiful fun-loving compassionate woman might consider worthy.

Why not rehearse it now? Here and now.

Just then the moment we waited for began. The sky with all its shadows proclaimed the majesty of the departing sun by turning all light into spun gold, every shadow, the entire sky, even the water we sat in.

It was beautiful. We sank into the warm gold water, wishing to make it last longer.

TIME STATUES

Night replaced it.

She had an idea and put it into words.

I laughed and put it into action. She did as well.

We naturally had first exited the hot tub, and now, relieved of our liquid, we admired from a distance our own newly golden-hued hot water.

We had rebirthed the Golden Pond. But smaller.

And then we signaled online for a flash mob of resort guests to join us at the majestic regal indoor resort pool.

Pool hours were over and the pool area was deserted when we got there.

Once the flash mob came, they were soon all relieving their bladders into the posh regal waters.

Next laughter and dispersal. Some photos.

That night we slept well, imagining the eventual discovery of our regal Golden Pond.

Yes, consternation and chaos would ensue.

Also: A special moment of color in our life.

Chapter 45. A Life Owed to the Dime Movie

It was a Saturday at the end of August in 1948. The place: Buffalo, New York. Great Lake cities this time of year were warm and humid. Sun peeked out through pervasive clouds. The endless summer was ending, school coming soon.

My father had finished a grueling week at work. He was in bed now, paying his sleep debt of deprivation from Monday thru Friday. As the sports reporters said, doing his job he had "left it all on the field" for his job. (This meant he had given all his energy to his work, though canines and felines would understand this as meaning you should watch where you step on that field.)

So he would recuperate by sleeping through the morning, arising rested in the afternoon.

My mother was a public school teacher with the summer off, at least for a few more days. She rushed breakfast for me, her only child, seven years old.

I had to leave to make it to the weekly noon Saturday matinee. She slipped me a dime for the ticket ($10 today?) and I was gone.

This was a wonderful way to spend a Saturday afternoon. A double feature, two new ninety minute movies, and also a cartoon, newsreel, and serial (how can the hero possible survive sure and certain death—find out next week).

Not to mention the flying popcorn in the audience (don't sit in the target area in front). Four hours right there. Play outside after until supper time.

Even the walk there seemed like an adventure. We lived in what was called the "Fruit Belt" in East Buffalo. No fruit trees to be found. Just streets named after the absent fruit. It was a challenging neighborhood.

Not so much for us kids though. We adapted just fine. Maybe there might be a body lying in the street from the night before. Drunk or dead, it was an adult and we took it in stride, moved on. A child our age lying there would have been a lot worse, but that we didn't see.

At the movie we stood in line to buy our ticket. My ten cents were ready. We looked appreciatively at the bullet holes in the movie building and signs. Made us feel tough and older.

Better yet, before entering the theater we were frisked for knives. They were not concerned about protecting us. It was the theater seats that they didn't want cut. Still, at age seven, being frisked for a knife also was part of the charm.

Meanwhile that afternoon with me away left my parents in a rare state of being rested and private. Contemplating the end of the summer. Soon both would be working, the weather cold and gray. But not that day. It never occurred to me then how they might use this opportunity.

Nine months later, on May 30th 1949, my brother was born. A welcome gift. I was no longer an only child. He owes his existence to the dime movie.

Note: Brother's response *"Well, speaking out of self-interest, it was a dime well-spent."* I agreed, saying it was worth at least twice what I paid. (Adding though that it was all I had in my jeans at the time.)

Chapter 46. Father's Day

Raising daughters as a single parent turned out to be more joy than anything else.

When they were in middle school, they both competed in a Father's Day Contest. The prize was a $100 savings bond.

The challenge was to write the best tribute to Dad in 25 words or less. This was a huge sum for children of that age in those days, many competed.

The older daughter wrote some beautiful words. They meant a lot to me when she shared them. Even though they didn't win.

The younger one submitted a few entries. She enjoyed writing and there was no limit on tries. One of hers won the contest:

"My father never spanks us. He just gives us a disappointing talk."

When she received the savings bond in a well-attended ceremony, the MC gave her a big condescending smile and said:

"Little girl. Didn't you mean to say 'disappointed?'"

She smiled back at him.

"No. I meant 'disappointing.'"

—

One of my college roommates was from Bermuda.

He told me that Bermudian males often had children from all over the island. He said that their favorite two things were food and sex. Not in that order. On Father's Day they hoped to get enough gifts to help with all the presents they needed to deliver all over the island on Christmas. Santas incarnate roamed the island that morning.

How many men everywhere else never really know how many children might honestly call them "father?" Just wait to see who sends them a card on Father's Day?

Lilly Tomlin was asked once if she had any children. She responded: *"None I know of."*

CHILDREN'S DAY

As a child I asked why there wasn't one. The answer: always a tired *"That's every day!"*

MOTHER'S DAY

On that day she is clear about this to her children: *"You're not ever going back there!"*

I used to suggest to my class that they find the day and date nine months before they were born and then ask their parents exactly what they were doing on that day. A great discussion gift for both Mother's and Father's Day. Or anytime.

TIME STATUES

MOTHERS DAY: NO RETURNS TO THE WOMB

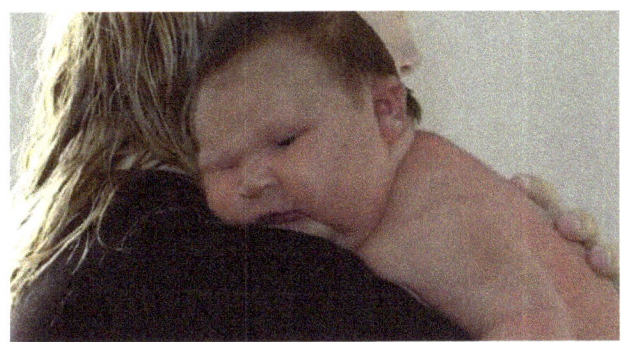

ROBERT F. MORGAN

Chapter 47. An Unpaid Bill

As soon as you're born, you've already won a lottery. In the midst of flocks of sperm, all competing for that egg, the egg chose you. Let you in. Nurtured you while you grew, and months later emerged into a very new world.

My first post-doc university teaching job was in 1967 at Saint Bonaventure University, miles south of Buffalo New York in a mountain town called Olean. In that first year there, a new university president began as well. In a grand welcome ceremony befitting a Pope, Father Reginald Redlon began his reign.

The President with a sweep of his robed arms promised that he would grant the faculty new rights. This gesture was somewhat deflected when Father Angelus, a priest from the Philosophy Department, stood and bellowed *"Rights are not granted! They are recognized!"*

Yet the ceremony went on. Seemingly for endless ritual and grandeur. Then, near the very close of the event, Reginald looked into the audience, appearing to look right at us, and proclaimed thusly: *"You will find the secret of life in these hills!"*

That was the October that my daughter Cinnamon was conceived.

Nine months later we drove to the hospital to let her out.

Her mother had already birthed three children before I met and married her. This suggested to me that she deserved a certain experiential deference that I lacked. So we went the traditional medical route she had done before. After all, then in my twenties, I had never been at a birthing before.

Nor this time either.

I was escorted to a third floor room full of smoking and anxious expectant fathers. The door was closed behind me. I sat down in the nicotine cloud and impatiently waited with the others.

The delivery room was on the main floor and I sat in this room on the third. Acoustically it would have been impossible to hear, but: Suddenly I heard a scream.

I recognized the voice and bolted from the room, heading down three floors as fast as I could. Stopping only to put on a discarded white doctor's coat I saw on the way.

On the main floor, a nurse stood in my way, blocking the hallway path to where the scream had come. Officiously she said *"Are you a Doctor?"* Three years from my psychology doctorate, I answered: *"Doctor Morgan and on my way to maternity!"* She gave way. I moved on.

Coming to the birthing room, I stopped to let a nurse wheel out a newborn baby wrapped in a pink blanket and flat on her back. The baby's skin was rosy as well, her hair more light red blonde fuzz. The baby looked at me alertly, unusual for a newborn. I knew who she was.

I quickly in my mind promised her I would be back soon, and throughout her life, but there was an emergency to go to first. She seemed to understand. I moved on.

TIME STATUES

The birthing room was empty except for the baby's mother. She lay on a table, eyes shut, shivering. Her face and hands were blue with shock. I put my hands on her forehead and gently said: *"You're safe now. Warmer. When you are ready, you can open your eyes."*

I found a blanket and covered her while I waited. Soon her eyes opened and I suggested she rest while I got a nurse to take her to her bed. Her color was back, but it was too soon to talk.

The birthing nurse was not far away. Walking back, I asked why her patient was left in shock there in the birthing room alone. Turned out that the doctor scheduled to provide the anesthetic had stayed away longer than expected so as to finish his golf game. Missed the birth. Mother in shock. Golfing medic still not there. No wonder the baby had been so alert, not knocked out by anesthetic.

I stepped away from the now sleeping mother to see my new daughter. Newborns were in a room with an outside glass viewing pane for fathers to see them. Cinnamon was still in a pink blanket but now she was crying.

I asked the nurse to bring her to her mother. My white coat was gone and with it went my authority. The nurse looked at me with mixed annoyance and compassion for my perceived ignorance. She explained *"Oh that crying is just reflex. We ignore it. Their cortex is nonfunctional until the age of two."*

I considered that the nurse may have maintained her own nonfunctional cortex well past its maturation date.

Soon I was leaving the hospital with both mother and baby, days ahead of scheduled departure.

Once at home, Cinnamon demonstrated a very effective cortex and her childhood all her days, without exception, was definitely a pleasure.

Days later at home, sure and certain as Sun in the desert, the mail brought a bill from the anesthetic-deficient medic. Full charge for the non-show.

I pay my bills. But not that one. Not then, not ever.

Chapter 48. A Mystery Even to this Day

She is of Cherokee/Choctaw and Irish descent. Known as Becky Owl, she grew up in the Great Smoky Mountains of North Carolina within the American Indian tribal nation of the Eastern Band Cherokee. As a young woman there she worked in the Cherokee Village as a guide for the many national and international tourists that visited, most in good weather months. They at times asked questions for which she had no matching answers. In that case she had learned to say in a quiet confidential whisper: *"That is a mystery even to this day."*

I always thought this to be a far more impressive answer than *"I don't know"* or *"research is in progress"* or *"it's a complex, inconclusive, and contradictory matter"* or *"here are some citations"* or *"you can find it online"* or *"read my book"* or *"I'll tell you later "*(8 ball response) or *"excuse me- nature calls."* Becky's response is a form of reframing. As we know, reframing is an essential intervention, useful in exchanges from psychotherapy to international progress.

Many Rest Stops

In 1991 Becky and I were new faculty at an eastern Montana University, she a librarian and me a psychology professor. We called our group of newcomers the Freshman Class.

I had been a single divorced dad for 13 years but my children were in college and I was open to something new and wonderful. Just seemed unlikely.

Becky and I were among the very few faculty newcomers to still be standing during a day long orientation. I wondered out loud to a friend, why in Indian Country, out of about two dozen of us none of the new hires were American Indians? That's how we met. Her nametag said "Becky Owl." I thought from her name that she was British. She set me straight right away. Cherokee-Choctaw (and Irish) and definitely American Indian. Still, the only one.

Even though she was not much more than fresh out of library school, she already had the reputation of being the best (only?) person for faculty or students to see if you needed something from the library. She was so good that I was warned about the risk of dating her, lest if it went bad I could lose her valuable and unique service.

Nah. She was too professional for that. Besides, what was more important anyhow? So we began dating.

She had a great sense of humor. Told me her "Indian Name" was *"Many Rest Stops."* A self-inflicted joke as we did stop at every opportunity for her to anoint fresh territory. Just well-hydrated I supposed. It was a dry cold there in Montana.

Becky was also strongly motivated to see the best in people, almost to a fault. She was very diplomatic. Even in sad situations she saw the glass as not empty but at least 5% full.

During a very early evening in our relationship, we visited a friend's party at her home. Not long after arrival, we naturally sought out a free bathroom so my date could liquidly mark the new territory as her own. (She now decades later has these claims established all over the earth.)

We were directed to a quiet place on the second floor. So quiet in fact that standing outside in the hall, all the internal sounds carried to my ears. She knew it too and was quietly embarrassed afterwards as she commented on the acoustics. I said I was glad to know that she always washed her hands at the end.

This seemed to make her uncomfortable so I resolved to find a way to destress the situation.

So I took a turn inside the bathroom while she waited outside the door, doing her best not to hear anything from within. Or comment.

I only had to void a moderate amount of liquid, albeit the sound undoubtedly carried in these acoustics just acoustically short of Niagara Falls. I imagined her standing outside in the second floor hallway, doing her best to ignore the music. Then I noticed a long hose attached to the sink faucet next to where I was standing. Just before I finished I had time to turn on the faucet and move the hose over to pour sink water into the toilet bowl. It was seamless and the torrent sound continued nonstop from the hose.

By my watch this continued for nearly ten minutes. Finally, from outside in the hallway, I heard her say *"**OH COME ON**!"*

My adult daughters and brother found her delightful. Full approval. My home version of an old song: *Nobody knows the trouble I've been. Nobody knows but Becky.* And yet thirty years later we are still together.

Chandigarh Wedding

My wife, in sickness and health, poverty or wealth. Speaking of wealth. We are pictured below as guests when we visited a ceremony of partially restrained wealth at a wedding in Chandigarh, India.

Irina Brar, my past graduate student and celebrated professional golf pro, married another top India golf pro and into his Singh family. Subsequently Irina became India's first Sports Psychologist.

The Three Tables of Development

When I was doing my internship at Hawaii State Hospital, the volunteer teacher and I put together an adolescent day program for the 30 children hospitalized there at the time. In a mental health treatment facility focusing primarily on 1000 adults, there was a genuine need for daytime activities. Since the only full-time hospital staffer was me, these thirty patients, aged 11-18, would necessarily need to develop a therapeutic community quickly.

We set out three tables for our first meeting, each with 10 chairs. I told the children that each of the three tables would become an activity group to meet daily with each other. Ten children sat down at a table immediately while the rest watched. These it turned out were high functioning adolescents misplaced in the hospital. They very soon were enrolled in a nearby public school during the day, sleeping in their ward at night.

Next: after a few minutes went by, a teen named Bobby marched to the second table and sat down at its head, beckoning imperiously to his selection of standing patients to join him. When all seats were full at his table, he let them know he was in charge. All had to dress as he did and follow his orders. He would take care of them.

The remaining ten patients had the most severe issues and never did sit at the remaining table—in this they defined themselves as the third activity group. As the weeks went by, it became clear that as children in this dysfunctional group left at or near the third table improved, they moved up to Bobby's group in table number two.

In his group there was always room for more since once anybody found the courage to disobey him, he exiled them... and then these exiles moved to join the high functioning group, table number one. Group one always had room for more since its members were regularly being discharged back into the community. This highest level might have best been described by psychologist Eugene Jacobson in his definition of democracy: when those most directly impacted by a decision made that decision.

This three table progression was clearly a developmental sequence, both for patients, typically for all children, and as a metaphor for anywhere in the human family. Once infants have a sense of themselves and their environment they move to attach themselves to a strong parental leader or authority; the next developmental step is to individuate and internalize their own sense of self and responsibility as they relate to authority, a healthy personal reframing.

Oh: a specific personal reframing example? I took the two higher functioning activity groups on a day trip to the city. All were quiet and extremely well behaved (atypical for non-hospitalized adolescents). At one store though, a patient named Eileen asked a clerk if she could try on a dress. The clerk refused, saying that she was afraid Eileen would try to steal it. Eileen considered this and before I could intervene said *"Watch it! I'm psychotic!"* The clerk looked to me and I nodded affirmatively but smiled. Eileen got to try on the dress. One of us bought it for her.

- On my first day as a Dean at the California campus of a freestanding school of professional psychology, I sat quietly under an old and beautiful tree, one in an inner courtyard that offices and classrooms looked down on. When I re-entered, I was summoned to the office of the Provost. *"Are you taking drugs?"* he asked. *"Not even an aspirin"* I answered. *"Why?" "You were seen sitting next to a tree doing nothing for an hour. We thought you might be stoned. What were you doing?" "It's called thinking"* I answered.

- In Thailand we sat in the first few rows of the movie theater as we usually do in our home country. Halfway through the movie, somebody came up and whispered to me that the front rows were reserved for the royal family. But seeing as the movie was not yet done, he said I could stay so long as I either sit up straight as a royal guest might or slouch further down as a clue-less foreigner might.

TIME STATUES

From this I may have learned: In Singapore, during the Chinese cultural celebration of the Hungry Ghosts, the front rows for an outdoor performance were covered by an unusual haze. I asked what would happen if I sat there and was told that these seats were reserved for the ancestral ghosts who were obviously there to enjoy the performance. I moved on.

In Thailand and other countries observing these annual ancestral visits, money is burned so the ghost can spend it in their afterlife; pragmatic Singaporeans participating in this ceremony burn non-currency paper knowing that the ghosts should appreciate the thrift as well as the intention.

- As related in an earlier chapter, in the 1960s African American psychologist Ermon Hogan was in the District of Columbia to work with me on evaluating the success of a federally funded grant awarded to Dr. Martin Luther King's SCLC.

Let's review this again so as to add what happened next.

We had decided to discuss our plans over dinner at an expensive Washington restaurant. The grant supported a very effective adult literacy program in Chicago, following earlier support for learning the effects, in Prince Edward County, Virginia, of what happened to thousands of children after four years of closed public schools (formal education or its lack turned out to profoundly impact measured intelligence; critical periods of learning were identified).

The Prince Edward County project led to a reading instruction method by Myron Woolman so powerful that it fit Adult Learning as well. This conversation lasted nearly an hour. We then realized that our waitress had cheerfully waited on every table but ours during that time.

All the other diners as well as the wait staff were white and we were inter-racial patrons. This was a time when apartheid laws prohibited inter-racial marriage. I got the waitress to our table.

Confronted with a very angry Dr. Hogan, the waitress manifested some body language often associated with lies. She said: *"I am a little slow today and I probably should apologize. My entire family died yesterday in, um, a car crash. And, um, my doctor said I should work today to get my mind off it. So you need to be patient."*

Dr. Hogan considered this and then said with quiet intensity: *"The last surviving member of your family will be gone if you don't take our order right now."*

The waitress took the order.

But in this chapter we learn what happened next.

Instead of food, the owner/head cook of the restaurant came to our table.

Loud enough to be heard by the patrons at other tables, he defended the waitress, saying she was only trying to protect the restaurant's reputation by not serving us. He insisted that had we not been "provoking" her by being inter-racial we would have been better served. After all, he addressed all the patrons listening, everybody knew that his restaurant had the best food in the region.

I got up to be better heard in the room since it was my turn.

"While we do not agree with your views, there IS that rumor that your food saved a life."

TIME STATUES

Now he was intrigued and asked for an explanation. I went on.

"There's a handicap called synesthesia in which one sense takes the place of another. This can be the basis of creativity at its best (or dyslexia if suppressed) but for one of your customers, it threatened his survival."

I paused. Swelling with pride, he insisted I continue. I did.

"This poor man had developed synesthesia recently focused on smell. All food, no matter how well prepared, smelled to him as though it were already digested, much like fecal matter, poop. Conversely, stepping into a fully used public bathroom generated only to him such succulent smells that it made him beyond hunger, made him ravenous. Consequently he could not manage to eat anything nourishing and his weight was shedding to life-threatening level. The poor man was desperate."

"But then he found your restaurant and, thanks to the steaming hot poop smell from you and your cooking, rotten enough to curl paint for three blocks, well, he ate here and lived. But Dr. Hogan and I, having normal smell and taste, will move on."

Scattered laughter from customers, then some applause.

Just for a moment he seemed to think that the applause was for him. In that, he looked puzzled long enough for us to leave.

We found a friendlier place to eat.

Maybe what I said is still a mystery to him today.

Psychologist Lee van den Daele later called this reframing "time-release humor."

Back to Becky

Compassionate Considerate Warm Creative Talented Intelligent Educated Fun Passionate Fair Cultural Competent International Traveled Ticklish Dancer Librarian Student Gifted Learner Spontaneous Sense Of Humor Loving Young Athletic Integrity Honest Successful FP Huggable Grandma Grant Coordinator Eastern Band Many Rest Stops Greatest Date Writer Helper Companion Brave Kind Justice Social Conscience Singer's Voice Vacations Restauranteur Home Care Hard Worker Reader Best First-In-Class Camouflaged Apology Adept My Heroine Collector Office Supplies Swimmer POAT Relentless Laugh Human Form Partner Vintage Movie Watcher Territory Friend Detective Boolean Music Mornings Ethnic Nights Curious George Movie Critic Navigator Cherokee Captain Choctaw Northern Irish Friend Owl Needs Assessment Fun Leader Lovely Fashion Plate Elegant Affectionate Keeper Miss-Fall-Festival Safe Smile Protected and Always Loved.

Best of Burque 2016 Alibi newspaper, April 7th 2016 "Abraham Lincoln once said, "The ballot is stronger than the bullet." While we seriously doubt he was referring to the election of Albuquerque's Best Parking Lot to Make You Lose All Faith in Humanity, Best Uber Driver, or Best Gay Bar, the

essence of his sage words still rings true. The Alibi's "Best of Burque" was created so you, dear readers, don't have to fight over or guess who are the royalty in this great dusty city. Congratulations to the winners, sympathies to the losers, and a massive thank you to our readers who showed up online in record-breaking numbers this year to share their opinions about who the best really are. The votes have been cast, the people have spoken. So without further ado, we give you the best that Albuquerque has to offer in the categories of arts, services, goods, kids, pets, night life, music, local flavor and life in Albuquerque." Best Category We Forgot By Our Readers: "Best Woman in ABQ: My Wife Becky "

Becky Owl became Becky Owl Morgan when she married me all those years ago.

Why she did so, and seems still happy doing so, can also be a mystery to this day.

Chapter 49. Young Love 2020

Covid beats Ovid.

Room to move
Becky Owl and Craig Menteer perform a modern dance at a Friday afternoon

She was having none of it

Chapter 50. Shaking Hands with Lincoln

"The history of the handshake dates back to the 5th century B.C. in Greece. It was a symbol of peace, showing that neither person was carrying a weapon. ... Some say that the shaking gesture of the handshake started in Medieval Europe. Knights would shake the hand of others in an attempt to shake loose any hidden weapons."
—<https://deepenglish.com/lessons/handshake-history-listening-fluency-116/>

In modern times, a handshake can signify greeting, agreement, or peace (GAP). Beginning in early 2020, the global Covid-19 pandemic discouraged the use of this historic gesture, a GAP or gap ignored by large minorities of the populace, ones believing the lethal pandemic a hoax or not concerning them. As time went by, the disease thinned out the numbers of these people to the point that handshakes looked to be perpetually forsaken. Once the pandemic came under full control though, following much time and demise, the handshake returned. Now it had a new additional meaning: asserted lack of contagion.

It was writer Alex Haley who said *"The death of an elder is like the burning of a library."*

Certainly, the contemporary drive to record oral histories is a useful attempt to connect the decades and centuries to a better future. Anyone over 100 is a living link with history. I met my first such person in 1950 at my elementary school assembly. A vigorous speaker, she was celebrating her 100th birthday at a time when this was a highly rare event. She chose to speak to us of being born into slavery in 1850:

"I was your age, about 8 years old I think, when my mother explained that in a few years I would be paired up with whomever the 'master' chose as husband for me. Any of our children could be sent away and sold. So she told me not to count on anything or anybody very much. Nothing lasts long around here, she said. Now I did not care to hear this at all. I had strong ideas about who I wanted to be with and I surely did not want my children sold! Just as I got to be about 13 or so, the war, the now so-called 'Civil' War, came along and, lucky me, I got ignored in all the fuss. So I did not have to be with some man I did not care for nor did I have any children to sell off. Then we got even more luck. Mr. Abraham Lincoln, our President, set us all free. He said slavery was over and it was. We were so happy with him that when the war ended, my mother and I set out to thank him personally in Washington. After a whole lot of travel, we got there and he came out to see us, busy as he was. What a tall man! His voice was a surprise: it was high pitch. But his handshake was warm (most men did not bother shaking a lady's hand) and his eyes smiled at us as much as his face. I thought I am never going to forget that hand on mine and I did not. Not even today, as you see. We thanked Mr. Lincoln and went home. I married a man I chose myself and we all came to the western frontier here in Buffalo, New York, where I have lived for 82 years. None of my children or their children or even

their grandchildren will ever be sold. We are free people. That is what I am really here to celebrate today."

After her talk, some of us children went up to congratulate her.

I asked her why she had a Republican Party button on, as the African American community in Buffalo was already very Democratic then. She said it was because *"He freed us,"* meaning Lincoln.

For her, this Lincoln time statue of the past was still very alive and it influenced her present.

Yet her emphasis on the powerful meaning of freedom schooled her children's children for the difficult future decades just ahead.

We were honored to shake the hand that shook Lincoln's hand and, in this way, this courageous elder had connected us to her history and ours.

As discussed in an earlier chapter, from 1964 to 1968, Robert Lee Green and I had the honor of providing psychological services to Dr. Martin Luther King Junior and his Southern Christian Leadership Conference (SCLC). My role was as a part-time graduate assistant to Dr. Green, Dr. King's full-time Education Director as well as the only ful- time psychologist at SCLC.

As part of my apprenticeship I evaluated SCLC's adult literacy programs in Chicago and assisted with the already noted evaluation of children blocked from their Prince Edward County, Virginia, schools for four years (Green & Morgan, 1969).

Dr. King was a respected "older" man in his late thirties, at least so it seemed to me in my mid-20s. As related in an earlier chapter, in 1967 I listened to Dr. King present his Invited Keynote Address to the American Psychological Association. Hearing his powerfully eloquent appeal for a new psychology to deal with the trauma of racism and oppression, a "Community Psychology," a liaison between social scientists and activists, was like hearing Olivier or Barrymore deliver a scientific paper. It was passionate, articulate, reasonable, and moving. Dr. King had taken our facts and suggestions, some literature references, and made a masterpiece for us all.

At the reception following the talk, Dr. King grasped my hand firmly in both of his and said "Thank you." It was an unforgettable reward.

Now that my hand has vicariously shaken hands with Lincoln, and directly with Martin Luther King a century later, I hope in my lifetime to be able to shake hands with somebody of equal stature to Lincoln or King.

Somebody who will lead the way to a better and trauma-free future for all this planet's inhabitants.

This person may only be a child today, so I wish to shake this hand before my hand just shakes.

Chapter Last. The Human Family Reunion

*"We stand in life at midnight; we are always on
the threshold of a new dawn."*
— Martin Luther King Jr.

*"The nation that draws too broad a difference between its
scholars and its warriors will have its thinking done
by cowards, and its fighting done by fools."*
— Thucydides, 431 B.C.E. *(History of the Peloponnesian Wars)*
as relayed by Benjamin Tong in 2007.

*At the large family annual gathering, the grandfather,
as the eldest, emerged to welcome his brethren:
"Hello to some of you" he said.*

All of our species on earth today are survivors that can be DNA-traced back over thousands of generations to a single specific parent (Oppenheimer, 2002, 2004; Wells 2003, 2004, 2007). Their descendants left East Africa and disbursed over the earth. Across the millennia of migration, surviving branches of our family settled into their own geographic regions. There they were shaped by the environment and life around them, including their skin color and other physical features, their food choices, and even their behavior. It is a mistake to overlook just how much what surrounds us shapes us, particularly over millennia (McDonald, 1998).

From these pockets of intergenerational humanity grew the gifts and challenges of varying cultures, languages, beliefs, inventions. These groups, mostly isolated from one another, developed important potentials for our family, more than a thousand flowers blooming. That is, until the most recent millennia of our family history.

Transportation revolutions, faster than climatic-inspired migrations, began connecting these disparate family branches. Bodies of knowledge reflected the diverse accomplishments of culture. Then electronic communication, ever accelerating in capacity, began reconnecting all the families. Some languages died out, others integrated many tongues into one. The new connectedness allowed music, the arts, and a growing shared sense of humor to strengthen family mental health, to bring productive healing change to new generations (Morgan, 2012abc).

We are now in an era when the gifts and challenges of the dispersion of our family are coming home to form a global culture. Much can be lost in this process, yet the contributions are immense. This is a consolidation phase for the human family- a coming home of ideas. Such a reunion can elevate us or destroy us. Families are like that.

A San Francisco Family Time Statue: Hoo Hah and the Dry Cleaner (1994)

That week, our catch phrase was the then street-current inexplicable phrase *"Hoo Hah"* which apparently now meant something of the female anatomy protected by feminine hygiene. "Careful of your *Hoo Hah*" was retrospectively a strange but then very funny thing to say when Becky was doing home exercises or lifting something. Couples married for more than a few anniversaries can begin to manifest this sappiness of phrase, a new one every week or so, to mutual hilarity. Umm. Often mutual.

We had just moved back to San Francisco, renting the same La Playa apartment at Ocean Beach. The Christopher Lee *"Burning Man"* film had inspired the actual night fires all along the beach to launch the original annual Burning Man ceremony.

To escape the unpacking, at least for a little while, we set out to find a drycleaner. Easier now since we no longer needed regular laundry done; Becky insists on washer dryer access. As we drove the neighborhood (no computer search first), on Geary I saw a small dry cleaning store with a soft glow around the entrance. "That's it" I said, and Becky pulled over, her brow sending a clear question mark, yet kindly unsaid.

Inside was the elderly and friendly co-owner, Mr. Ng. He had come to San Francisco from China when, as he put it, the city was still young. Young enough for his new San Francisco bride to buy their dry cleaning store for very little money, perhaps with some help from her family. They not only owned the store, they were the complete staff. She did the books and he was the talent. Soon we were both impressed by his wizardry. No stain survived his action (and I am definitely a cereal spiller). The cost was always reasonable, especially for this city.

One day we dropped off the weekly dry cleaning only to find Mr. Ng hunched over and limping in pain to the counter. He was pleased to tell us why. (Sometimes when you say "How are you?" to an elderly citizen, you get much more than a "Fine," maybe half an hour more of medical specifics. An elderly woman who was used to this called it "an organ recital.")

In this case we really cared about what had happened to the endearing Mr. Ng.

Turned out he and his wife had been arguing about the business (we didn't ask).

Shortly after this, he climbed a ladder to step out on a ledge and change a light bulb. Task complete, he stepped backwards to the ladder that he had climbed up on.

It was no longer there. He fell. Back still hurt. His wife had apologized for moving the ladder but he said she seemed strangely happy when she did.

Following our genuinely expressed sympathy, Mr. Ng began sorting through our dry cleaning pieces, slowly, one at a time. He always checked the pockets before taking in any work. Out of a pocket in one of Becky's shirts fell a note I had put there for her to find. Which she had not. But Mr. Ng did. And said: "*Vass iss zis HOO HAH?*"

Becky flushed, smiled, and flourished a palm up gesture to me, meaning "*You* explain!"

I knew that the paper messages in fortune cookies were first used to signal the day of a coming rebellion against the Mongol invaders in a language they couldn't read; if they asked what it said, the Mongol was told "It says you have good fortune coming" (thanks Ben Tong).

I used the fortune cookie defense.

"*Good luck: It means you will have no pain soon*" I said.

He looked over his shoulder at his wife in the back room. I think he interpreted his pain-free fortune as a warning of a swift death from behind. We left quickly.

We still smile when one of us says "Vass iss zis *HOO HAH?*

Especially since Mr. Ng actually went on to survive and thrive.

Difficult Relatives

Behavioral therapists are now advertising on our communications media. As a public service this can be family-healthy but if the profit is key, then other things happen.

One oft-repeated radio ad promising "total transformation" begins: ***"I will never forget the day my son Jeremy said 'I hate you!' and slammed the door in my face."*** The day her son Jeremy slammed the door in her face may be the day he heard this ad. Jeremy is probably a well-behaved adult now and may resent his mother reminding him and the whole listening human family of his past childhood bad behavior. Solely to build a business on dealing with miscreants like him.

TIME STATUES

And then there is the explanation currently circulating across our global economic network as to why many of our elder family members, due to global economic depressions, are too often forced to leave retirement and apply for a job, with mixed success.

Their resources of extensive experience and the confidence of longevity may be somewhat diverted by the less inhibited tendency of some to favor candor over diplomacy. A mark of awareness of impending expiration dates that comes with great longevity.

With few resources outside the military base, people of Guam made do with the best they could find. For some, this meant Christmas was a lean time.

I am reminded of that earlier era in Nova Scotia when many middle school age children I tested did not know their birthday. Parents withheld this basic information so nobody would have to have a birthday without presents: birthdays were celebrated for everybody at Christmas. In Guam though there was more of a community feeling. Holidays were ongoing and neighbors made sure they were fun.

The Shaking Artist

He had black polish on his fingernails and very long hair. James was in his thirties and was calmly discussing his art and his communal life in his new San Francisco home.

James had left Buffalo, New York, the month before although he could not say exactly why. He was in my clinic office because, for no apparent reason, he would from time to time start shaking uncontrollably.

He was tall and athletic, self-assured, and utterly mystified by these shakes. He wanted me to solve the mystery for him and banish the problem.

When I asked him to do some deep breathing and to visualize what was causing the anxiety, he complied but in seconds was vibrating in a near epileptic fit.

I changed the focus and asked him to visualize his best art. The shaking stopped.

I decided to work on rapport first, being clear that we would not address the cause any more that session. He relaxed completely. Rapport was easy- we had grown up in the same city and he had sought me out after reading a light novel I once wrote about it. He agreed to return the following week at the same day and time.

Using visual and relaxation exercises over several sessions, and a distancing technique (client asked to imagine a photograph of a painting of the problem) he was able to realize he had left his home at the other end of the country because he was running away from something traumatic. Something "lethal." Each session we gave a little more time to these exercises but none were devoid of shaking.

He did eventually feel safe enough (a key trauma basic) in my office to visualize a photograph of a document that underlay his trauma. It was a medical document and the words standing out above the rest were "**terminal cancer**."

Now we could begin the reality phase of our work.

He was able to fully recall the diagnosis and his running away from it. Now he no longer shook because he knew what the catastrophic fear was based on. With my support he agreed to get an immediate and complete medical examination. Somewhat embarrassed, he brought me the report. The cancer was in complete remission. He was healthy.

And if he had not confronted his catastrophic fear, he would have lived out a full life with constant anxiety attacks. Facing trauma's origin works.

APPLICATION: David Cheek's discovery recalled once more

David Cheek, in his many years as a gynecologist, was told by a teenage patient that she was having nightmares about people laughing at her and she had no explanation.

David had taught her autohypnosis, as he did all his patients, and she willingly went into a light trance. With David's guidance she recalled a conversation from her recent appendectomy.

She was under general anesthetic and unconscious but the memory was clear. She had a weight problem and the surgeon was joking about her appearance to his operating room nurses. The operation went well but the patient left with unconscious trauma.

It was one of David's greatest contributions to us all: we can remember what is said while we are under general anesthetic. More than that, we are in an emergency state of crisis which means we are in a highly suggestible level of hypnosis. Helpful words can aid a patient's healing and the wrongs ones could kill (Cheek 1968; Rossi & Cheek 1994).

In the case of David's teenaged patient, she now knew the origin of her nightmares and could confront them. She scheduled and held an appointment with her surgeon.

He was stunned that she was aware of his misplaced sense of humor. Confirming her memory, he apologized. No more nightmares.

*   *   *

"People don't want to go to war.... But, after all, it's the leaders of the country who determine the policy, and it's always a simple matter to drag the people along whether it's a democracy or a fascist dictatorship or a parliament or a communist dictatorship.... Voice or no voice, the people can always be brought to the bidding of the leaders. That is easy. All you have to do is tell them they are being attacked and denounce the pacifists for lack of patriotism and exposing the country to greater danger. It works the same way in any country." (Hermann Goering, during the Nuremberg trials, 1946).

Goering was convicted of crimes against humanity and sentenced to death by hanging. Two hours before the scheduled execution, he committed suicide with potassium cyanide (Frank 2007).

Psychologist Gene T. Orro's Emphatic Memorial Day Tribute remarks, the year 2000:

"As the search for peace remains in vain

The thought of war and heroes give me pain

So I dare to be so rude

As to wish the ants your picnic food

And pray the clouds obscure your sun with shade

And rain water, cats and dogs, on your parade."

It was read at his own memorial not long after.

> Dear God, Instead of Letting people die and haveing to make new ones why don't you just keep the ones you got now?
>
> Jane

"Sometimes a play or movie or performance is abysmal, so deadening that we mourn the loss of the time spent watching it as a piece of our life that we can never get back. If then we are asked 'How was it?' a San Francisco ACT reply is often 'It had its moments.' We are now living through such moments." (Tong 2006).

Brain Trauma as an Opportunity, or Where the Rock of Probability Theory Went Wrong

My younger brother and I have always been close friends. When I ask him why we never argued like so many brothers and sisters do, he just smiles and says "You were always bigger."

It could also be because he was and is the best man I know, brilliant, kind, and full of fun. With an 8-year age difference between us, I more often had the role of parent than brother.

TIME STATUES

Our mother and father had survived economic depression and both came from large families (9 and 14 respectively). That may explain why birthday and Christmas gifts were always very practical: mostly socks, underwear and shoes. I took it on myself then to work at door-to-door sales and other jobs a mobile child can do, long enough to buy genuine toys for my only brother.

A tape recorder was one such gift although I do remember using it more than he did (well, I *was* bigger). Given all of that, I still feel uncomfortable about a few things I did, at times more a child than a parent. Like the time I was told I had to play hide and seek with him at home when I usually went to the movies with friends. That particular Saturday, once he finished counting, he never found me. Even after hours of scouring the large house. Probably because I was at the movies.

But there was something worse.

When I was 15 and my brother was 7, we were left to fend for ourselves on a family holiday in the mountains. Our parents were asleep in the isolated cabin. The quiet Sunday afternoon would have been heaven for bird and tree watchers, so we were profoundly bored.

We decided to toss rocks over the cabin and see how near we could get to a small target circle we had set up on the ground on the other side. So we took turns throwing rocks over the roof and racing around to see exactly how close we had come to the target. Not very close. Of course, throwing blind over a cabin to a target the size of a dinner plate was not easy.

My brother, seeing me discouraged, suggested that maybe our rocks had actually hit closer than it seemed and then rolled away. Hmmm. I suggested he go to the other side of the cabin and see exactly where the rock hit before it rolled. You see where this is going.

I did *not* want the rock to hit him, so I told him that I wanted him to spot my throws in a very safe place. He asked where the safest place was. This is when I explained my understanding of probability theory to him.

Although a teenager, I did subscribe to science fiction magazines after all and Isaac Asimov had recently explained clearly that we all live in a world where every action can have many different outcomes, a probabilistic world is our way of navigating reality, reality being a consensus.

What this meant for my brother is that I wanted him to stand in the place my rock was least likely to hit him: the one place, given how hard a shot it was (blind over the roof to a small target), that my rock was least likely to hit. He should stand on the target circle itself.

What were the odds that I could possibly hit that tiny a target? Highly unlikely, based on our past shots. Then from there he could see very easily how close my rock came. Made sense to him. So he ran around and stood on the target dish, yelling ready when he was there.

Well, you saw this coming and you were right.

He saw it coming too and stood his ground, relying on the probability theory his big brother had given him. A doubter would have ducked, not him. I heard a *"thunk"* and an *"Oh!"*

Running around the cabin, I saw him lying on the ground next to the target dish, blood running from his scalp. He seemed to be unconscious or in shock. He wasn't moving.

I started to run over to him but out of the cabin came our father, a very strong and angry man. Worse, he had been mercilessly oppressed as a child by his eldest brother. Now, what he saw before him was a biblical scene: Cain and Abel all over again. Ignoring my brother he took off after me. That was the day I knew how very gifted I was at running fast.

Eventually, after dark, I circled back. Hours had gone by, my brother was up and apparently okay. As was his nature, he forgave me instantly as he and I both knew I had not meant for that to happen, right? (Will the psychologists reading this please not read anything into it?) Given my brother's apparent full recovery, my father decided to let me live, my mother's vote as well.

Of course, they did blame that rock from then on for any aberrant illness or behavior on my brother's part. This included his years as a hippie at Haight/Ashbury, and his early departure from high school without graduating.

This so he might, at the age of 15 and, with my assistance, begin college at the University of Chicago (his perfect SAT Math and near perfect SAT English helped).

He did show some evidence of lasting trauma now and then. For one, he got a doctorate in Engineering and Physics at the University of California Berkeley.

Worse, after years of distinguished research as a professor at this university, he agreed to take on an administrative job as Director of their affiliated International Computer Science Institute which continued for decades.

Today he is a founder of UPRISE, designed to aid candidates for election whose talent is not supported by adequate funding. He is also a successful father, grandfather, uncle, husband, musician, and friend.

Our parents were convinced to the day they died that my rock had given their younger son brain trauma and was responsible for changing his life thereafter.

Maybe they are right.

Okay brother, no need for thanks.

* * *

Back to Guam.

WHERE DID THEY GO?

Found in Guam's jungle is the Monitor Lizard.

While it does have a venomous bite, its main defense is bacterial infection. As it's crawling with lethal disease, Chamorros warn their children to stay as far away from them as possible.

The bacterial defense has also been a major cause of the disappearance of human populations.

Historically, Europeans in the middle ages believed that deadly pneumonia or plague was brought on by bathing. Royalty typically were bathed only twice in their life, at birth and at death. Hence the heavy use of perfume. This of course brought on epidemics of disease. The Black Plague of medieval times wiped out a third of the population. Survivors had immunity and continued to carry lethal bacteria from the unbathed lifestyle. This was a defense as strong as the Monitor Lizard had. The indigenous peoples of North America had little or no protection against the bacteria crawling on European pioneers. The majority died.

Whole civilizations, per archeological digs, seemed to disappear in a generation. Where did they go? Epidemics may well be the cause. Epidemics from contact with people or animals carrying disease for which they had no protection.

Was this another reason for the Great Wall of China? Defense against foreign plague?

Going much farther back in time, what happened to the Neanderthal? Where did they go?

They had lived for eons in Europe before our branch of the human family made it out of Africa to settle in their territory. The fact that modern people of European descent usually show Neanderthal DNA of one or two per cent gives evidence that the contact was often close and intimate.

The Covid-19 pandemic has sensitized us to the lethal history that viruses and bacteria may well have played in our erratic patterns of survival.

Science today has noted that the Covid-19 plague turned out to be more dangerous for those with traces of Neanderthal DNA. Where did the Neanderthal go? Into the ground apparently. And into our DNA.

Our human family has branches that may have been and continue to be as dangerous as the Monitor Lizards in Guam's jungles.

The Day of the Hobbit

It was May of the year 2000 in Guam, entrance to the 21st century and a new millennium.

Somewhere in that month I passed out on the stairs on my way to teach my class.

I was only out for a minute or two, fast getting up, saying I was fine, pretending that I was.

After my class, the Dean wanted to see me. He said that sometimes people like me, walking to the university on a hot day like that day, well, they just fainted. But I knew that wasn't the problem. I never faint. Maybe I needed a checkup for my heart. Soon.

Still, the next afternoon I set out again for the walk to my campus. I wore heavy shoes and asked my feet to stand tall, not let me pass out. I could feel *"trouble be knocking at my door"* as some Pacific islanders like to say.

I got about halfway to campus when I saw her. She was barefoot yet walked out of the jungle with ease. Nobody walked into the jungle barefoot, the snakes alone … yet there she was. She looked like a child with an older person's face. She was about three and a half feet tall. She wore a yellow dress and had a yellow ribbon in her hair.

She calmly started walking next to me. Said *"What would you like to know?"*

Years after I still think of all the questions I should have asked. At the time though, we were approaching that massive usually vicious dog chained to a pillar, a chain keeping it just short of the road. It always tried to bite anybody passing, more like wanting to tear somebody apart, not a great part of my daily walk.

But today! When I walked by the dog it quietly watched me, not even rising. Still wasn't friendly. But smiled the way dogs can smile, mixed both hateful and happy it seemed.

I asked the girl *"Why is that dog so full of rage? From being chained up?"*

She regarded the dog a second. Said *"No. She had only one litter and it was drowned in a sack. She has wanted to kill people ever since. Chaining her up is necessary and she knows it."*

I asked a second question: *"Why is she so quiet then with me today?"*

"She can sense your heart is stopping and starting. She knows you are dying. It makes her happy."

We walked quietly for a bit while I digested that.

I objected *"I wasn't the one who drowned her puppies. Why so hateful with me?"*

Yellow Dress shook her head. *"She sees all humans, your kind, as the same. Being around humans for so long changed her. Humans are like that too you know."*

We got to a shelter, a bus stop with seats and a narrow roof.

It was beginning to rain. Windy horizontal Pacific rain, intense, but short. Tourists asking about the weather in Guam are a joke. It's always raining somewhere and the sun is always shining everywhere else.

To the Chamorro of Guam, there are usually only two locations on earth: Guam and "off-island."

Not counting the locations lost in time: *"Take the east road and turn past where the post office used to be."* We waited. When the rain stopped, not a long wait, we continued on our way.

Clearly, she did not seem used to such a lack of questions. She stopped as the jungle on our left came to its end and the campus began.

She smiled and said *"Well, what do you have for me today?"*

I used to carry edibles for children but that day I had nothing. I shrugged and said *"Nothing today. Maybe another day."*

She looked stunned, as though nobody had ever said that to her before. She then turned and walked back into the jungle.

I got a little closer to work, opposite a high school playing field, before I lost consciousness.

I woke on the ground not long after. Noticed my left ankle was broken at a right angle to the leg. Shoe was trying to do its job.

I reached down and snapped the foot back into place at the ankle.

When I woke again, the paramedics were there. The high school student that had called them was saying *"When his leg snapped, the crack sounded like a rifle or an explosion. So loud!"*

Apparently my heart block was expected to be fatal and soon. So they called the only cardiologist on the island (excluding the military base which was off limits).

There had been two cardiologists but this one was at the funeral of the other. He got there just in time to put in a pacemaker, a more current model I still use now 20 years later. That first pacemaker was the last one on the island. Saved my life.

A year later, veteran of two open heart surgeries, I was well enough to be back in class. Being in a wheelchair then, my class was held in my leased hotel apartment, in the long living room with six tables and chairs.

Since the hotel was at the edge of the campus, students were pleased to come there. Not only was it better than the usual classroom but my hotel had covered parking, great for the episodic rain torrents.

The first thing my students wanted was a complete update. So I told them about the girl in the yellow dress with the yellow bow in her hair. They called her *"Tautaumona."*

They said *"You should have given her a gift!"*

Note: Not long ago, they found evidence in Indonesia of an ancient separate branch of humanity, termed "the Hobbit." This is a label annoying diminutive Indonesians on the Island where they found the skeleton. Here is a better description of what they found: *"Homo floresiensis ("Flores Man;" nicknamed "Hobbit") is a small species of archaic human which inhabited the island of Flores, Indonesia until the arrival of modern humans about 50,000 years ago. The remains of an* *individual who would have stood about 1.1 m (3 ft 7 in) in height were discovered in 2003 at Liang Bua on the island of Flores in Indonesia."* Phys.Org, Feb 2016. https://phys.org/news/2016-02-mystery-hobbits-humans.html

Stories of the "little people" abound in cultures around the world. Menehunes in Hawaii, Leprecauns in Ireland, Yunwi Tsunsdi for the Cherokee, Tautaumona in Guam and the surrounding islands.

Are they still around, this alternate branch of humanity? Well, Pygmies still live in Africa.

Was the person walking with me that day a "hobbit?"

Staff at the Smithsonian reconstructed a face from the skull they found in Indonesia.

Here it is.

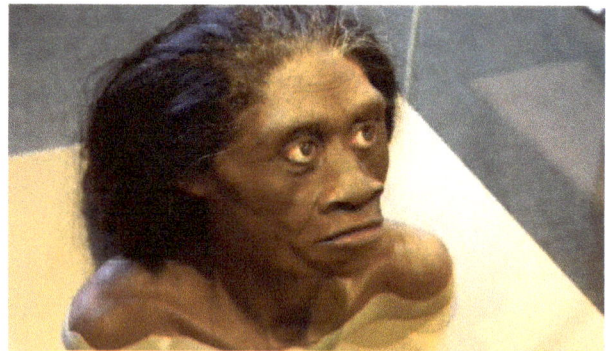

Yes.

Add a yellow bow. That's her.

Back to Now

TIME STATUES

I walked through a neighborhood characteristic of the earliest years of the 21st century.

The scenery in the Sierras was breath-taking, full of energy. Leaves on the trees blazed with reds, yellows, orange, blue and green. The air was crisp, and the sky a darkening navy blue. A few dozen hawks circled to the south, considering a move to warmer skies.

As to the human scenery back in the city, at this writing I am seeing a divided world fighting to retain its vibrant color—too much endless silver, black, white, and gray. Metal metaphor for an increasingly politicized era, one too often devoid of nuance and unity, an era of trauma and war, abandonment of so many victims of Racism, Covid, Climate Change, Corruption (the RCCC). A "risk shift" where health care and retirement are increasingly absent from government or employer (Hacker 2006), sanctification of trauma and torture, and authoritative proclamations of fascist danger at every corner.

Many of the more recent years of our new millennium might well have been called the *Propane Decades*: toxic, explosive, colorless, and odorless, but with a bad smell added to let you know it's there. What grayness of spirit in contrast to the pervasive beauty of nature disappearing all around us as the climate deteriorates our habitat.

How did it happen by the end years of the second decade that suddenly *"the end justifies the means"* was the basis for so many living with others or, sheltering in place, living or even dying alone?

Had we lost knowing that the means is an essential end in itself? Did our entry into a new millennium so frighten so many of our global decision makers that they jumped us back in time, stopping briefly for breath in the 1950s, and then race in reverse eight more centuries to despotic medieval times. Was this to rerun the Crusades and void the Magna Carta? The hateful despotic days replaying what led up to the Second World War? Was it safer living our life in the past lane?

How was it that such a large fraction of our human community were willing to turn their back on the beauty and promise of a new century, working against their own best interests? Was it manipulated fear? We had so many false alarms, the real dangers magnified many times, until we became used to the rhetoric of danger. Each new RCCC traumatic crisis left people still shaken, but not stirred. So: How did such large numbers of people in the early 21st century allow themselves to become so devastatingly traumatized as to turn their backs on the boundless resources and opportunity available to a new millennium?

But wait. Possibly this is the reactionary turbulence prefacing and catalyzing a transition to a truly advanced nonlinear future. At this writing change may be coming, change for the better. Look at the millions of people marching in the street, when not under semi-voluntary home arrest to avoid pandemic. Around the world people of all ages are demanding progress. The younger generation particularly is more involved than ever in creating a better future. We have the opportunity to enter these newer decades, ones fresh, untouched. If we succeed it can truly be the threshold of a new dawn. It will not be easy. Struggle ahead.

TIME STATUES

The New Address

Our family home: now the entire earth. Maintenance responsibility to come. Hopefully.

References

Adams, H. F. (1912). Autokinetic sensations. *Psychological Monographs*, 14, 1-45. American Psychological Association (2019) Petition for Recognition of Post-Doctoral Specialty in Serious Mental Illness (SMI). Washington DC: American Psychological Association.

American Psychological Association & Jansen, M.A. (2014) Recovery to Practice Initiative Curriculum: Reframing psychology for the emerging health care environment. Washington DC: American Psychological Association.

Archer, L.A. (2013) *Verbal Aikido - Green Belt: The art of directing verbal attacks to a balanced outcome*. North Charleston, SC: CreateSpace.

Bandler, R. & Grinder, J. (1982) *Reframing: Neuro-Linguistic Programming and the Transformation of Meaning*. Boulder, CO: Real People Press.

Bartley, W. W. (1988) Werner Erhard: the transformation of a man, the founding of EST. New York: Clarkson Potter (Crown/Random House).

Barch, A.M., Ratner, S.C., & Morgan, R.F. (1965) Extinction and latent reacquisition. *Psychonomic Science*, $\underline{3}$, 495-496.

Battino, R. (2006) *Expectation: the very brief therapy book*. Norwalk, CT: Crown House.

Beier, E. G. & Young, D. M. (1998) *The Silent Language of Psychotherapy*. NY: Aldine.

Bickford, J. (2002) *Delancey Street Foundation: American Dreams*. Las Vegas, Nevada: American Dreams.

Bonastia, C. (2012) *Southern stalemate: Five years without public education in Prince Edward County*. Chicago: University of Chicago Press.

Booth, M. (1997) *The Doctor and the Detective: a biography of Sir Arthur Conan Doyle*. New York: Thomas Dunne/St. Martin's Minotaur.

Bousfield W.A., Sedgewick C.H.W. (1944) An analysis of sequences of restricted associative responses. *Journal of General Psychology. 30*:149–165.

Brandt, D. (1973). *Play Therapy with Adults: Effects on Child Rearing and Self Concept*. Ph.D. dissertation, California School of Professional Psychology, San Francisco.

Braud, W. & R. Anderson (1998). *Transpersonal Research Methods for the Social Sciences: Honoring Human Experience (Progress in Neural Processing; 7)*. Thousand Oaks, CA: SAGE.

Braud, W. & L. Dossey (2003) *Distant Mental Influence: Its Contributions to Science, Healing, and Human Interactions (Studies in Consciousness).* Newburyport, Massachusetts: Hampton Roads; Russell Targ Editions.

Breggin, P.R. (1994) *Toxic psychiatry.* New York: St. Martins

Breggin, P.R. (2007) *Your drug may be your problem.* New York: HarperCollins

Breggin, P.R. & Cohen, D, (2007) *Your drug may be your problem.* New York: HarperCollins.

Buckley, K. W. "Misbehaviorism: The Case of John B. Watson's Dismissal from Johns Hopkins University." In J.T. Todd & E.K. Morris, *Modern Perspectives on John B. Watson and Classical Behaviorism.* Greenwood Press, 1994.

Burr, T. (1965) *BISBA.* Trenton NJ: Hercules.

Bütz, M.R. (1997). *Chaos and complexity: Implications for psychological theory and practice.* Washington, D.C.: Taylor & Francis.

Bütz, M.R. and Schwinn, R. (2004) "Transforming Crisis Theory in Behavioral Healthcare: Moving from stasis to developmental adaptation." Paper presented to the Society for Chaos Theory in Psychology and the Life Sciences, Marquette University, July 16, 2004.

Cardeña, E., S.J. Lynn, & S. Krippner (Eds.). (2000). *Varieties of Anomalous Experience: Examining the scientific evidence.* Washington, DC: American Psychological Association.

Cardeña, E., & K. Croyle (Eds.) (2005). *Acute reactions to trauma and psychotherapy: A multidisciplinary and international perspective.* New York: Haworth Press. Also published as special issue of the *Journal of Trauma and Dissociation*, 6(2).

Cardeña, E., & M. Winkelman (2011a). *Altering consciousness. Multidisciplinary perspectives. Volume I. History, culture, and the humanities.* Santa Barbara, CA: Praeger.

Cardeña, E., & M. Winkelman (2011b). *Altering consciousness. Multidisciplinary perspectives. Volume II. Biological and psychological perspectives.* Santa Barbara, CA: Praeger.

Cardeña, E., S.J. Lynn & Krippner, S. (Eds.). (2014). *Varieties of Anomalous Experience: Examining the scientific evidence. 2nd ed.* Washington, DC: American Psychological Association.

Cardeña, E. (2014) ""What do anomalous experiences tell us about the potentials of consciousness?" International Workshop on East-West Approaches to the Nature of Mind, Consciousness and Self Lecture on extraordinary experience: https://www.youtube.com/watch?v=APcVsHdBkfY

Cheek, D. B. (1968) *Clinical hypnotherapy*. New York: Grune & Stratton.

Cheek, D.B. (1993) *Hypnosis: the application of ideomotor techniques*. New York: Allyn & Bacon.

Cheek, D. B. & L. LeCron (1968) *Clinical hypnotherapy*. New York: Grune & Stratton

Clavell, J. (1986) *Shogun*. New York: Dell.

Corsini, R. & Wedding, D. (2010) *Current Psychotherapies*, 9th edition. New York: Brooks-Cole.

Consortium for Longitudinal Studies (1983) *As the twig is bent: Lasting effects of preschool programs*. Lawrence Erlbaum: Hillsdale, New Jersey.

Cochran, M. (2004) *Impact of Reported Encounters with a Ghost: An Examination of 12 Experiences*. Ph.D. dissertation at Sofia University, Palo Alto, California.

Coon, D. J. "'Not a Creature of Reason': The Alleged Impact of Watsonian Behaviorism on Advertising in the 1920s." In J.T. Todd & E.K. Morris, *Modern Perspectives on John B. Watson and Classical Behaviorism*. Greenwood Press, 1994.

Craine, J.F. & Gudeman, H.E. (1981) The Rehabilitation of Brain Function: Principles, Procedures and Techniques of Neurotraining. Springfield: Thomas.

Crowley, T. (1958) Personal communication.

Duran, E. (2006) Healing the soul wound: counseling with American Indians and other native peoples. New York: Teacher's College Press.

Edwards, W. (2013) *The Real Life Sherlock Holmes: A Biography of Joseph Bell - The True Inspiration of Sherlock Holmes and the Pioneer of Forensic Science*. North Charleston, SC: CreateSpace.

Elkind, L. (1972) *Effects of hypnosis on the process of aging*. San Francisco, CA: California School of Professional Psychology. Unpublished doctoral dissertation.

Elkind, L. (1981) Hypnotic intervention: Elkind's contribution. Chapter 2 in R. F. Morgan *Interventions in applied gerontology*. Toronto: Kendall/Hunt, 33-58.

Elkind, L. Personal communication.

Ellis, A. (1984) Personal communication at an APA convention meeting on the prevention of Iatrogenic practice.

Erickson, M.H., Rossi, E.L., and Ryan, M.O. (1984) *Life reframing in hypnosis*. Manchester, NH: Irvington.

Farber, S. (1956) Personal communication from Dr. Sidney Farber, founder of the Dana-Farber Hospital in Boston and discoverer of the first successful childhood leukemia treatment.

Farber, P.H. (1999). MDMA and Hypnotic Anchoring. In T. Lyttle (Ed.). *Psychedelics Reimagined* (pp.87-90). Brooklyn: Autonomedia.

Fouts, R. ((1997) *Next of Kin: My conversations with Chimpanzees*. New York: Quill/HarperCollins.

Fraisse, P. (1963) The Psychology of Time. NY: Harper & Row.

Freud, A. (1979) The ego and the mechanisms of defense: revised edition. Madison, CT: International Universities Press (original work 1936).

Galton, F. (1907) *Inquiries into human faculty and its development*. 2nd edition, New York: Dutton.

Green, R.L. (Ed.) (1969) *Racial Crisis in American Education*. Chicago: Follett.

Green, R.L., Hoffman, L.J., & Morse, R.J. (1964a) *Educational Status of Children during the First Year Following Four Years of Little or No Schooling: CRP 2498*. Washington, D.C.; U.S. Office of Education.

Green, R.L., Hoffman, L.J., Morse, R.J. & Hayes, M. (1964b) *Educational Status of Children in a District without Public Schools: CRP 3221*. Washington, D.C.: U.S. Office of Education.

Green, R.L., Morgan, R.F. & Hoffman, L.J. (1967) Effects of deprivation on intelligence, achievement, and cognitive growth: A review. *Journal of Negro Education,* 36, 5-14.

Green, R.L. & Morgan, R.F. (1969) The effects of resumed schooling on the measured intelligence of Prince Edward County's black children. *Journal of Negro Education*, 38, 147-155.

Gudeman, H.E. (1982) Clinical Neuropsychology. J. Nervous and Mental Disease, 170, 124.

Gudeman, H.E. (1984) At the Interface between Ethics and Neurobiology. Contemporary Psychology: A Journal of Reviews, 11, 878-879.

Gustavson, C.R. & Gustavson, J.C. (1985) Predation control using conditioned food aversion methodology: theory, practice and implications. *Annals of the New York Academy of Sciences*, 443, 348-356. Published 2006: *linelibrary.wiley.com.*

Hastings, A. (1980) *Health for the Whole Person: The Complete Guide to Holistic Medicine* 1st

Hastings, A. (1994). Some observations on MDMA experiences induced through posthypnotic suggestion. *Journal of Psychoactive Drugs, 26* (1), 77-83.

London: Routledge.

Hastings, A. (2000). Paper presented at Tucson IV 2000 "Toward a Science of Consciousness" Conference: An extended non-drug MDMA-like experience evoked through hypnotic suggestion. *Bulletin of the Multidisciplinary Association for Psychedelic Studies* [Online], *10*(1), 10.

Hastings, A. (2006) An Extended Nondrug MDMA-Like Experience Evoked Through Posthypnotic Suggestion. *J. Psychoactive Drugs*, 38 (3): 273-283.

Hastings, A, I. Berk, M. Cougar, G. Ferguson, S. Steinbach-Humphrey, K. McLellan, C. Mitchell & B. Viglizzo (2000). An extended non-drug MDMA experience evoked through posthypnotic suggestion. (Abstract from *Toward a Science of Consciousness Conference Proceedings*. Tucson. AZ). *M A P S B u l l e t i n* 10 (1): 10.

Hastings, A., Ferguson, E., Hutton, M., Goldman, A., Braud, W., Greene, E., Bennett, C., Hewett, M., Berk, I., Lind, V., Boynton, T., and McLellan, M. (2002). Psychomanteum research: experiences & effects on bereavement. *Omega J. Death and Dying, 45* (3), 211-228.

Healy, D. (2006) Lifetime suicide rates in treated Schizophrenia: 1875-1924,1994-1999 cohorts. *British J. Psychiatry, 118*, 223-228.

Herink, R., ed. (1980) *The Psychotherapy Handbook*. New York: Meridian.

Hoehn, A.J. & Woolman, M. (1969) Operational context training in individual technical skills: ED041233 . Clearinghouse for Federal Scientific & Technical Information: Springfield, Virginia.

Hogan, E. O. & Green, R. L. (1971) Can Teachers Modify Children's Self-Concepts? Teachers College *Record*, 72 (3) 423-426.

Jacobson, E. (1964) Personal communication. Michigan State University, East Lansing, Michigan.

Karon, B.P. (1975) *Black scars: rigorous investigation of the effects of discrimination, with an appendix on the Southern white*. New York: Springer.

Karon, B.P. & Vandenbos, G. ((1981) Psychotherapy of Schizophrenia: the treatment of choice. New York: Aronson.

Karon, B. P. & Widener, A.J. (1999) The tragedy of Schizophrenia: its myth of incurability. Ethical human services and sciences, 1 (no 3), 195-211.

Kay, P. and Kempton, W. (1984). "What is the Sapir-Whorf Hypothesis?" *American Anthropologist* 86(1): 65-79.

Kimble, G.A., Wertheimer, M., and White, C. (2013). *Portraits of Pioneers in Psychology*. Psychology Press.

King, M.L. (1968) The Role of the Behavioral Scientist in the Civil Rights Movement. *J. Social Issues* 24 (1).

Kozol, J. (1967, 1985) *Death at an Early Age: The Destruction of the Hearts and Minds of Negro Children in the Boston Public Schools*. NY: Houghton-Mifflin, Plume.

Kozol, J. (2006) *The Shame of the Nation: The Restoration of Apartheid Schooling in America*. New York: Three Rivers Press.

Krippner, S. (1980) *Human Possibilities: Mind Research in the USSR and Eastern Europe*. New York: Anchor/Doubleday.

Krippner, R. (2016) *Shamanic Powers of Rolling Thunder* (with Sidian Morning Star Jones). Rochester, VT: Bear & Co.

Krippner, S. & H. Friedman (2010) *Debating Psychic Experience: Human Potential or Human Illusion?* Westport CT: Praeger.

Krippner, S. & I. Taitz (2018). Psychotherapeutic approaches for posttraumatic stress disorder nightmares. *International Journal of Dream Research,* in press.

Kuhn, T. S. (1996) *Structure of Scientific Revolutions*. 3rd ed. Chicago, IL: University of Chicago Press. (1st edition was in 1962).

LaBarre, W. (1961) *The human animal*. Chicago: University of Chicago Press.

Lazar, I., Darlington, R., Murray, H., Royce, J. Snipper, A., & Ramey, C.T. (1982) Lasting effects of early education: A report from the Consortium for Longitudinal Studies. *Monographs of the Society for Research in Child Development, 47 (2/3),* 1-151.

Lederer, R. (2005). *The revenge of anguished English*. New York: St. Martins.

Lewis, J.E., & S. Krippner (Eds.). (2016). *Working with dreams and PTSD nightmares: 14 approaches for psychotherapists and counselors*. Santa Barbara, CA: Praeger.

London, J. (1916/1986) Kanaka Surf. In *Stories of Hawaii*. Honolulu: Mutual.

McDonald, A. (1998) "On where we live as a primary determinant of who we are." Comment at the Senior Psychologists Session, American Psychological Association, San Francisco.

McKay-Riddell, Valentine (2014). Personal communication on use of the word "Epiphany."

McMullin, R.E. (2005) *Taking Out Your Mental Trash: A Consumer's Guide to Cognitive Restructuring Therapy*. New York: W.W. Norton.

McReynolds, P. (1997) *Lightner Witmer: his life and times*. Washington, D.C.: American Psychological Association.

May, R. (1986) Personal communication.

Morgan, A. K. (2011, March). The Malaysian people of the dream and traumatic nightmare intervention. *Journal of Tropical Psychology. 1*(1), 15-16. 10.1375/jtp.1.1.15 Cambridge University Press: http://dx.doi.org/10.1375/jtp.1.1.15

Morgan, A. K. (2014, December). Dream sharing as a healing method: Tropical roots and contemporary community potential. *Journal of Tropical Psychology,* 4(e12). doi:10.1017/jtp.2014.12. Cambridge University Press: http://dx.doi.org/10.1017/jtp.2014.12

Morgan, A. K. (2016). Dragons, angels, and rites of passage: The universal language of children's dreams. In C. Johnson & J. Campbell (Eds.), *Sleep monsters and superheroes: Empowering children through creative dreamplay* (pp. 69-87). Santa Barbara, CA: Praeger.

Morgan, A. K. (2018*). Dreamer's powerful tiger: A new lucid dreaming classic for children and parents of the 21st Century.* Ashland, OR: The Dreambridge.

Morgan, R.F. (1964a) The M/I frequencies: A quick and computation-free non-parametric method of test item evaluation. *Psychological Reports,* 14, 723-728.

Morgan, R.F. (1964b) A galvanic skin response technique for the sensory evaluation of annelids. M*ichigan Academy of Science Papers,* 50, 337-342. (Cf. M.A. thesis, Michigan State University, 1964.)

Morgan, R.F. (1964c) The adaptational behavior of chicks in a spinning environment. *Psychological Record, 14,* 153-156.

Morgan, R.F. (1965a) Do-it-yourself hallucinations. *Science Digest, 57,* May, 41-43.

Morgan, R.F. (1965b) Temporal conditioning in humans as a function of intertrial interval and stimulus intensity. *Dissertation Abstracts,* 37, No. 66-6153. From R. Morgan's Ph.D. dissertation, Michigan State University, 1965.

Morgan, R.F. (1965) Note on the psychopathology of senility: senescent defense against the threat of death. Psychological Reports, 16, 305-306.

Morgan, R.F. (1967) Memory and the senile psychoses: A follow-up note. Psychological Reports, 20, 733-734.

Morgan, R.F. (1968a) The Adult Growth Examination (AGE): preliminary comparisons of physical aging in adults by sex and race. *Perception & Motor Skills,* 27, 595-599.

Morgan, R.F. (1968b) The need for greater use of efficiency percentages to supplement reports of statistical significance. *Perceptual & Motor Skills,* 27, 338.

Morgan, R.F. (1968c) The definitive method for assessing the genetic basis for behavioral differences between the sexes. *Perceptual & Motor Skills*, 37, 90.

Morgan, R.F. (1969a) "Compensatory education and educational growth." Chapter 9 in Robert L. Green (Ed.), *Racial Crisis in American Education*. Chicago: Follett, 186-219.

Morgan, R.F. (1969b) How old are you? *London Sunday Times*, October 19th, 39.

Morgan, R.F. (1970) Techniques for assessing differential aging: How old are you? *Canadian Magazine*, February 28, 2-4.

Morgan, R.F. (1972a) The Adult Growth Exazination (AGE): validation, analysis, and cross-cultural utility of a compact brief test of individual aging. *Inter-American Journal of Psychology*, 6, 245-254.

Morgan, R.F. (1972b) Reliability of the Adult Growth Examination: a standardized test of individual aging. *Perceptual & Motor Skills, 34,* 415-419.

Morgan, R.F. (1976) *Conquest of Aging: Modern Measurement & Intervention. An Assessment-Centered Textbook of Applied Gerontology for the Behavioral, Social, Life, & Health Sciences*. Pueblo, Colorado: Applied Gerontology Communications.

Morgan, R.F. (1977a) The Adult Growth Examination: A follow-up note on comparisons between rapidly aging adults and slowly aging adults as defined by body age. *InterAmerican Journal of Psychology (Revista InterAmerican de Psicologia)*, 11, 10-13.

Morgan, R.F. (1977b) An introduction to applied gerontology. *Long Term Care & Health Services Administration Quarterly,* Summer, 1, 168-178.

Morgan, R.F (1981a) *Interventions in Applied Gerontology*. Dubuque, Iowa: Kendall/Hunt.

Morgan, R.F (1981b) *Measurement of Human Aging in Applied Gerontology*. Dubuque, Iowa: Kendall/Hunt.

Morgan, R.F. (1982) Balloon therapy. *Canadian Psychology*, 23, 45-46.

Morgan, R.F. (1983) Community dispersion or problem resolution?: hypothetical plight of community residential patients with appendicitis. *Psychological Reports, 53,* 353-354.

Morgan, R.F. (1994) "Human Biologic Age Determination: Adult Growth Examination" (Ch. 12). In A. Balin (Ed), *Human Biological Age Determination*. Boca Raton, Florida: CRC, 181-211.

Morgan, R.F. (Ed)(1999, 2005a) Electroshock: the Case Against. N. Charleston, SC: Booksurge & Chico, CA: Morgan Foundation. (Chapter IV reprinted in Brent Slife's *Taking Sides: Psychological Issues, 13th edition,* Guilford,

CT: McGraw-Hill/Dushkin, 2004 and in Richard P. Halgin's *Taking Sides: Abnormal Psychology, 2nd edition,* Guilford, CT: McGraw-Hill/Dushkin, 2002.)

Morgan, R.F. (2000, 2005b) Training the Time Sense: Hypnotic & Conditioning Approaches. (With Linn Cooper, Elizabeth Erickson, Milton Erickson, Gary Marshall, Christina Maslach, Paul Sacerdote, & Phillip Zimbardo.) Albuquerque, NM: Morgan Foundation.

Morgan, R.F. (2005c) The Iatrogenics Handbook: A Critical Look at Research & Practice in Helping Professions. Santa Cruz, CA: Morgan Foundation. (With Robert Alexander, Peter Breggin, Jeffrey Buck, David B. Cheek, Juanne Clarke, Frank Epling, Stanley Fevens, David Frey, John Friedberg, Glen Gabbard, D'Arcy Helmer, Lenore Jacobson, Mark Kamlet, Richard Mason, Michael Miller, Geoffrey Nelson, Carl Rogers, Robert Rosenthal, Jalal Shamsie, Thomas Szasz, Benjamin R. Tong, Stuart Twemlow, Kenneth Walker, J.B. Woodward). (Canada edition with Toronto: IPI.)

Morgan, R.F. (2008) *Opportunity's Shadow and the Bee Moth Effect: When Danger Transforms Community: an existential psychologist's approach to chaos and choice in social, community, clinical, and iatrogenic contexts.* Fairbanks, AK: Morgan Foundation.

Morgan, R.F. (2011a) Guam: the Brown Tree Snake invasion, and suicide prevention. *Journal of Tropical Psychology, 1,* 2011, 11-14.

Morgan, R.F. (2011b) Nations within Nations: A Maidu Murder Mystery. *Bulletin of the International Association of Applied Psychology*, January/April 2011, *23(1-2),* 63-64. Supplement to *Applied Psychology: an International Review.*

Morgan, R.F. (2012a) *Trauma Psychology in Context: International Vignettes and Applications from a Lifespan Clinical-Community Psychology Perspective.* Santa Cruz, CA: Morgan Foundation.

Morgan, R.F. (2012b) "Intuitive humor." Chapter in R. A. Neimeyer (Ed.) *Techniques of Grief Therapy: Creative Practices for Counseling the Bereaved.* Pp. 50-52. London/New York: Taylor & Francis/Routledge.

Morgan, Robert (2012c) "Group treatment of anticipatory grief in senior pseudo-psychosis." In Robert A. Neimeyer (Ed.) Techniques of Grief Therapy: Creative Strategies for Counseling the Bereaved. Section XIV Grieving with Others. Routledge: London/New York. Pp. 336-337.

Morgan, R.F. (2012d). "Anticipatory grief through visualization technique: the shaking artist." Chapter in Robert A. Neimeyer (Ed.) *Techniques of Grief Therapy: Creative Practices for Counseling the Bereaved.* Section I: Modulating Emotion. Pp. 48-49. Taylor & Francis/Routledge: London/New York.

Morgan, R.F. (2012e) "Treating traumatic bereavement in conflicted and intergenerational families." Chapter in R. A. Neimeyer (Ed.) *Techniques of Grief Therapy: Creative Practices for Counseling the Bereaved.* Pp. 106-108. London/New York: Taylor & Francis/Routledge.

Morgan, R.F. (2015) Climate change in a multinomial world. *Journal of Tropical Psychology, 5,* Cambridge University Press.

Morgan, R.F. (2017) Time statues. *Bulletin of the International Association of Applied Psychology*, *29(2),* 99-128. Supplement to *Applied Psychology*: *an International Review.*

Morgan, R.F. (2018a) The story of Chort. *Four Winds Journal,* April 2018 (Spring) 21-29. Santa Fe, NM: Orenda Healing International/Winds of Change Press.

Morgan, R.F. (2018b) Actualizing democracy. *Bulletin of the International Association of Applied Psychology*, January 2018, *30(1),* 58-81. Supplement to *Applied Psychology*: *an International Review.*

Morgan, R.F. (2018c) Close encounters of the anomalous kind. *Bulletin of the International Association of Applied Psychology*, July 2018, *30(2),* 44-64. Supplement to *Applied Psychology*: *an International Review.*

Morgan, R.F. (2020a) Opening Day. *Four Winds Journal.* Summer 2020, 17.

Morgan, R.F. (2020b) Elders with Anticipatory Trauma. *Ethical Human Psychology and Psychiatry.* June 2020, 21 (2), 127-136.

Morgan, R.F. and Bakan, P. (1965) Sensory deprivation hallucinations and other sleep behavior as a function of position, method of report, and anxiety. *Perceptual & Motor Skills*, *10,* 19-25.

Morgan, R.F., Ratner, S.C., & Denny, M.R. (1965) Response of annelids to light as measured by the galvanic skin response. *Psychonomic Science*, 3, 27-28.

Morgan, R.F and Wilson, J. (1982, 2005*) Growing Younger: Adding Years to Your Life by Measuring & Controlling Your Body Age.* Toronto: Methuen, 1982. (Reprinted New York: Stein & Day, 983.)

Morgan, R.F. & Toy, T.B. (1970). Learning by teaching: a student-to-student compensatory tutoring program in a rural school system & its relevance to the Educational Cooperative. *Psychological Record*, 20, 159-169.

Morgan, R.F. & Elkind, L. (1972) National Institute of Mental Health Children's Community Mental Health Center Grant for the John Hale Health Foundation, National Medical Association, Bayview-Hunters Point, San Francisco. Empowerment model: Coordinated by single-parent interns for their own children and for prevention intervention with community children.

Morgan, R.F. & Toy, T.B. (1974) "Learning by teaching: A student-to-student compensatory tutoring program and the educational cooperative." In J.G. Sherman (Ed.), *Personalized System of Instruction (PSI) Germinal Papers: Selected Keller Plan Readings*. Menlo Park, CA: W.A. Benjamin, Inc., 1974, 180-188.

Morgan, R.F. & Fevens, S.K. (1981) Transcending the iatrogenic approach to treating mentally retarded and learning disabled persons. *Psychological Reports*, 49, 47-54.

Morgan, R.F. & Dean, W. (1988) In defense of the concept of biological aging measurement - current status. *Arch. Gerontol. Geriatr.* 7, 191-210.

Morgan, R.F. & Wilson, J. (2005) *Growing Younger: How to Measure & Change Body Age*. N. Charleston, SC: Booksurge & Chico, CA: Morgan Foundation. (First edition with NY: Stein & Day/Toronto: Methuen.)

Neimeyer, R.A. (Ed.) (1994) *Death Anxiety Handbook: Research, Instrumentation, and Application*. New York: Taylor & Francis.

Neimeyer, R. A. (Ed.) (2012) *Techniques of Grief Therapy: Creative Practices for Counseling the Bereaved*. London/New York: Taylor & Francis/Routledge.

Neill, A.S. (1978) *Freedom-not license!* London: Pocket.

Neill, A.S. & Lamb, A. (1995) *Summerhill School: A new view of childhood*. New York: St. Martin's Griffin.

Oppenheimer, S. (2002) *The Real Eve: Modern man's journey out of Africa*. Santa Monica, CA: Discovery. DVD narrated by Danny Glover, directed by Andrew Paddington.

Oppenheimer, S. (2004) *The Real Eve: modern man's journey out of Africa*. New York: Carroll & Graf.

Patterson, F. (1987) *Koko's Story*. New York: The Gorilla Foundation/Scholastic.

Petterson, F. (1999) *Conversations with a signing Gorilla*. New York: Dutton.

Patterson, P. & Schroeder, B. (2010) Koko: A Talking Gorilla. Culver City, CA: Sony Pictures DVD.

Popenoe, C. (1977) Wellness. New York: Random House. Supplements through 1982.

Ratner, S.C. & Denny, M.R. (1964, 1970) *Comparative Psychology: Research in Animal Beh*avior. Belmont, CA: Dorsey.

Reich, W. (1981) *Record of a friendship: The correspondence between Wilhelm Reich and A.S. Neill 1936-1957*. New York: Farrar, Strauss, Giroux.

Rhine, J. B. (1934). *Extra-Sensory Perception*. Boston, MA, US: Bruce Humphries.

Rhine, J. B., & J.G. Pratt (1957). *Parapsychology: Frontier Science of the Mind.* Springfield, IL, US: Charles C. Thomas.

Rogers, R. (1995) *Destiny's Landfall: a history of Guam.* Honolulu: University of Hawaii Press.

Rosenthal, R. & Jacobson, L. (1966) Teacher's expectancies: Determinants of pupils' I.Q. gains. *Psychological Reports,* 19, 115-118.

Ross, L. (2006) Teenscreen & Universal Mental Health Screening: ICSPP Task Force. *International Center for the Study of Psychiatry & Psychology ICSPP Newsletter, 4,* 7-9.

Rossi, E.L. & Cheek, D.B. (1994) *Mind-Body therapy: methods of ideodynamic healing in hypnosis.* N.Y.: Norton.

Salzer, M. S., Brusilovskiy, E. & Townley, G. (2018) National Estimates of Recovery-Remission from Serious Mental Illness. Psychiatric Services 69 #5. https://doi.org/10.1176/appi.ps.201700401.

Schweitzer, G. (1857). Über das Sternschwanken. *Bulletin de la Société impériale des naturalistes de Moscou.* 30: 440-457; *31*: 477-500. Source: *Skeptic*, Volume 17. No. 2 2012, pages 38–43.

Schmeidler, G. (1945) Separating the sheep from the goats. *Journal of the American Society for Psychical Research,* 1945, 39, 46-49.

Schmeidler, G. & G. Murphy (1946) Influence of belief and disbelief in ESP upon individual scoring levels. *Journal of Experimental Psychology,* 36, 271-276.

Shapiro, J. (1970*). Investigating the effectiveness of sensitivity training of nurses on the progress of their patients.* Unpublished PhD dissertation at the University of Waterloo, Ontario, Canada.

Sheikh, A.A. (2003) *Healing images: the role of imagination in health.* Amityville, New York: Baywood.

Sherif, M. (1935). A study of some social factors in perception. *Archives of Psychology, 27*(187).

Slattery, U. (2005), *Unfortunate baby names: Slattery's complete collection of the most notable ten thousand for dramatic or other usage.* N. Charleston, SC/ Grass Valley, CA: Morgan Foundation.

Stevenson, A. & Waite, M. (Editors, 2011*) Concise Oxford English Dictionary.* Oxford: Oxford Univ. Press.

Tart, C. (1969) *Altered States of Consciousness: A Book of Readings.* New York: Doubleday.

Tart, C. (1975) *Transpersonal Psychologies.* El Cerrito, CA: Psychological Processes.

Tart, C. (1976) *Learning to Use Extrasensory Perception*. Chicago: University of Chicago Press.

Tart, C. (1977) *Psi: Scientific Studies of the Psychic Realm*. New York: E.P. Dutton.

Tart, C. (1986, 2001) *Waking Up: Overcoming Obstacles to Human Potential*. Boston: New Science Library.

Tart, C. (1989) *Open Mind, Discriminating Mind: Reflections on Human Possibilities*. New York: Harper & Row.

Tart, C. (2001) *Mind Science: Meditation Training for Practical People*. Napa, CA: Fearless.

Tart, C. (2009) *The End of Materialism: How Evidence of the Paranormal is Bringing Science and Spirit Together*. Oakland, CA: New Harbinger.

Tart, C., H. Puthoff, & R. Targ (1979) *Mind at Large: Institute of Electrical and Electronic Engineers Symposia on the Nature of Extrasensory Perception*. New York: Praeger.

Teague, R. (1973). *Experimental Exploration into C.G. Jung's Concept of Synchronicity: The Role of Meaningfulness in Parapsychology*. Unpublished Ph.D. dissertation at the California School of Professional Psychology, San Francisco.

Thomson, G. (2002) *On Gurdjieff*. Independence, KY: Wadsworth Philosophers.

Titus, J. (2011) *Brown's battleground: students, segregationists, and the struggle for justice in Prince Edward County, Virginia*. Chapel Hill: University of North Carolina Press.

Toch, H. (1980) T*herapeutic communities in corrections*. New York: Praeger.

Toch, H. (1995) "Inmate involvement in prison governance." *Federal Probation*, 59, 34-39.

Toch, H. ((1997) *Corrections: A humanistic approach*. Albany, N.Y.: Harrow & Heston.

Toch, H. (2017) *Violent Men: An Inquiry into the Psychology of Violence*. 25th Anniversary Edition. Washington, DC, American Psychological Association.

Tong, B.R. (2005) On the confusion of psychopathology with culture: Iatrogenesis in the treatment of Chinese Americans. In R. F. Morgan (Ed.) *The iatrogenics handbook: a critical look at research and practice in the helping professions*. N. Charleston, SC/Grass Valley, CA: Booksurge & Morgan Foundation.. Pp. 355-374.

Tompkins, P. & C. Bird (1989) *The Secret Life of Plants: a Fascinating Account of the Physical, Emotional, and Spiritual Relations between Plants and Man*. New York: Harper & Row.

Tondow, M. (1974) Personal communication.

Ulrich, R., Stachnik, T,, & Mabry, J. (1966), *Control of human behavior.* Glenview, IL: Scott, Foresman.

Wallace, R. K., Jacobs, D.E., and Harrington, B. (1982) The effects of the Transcendental Meditation and TM-Sidhi program on the aging process. International Journal of Neuroscience 16: 53-58. (CF *Journal of Personality and Social Psychology* 57 (1989): 950-964.; *Journal of Behavioral Medicine* (1986): 327-334.)

Watson, J. B. (1913). "Psychology as the Behaviorist Views it." *Psychological Review*. 20: 158–177. doi:10.1037/h0074428.

Watson, J. B.; Rayner, R. (1920). "Conditioned emotional reactions." *Journal of Experimental Psychology*. 3: 1–14. doi:10.1037/h0069608.

Watson, J. B. (1930). *Behaviorism* (Revised edition). Chicago: University of Chicago Press.

Wearden, G. (2014) "Oxfam: 85 richest people as wealthy as poorest half of the world." theguardian.com, 20 Jan.

Wells, S. (2003) *Journey of Man*. DVD narrated by Spencer Wells and directed by C. Maltby. Washington, D.C.: PBS.

Wells, S. (2004) *Journey of Man: A Genetic Odyssey*. New York: Random House.

Wells, S. (2007) *Deep ancestry: Inside the Genographic Project*. Washington, D.C.: National Geographic.

ROBERT F. MORGAN

Robert F. Morgan, Ph.D., is a Life Member of the American Psychological Association. An NIMH Pre-Doctoral Fellow at Michigan State University, he continued with more than 55 years of post-doctoral practice and teaching experience. A former speech collaborator and project consultant for organizations including the Peace Corps and Dr. Martin Luther King Jr., he was founding editor of the Cambridge University Press Journal of Tropical Psychology, founder of the Division of Applied Gerontology in the International Association of Applied Psychology (IAAP). He has overseen 126 psychology doctoral dissertations in California, Singapore, and Australia. He most recently taught a trauma psychology seminar at the University of New Mexico. He has published more than a hundred articles and 14 books on topics including life span psychology, trauma psychology in context, applied gerontology, international psychology, and unfortunate baby names. Only semi-retired he avoids a lethargic status he regards as "retireded" by continuing to think and write. He also hopes to avoid that opposite error exemplified by misleading voices of our era and, of course, Lincoln's prescient warning from a long past time: "It is better to be silent and thought a fool than to open one's mouth and remove all doubt." Well, readers of this book will be the judge of that.